Books should be returned or renewed by the last
date above. Renew by phone **03000 41 31 31** or
online *www.kent.gov.uk/libs*

D1336934

C334373763

JOHNY PITTS

Afropean

Notes from Black Europe

ALLEN LANE
an imprint of
PENGUIN BOOKS

ALLEN LANE

UK | USA | Canada | Ireland | Australia
India | New Zealand | South Africa

Allen Lane is part of the Penguin Random House group of companies
whose addresses can be found at global.penguinrandomhouse.com.

First published 2019
001

Copyright © Johny Pitts, 2019

The moral right of the author has been asserted

The extract on p. 7 is by permission of Aimé Césaire, *Cahier d'un retour au
pays natal* © Présence Africaine Editions, 1956

Set in 10.2/14.25 pt Sabon LT Pro
Typeset by Jouve (UK), Milton Keynes
Printed and bound in Great Britain by Clays Ltd, Elcograf S.p.A.

A CIP catalogue record for this book is available from the British Library

ISBN: 978-0-141-98472-8

www.greenpenguin.co.uk

MIX
Paper from
responsible sources
FSC
www.fsc.org   FSC® C018179

Penguin Random House is committed to a
sustainable future for our business, our readers
and our planet. This book is made from Forest
Stewardship Council® certified paper.

To my parents, Richie and Linda,
and my siblings, Richard and Chantal

'They live in a sort of frontier zone criss-crossed by ethnic, religious and other fault lines. But by virtue of this situation – peculiar rather than privileged – they have a special role to play in forging links, eliminating misunderstandings, making some parties more reasonable and others less belligerent . . . And that is precisely why their dilemma is so significant: if they themselves cannot sustain their multiple allegiances, if they are continually pressed to take sides . . . then all of us have reason to be uneasy about the way the world is going . . .'

– Amin Malouf, *Les Identités meurtrières*, 1998

Contents

Introduction	1
Prologue: Sheffield	11
Paris	31
A Tour of Black Paris	33
An Afropean *Flâneur*	52
Four Days in Clichy-sous-Bois	64
Brussels	83
Matongé	85
Tervuren Uncensored	102
A Meeting with Caryl Phillips	116
Amsterdam	127
Fight the Power	129
Berlin	165
Whitegeißt	167
Germaica	181
Stockholm	205
Let the Right Ones In	207
Rinkeby Swedish	223
Moscow	245
I Worry as I Wander	247
Strangers in Moscow	264
Marseille and the French Riviera	283
Interlude in Rome	285
Joseph Mobutu's Roquebrune-Cap-Martin	290

CONTENTS

James Baldwin's Saint-Paul-de-Vence   298

Frantz Fanon's Toulon   306

McKay's Marseille   313

Lisbon   337

The Night Train to Lisbon   339

A European Favela   354

An Afropean Odyssey   373

Notes   383

Acknowledgements   389

Resources   393

NEW EUROPE
[redacted]
[redacted] A VOYAGE OF DISCOVERY OUT NOW I[redacted]

Introduction

When I first heard it, it encouraged me to think of myself as whole and unhyphenated: *Afropean*. Here was a space where blackness was taking part in shaping European identity at large. It suggested the possibility of living in and with more than one idea: Africa and Europe, or, by extension, the Global South and the West, without being mixed-this, half-that or black-other. That being black in Europe didn't necessarily mean being an immigrant.

Labels are invariably problematic, often provocative, but at their best they can sing something into visibility. From my stymied vantage point – growing up in a working-class area of Sheffield ravaged by the external forces of free-market economics and the internal, protective force of local insularity that took shape in postcode wars – I began to notice a world that had been invisible to me before, or at the very least implausible; in my small corner of Britain, I had felt I was being forced to react against one culture or overidentify with the other.

Originally coined in the early 90s by David Byrne and Belgian-Congolese artist Marie Daulne, front woman of music group Zap Mama, I first encountered this notion of 'Afropean' in the realms of music and fashion. Among many others, Les Nubians, soul sisters from Chad by way of France, exuded it, as did Neneh Cherry, whose roots are Swedish and Sierra Leonean, Joy Denalane from South Africa via Germany, and Claude Grunitzky's *Trace* publication. 'Transcultural Styles and Ideas' was the magazine's tagline and reflected Grunitzky's own Afropean identity: he had a Polish grandfather on his mother's side, was born in Togo, raised in Paris and launched his magazine in London. This was a very attractive scene I was tapping into: beautiful, talented, successful black Europeans effortlessly articulating their cultural influences in coherent and creative ways. It was particularly attractive to me because the sense was that this iteration of blackness existing in Europe appeared as if it wasn't going to be going anywhere any time soon, felt closer to home than the sometimes overbearing cultural and political language emerging out of America, and more encompassing and nuanced than the Black Britain club, whose sense of itself was starting to feel outdated, often packaged exclusively as an embodiment of the Windrush Generation.*

Initially, then, I saw 'Afropean' as something of a utopian alternative to the doom and gloom that has surrounded the black image in Europe in recent years and an optimistic route forward. I wanted to work on a project that connected and presented Afro-Europeans as lead actors in our own story and, with all this glorious Afropean imagery in mind, I imagined this would result in some kind of coffee-table photo-book with snippets of feel-good text to accompany a series of trendy photographic portraits. There would be images of the 'success stories' of black Europe: young men and women whose street style effortlessly and elegantly articulated an empowered black European mood.

It was a visit to the 'Jungle' in Calais in 2016 that encouraged me to reconsider this approach. Over some fragrant, milky Arabic tea, Hishem, a young man from Sudan who ran one of many small, remarkably organized cafés and had been living in the Jungle for ten months, told me how he'd lost everything, had no surviving family members, had painful memories of the past and tremulous visions of the future and was stuck in this limbo land between Africa and Europe, home (a little of which he'd miraculously fashioned in his cushion-covered café) and anonymity. As I left his creaking plywood premises, he suggested that I write about his story and about life in the Jungle, a request I was nervous about. This man was intelligent,

---

* In the last national census, for the first time more black Brits identified themselves as black African than Afro-Caribbean.

articulate and literate: wouldn't it be better that he write about the Jungle himself? Maybe I could help attract attention to his writing, or publish his story on the website that I run, but what did I personally know about seeing friends massacred, fleeing war, hiding for my life in shipping containers or on ill-equipped boats in order to arrive penniless at a bunch of cold, windswept shacks in the hinterlands of northern France, apart from what he was telling me?

After exchanging contact details, I left the Jungle on my bicycle and slowly realized that I was being watched and followed through the blustery streets of Calais by the French military police, the Gendarmerie. Attempting to enter the white gates of the port to catch my ferry back to the UK, I was stopped before I could even get to passport control, searched, asked for my ID, where I was going, where I'd come from, how long I'd been away, and why. Finally, after more questioning and looks of suspicion, I was allowed to enter an official compound I'd seen other brown-skinned men of my age look longingly at from a distance. I was in; they were out.

Unlike the people I met in the Jungle, I wasn't so much living in limbo as living with liminality. I was 'in' because I had ID. I had ID because I was born and raised in England, had a history connected to Europe, knew how things ran. And yet, within this piece of geography, this idea of Europe, I was frequently reminded that I wasn't all the way in; one Remembrance Day – a day I've come to dread for the way it spikes an ugly nationalism which I sometimes find myself on the receiving end of – I was hit with that old chestnut and told 'go back to where you came from' by a middle-aged man, red-faced with rage and racism. My skin colour had disguised various facts, such as my grandfather having fought for Britain behind enemy lines in the Second World War and winning a medal for doing so. My skin had disguised my Europeanness; 'European' was still being used as a synonym for 'white'.

If 'Afropean' was something that could attempt to address this issue, I needed to find out what lay behind or beyond its brand. A brand largely black-spun and authored, yes, but that's all it was for now, a pleasant idea that was being sold to me and involved PR companies, stylists, fashion photographers and art direction. In Britain, it was this sort of vision of corporate multiculturalism, this veneer of inclusion, that Tony Blair's New Labour had used in an attempt to make Britain appear international, open-minded, forward-thinking and ready for business in the global economy, without affecting policies for long-term change in the way Britain treated its immigrants. Did Afropean include only beautiful, economically successful (and often light-skinned) black people?

'Afropean' as aspiration was one thing, but as I was writing about an interplay between black and European cultures, I realized this utopian vision of a black European experience would mean wilfully ignoring realities shared by a majority of black people living in Europe. It would mean making the numerous groups of unemployed black men I saw at train stations, or the African women cleaning toilets, or the disenfranchised communities struggling in the hinterlands of cities, completely invisible. It also seemed disingenuous to leave out my own culturally rich – if also less glamorous – experience of growing up mixed-race in Britain, and how it felt to travel Europe as somebody who identifies as black. It became apparent that I should let the reader know where I was coming from, in order that they might better understand where I was heading, that is, the under-documented areas of Europe that often contradict the homogenized monocultured depictions suggested by tourist boards and pocket-sized travel guides. I was also travelling during a time when a 'multicultural backlash' suggesting that the likes of me represented some sort of failed temporary experiment was sweeping across the continent and felt it was time to regroup and reassert my own plurality as part of a larger mission to suggest how multiculturalism might work beyond the pages of a reactionary press, in the very real multiculturalism embedded in my own heritage and in the streets of European cities. 'Afropean' had to be more than, to paraphrase Labour MP Jon Cruddas, an obsession with an authentic search for the self, and something more like a contribution to a community, with its trade-offs and compromises. It had to build a bridge over that dividing fence that says whether you're in or out and form some sort of informal cultural coalition.

I read a lot of valuable academic research and sociological theory, but all too often this was gathering dust in universities, or preaching to the converted, written or cited more often by wealthy, educated white scholars than the people being written about and couched in a stand-offish academic vernacular. Formal education is often driven by someone else's knowledge: who authorized and shaped its rhetoric? Whose knowledge is it? Who has access to it? What about black Europe beyond the desk of a theorist, found in the equivocal and untidy lived experiences of its communities? Black Europe from the street up?

I had no choice but to let a subjective light slip between the cracks and remind myself that I wasn't trying to insert this word that resonated with my experience – 'Afropean' – as some authorized new discourse in racial politics. It seemed to me that many 'big picture' books about race were being produced at a time when day-to-day dialogue and conversation were breaking down, when interactions on social media lacked goodwill and humour, with authors and bloggers presenting themselves as infallible spokespeople. This work is an attempt to use on-the-ground travel reportage as a way to wriggle free from the pressures of theory and honestly reveal the secret pleasures and prejudices of others as well as myself, by which I mean the human self; learning to be comfortable with being black and imperfect in depictions on a page. An effort to begin with the personal in order to arrive at the universal.

So while there are encounters with movers and shakers – artists, thinkers, fashionistas, intellectuals, writers and academics – many of the stories I found are about as far away as you can get from that coffee-table sheen: those of addicts, homeless people, thieves, drug dealers and militants. But there is something else, too. Hip-hop artist Mos Def once wrote of the depiction of black culture in the media that 'we're either niggas or kings, we're either bitches or queens',[1] and in contemporary Europe it seemed to me that black people were either presented as über-stylized retro hipster dandies in thick-rimmed glasses and a bit of kente cloth, or dangerous hooded ghetto-yoot. In the middle of these high and low superlatives of blackness is perhaps the most important inclusion in this book: chance meetings with regular folk and casual encounters with shop workers, hawkers, tour operators, students, bouncers, activists, musicians, youth workers and those I simply made friends with in cafés, bars, community clubs and hostels, who all unveiled the experience of the everyday, set slightly aside from a grand narrative: beauty in black banality. As my travels weren't funded or reviewed by an academy and for the most part I didn't (couldn't) swan around Europe's swankier hotels, this style of working also suited practical considerations. The book is forged by independent black budget travel; it is an independent black working-class journey.

The view I was left with, then, was something of a sullied utopia. A place of struggle and hope, of high drama and quiet nuance, of conclusions and ambiguity, connections and disjuncture, but always there were humour and humanity in my encounters and interactions. To paraphrase Robert Frost, my quarrel with the continent is a lover's quarrel. I've travelled extensively across the planet, including in West Africa, where my blackness is rooted, and Brooklyn, that hotbed of black culture that has infinitely inspired me and where my father was born, and still, nowhere else feels quite as much like home as Europe. I was taught how to read and write here, not always the right things necessarily, but I speak its languages, engage in some of its customs. I make use of the intricate and sometimes faded beauty of its old architecture, the free museums and galleries, often in existence thanks to the blood and toil of black men and women under exploitative empires. As Martinican poet and politician Aimé Césaire wrote beautifully:

Et je me dis Bordeaux et Nantes et Liverpool et New York
et San Francisco
pas un bout de ce monde qui ne porte mon empreinte
digitale
et mon calcanéum sur le dos des gratte-ciel et ma
crasse dans le scintillement des gemmes!

(I tell myself Bordeaux and Nantes and
Liverpool and New York and San Francisco
Not one inch of this world doesn't bear my digital imprint
And my calcaneum on the back of skyscrapers and my squalor
in the sparkle of gems!)[2]

As a member of Europe's black community, this Europe I speak of is all part of *my* inheritance, too, and it was time to wander and celebrate the continent like I owned it. A continent that has frequently, to quote Césaire's protégé Frantz Fanon, 'woven me out of a thousand details, anecdotes [and] stories . . .'[3] A Europe that, as I would see, was populated by Egyptian nomads, Sudanese restaurateurs, Swedish Muslims, black French militants and Belgo-Congolese painters. A continent of Cape Verdean favelas, Algerian flea markets, Surinamese shamanism, German reggae and Moorish castles. Yes, all this was part of Europe, too, and these were areas that needed to be understood and fully embraced if Europe wanted to enjoy fully functional societies. And black Europeans, too, need to understand Europe and to demand participation in its societies, to demand the right to document and disseminate our stories.

That said, there are various omissions here that are intimately linked to the black European experience, and this may frustrate some. Namely, the role of the Church in keeping black communities together. As somebody who embraces spirituality but is not religious, I decided that a separate book, written by someone more closely connected to the direct issues raised by religion, might dedicate itself solely to that theme. For similar reasons, there isn't as much about Islam as there might have been; it, too, seemed beyond the scope of this journey.

As a black northerner frustrated by what I sometimes call the Brixtonization of black Britain – that is, the reduction of the black British experience into a single, neat, London-oriented narrative – it is lamentable that, because of time and money constraints, I had to restrict my circumnavigation around the continent mostly to each country's biggest cities. For instance, there is nothing about Liverpool, Cardiff, Southampton or Bristol in the UK (Bristol is likely where my second name derives from – a Bristolian called Robert Pitts who owned plantations and slaves in the areas of South Carolina to which I can trace my black American roots) or similar areas across the continent with important, historical connections to the centuries-old black presence in Europe. Big cities are dynamic meeting places for people from all backgrounds, often have the oldest, most established black communities and suited the mood of a book tilted towards second-, third- and new-generation black Europe which, in turn, aims to present a connective history and knowledge base for newer arrivals, such as Hishem.

Some big capital cities, particularly in Eastern and southern Europe, such as Vienna, Warsaw, Rome and Madrid, are also absent or constitute a disproportionately much smaller part of the work than I would have liked, and I'd have loved to have explored the history of the Moors of Montenegro, for instance, or delved into the former Yugoslavia's link with Africa through the non-aligned movement, which attempted to create transnational friendship among countries resistant to the hegemony of Eastern or Western powers. I have tried my best to produce a fair and even picture of contemporary life in black Europe, but I couldn't let myself be crushed under what James Baldwin called the 'burden of representation'. I can only hope that readers find virtue in a black document produced largely independently of any official organizations, bodies or academic institutions. I also encourage anybody dissatisfied with the voids I was unable to fill to

contribute to the ongoing conversations on Afropean.com, where we've so far had essays from writers with first-hand Afropean experiences growing up in places including Slovakia, the Isle of Wight, Barcelona, Geneva and Vienna, as well as from the African continent. And finally, it may be asked, 'So where is the European part in this "Afropean"?' in the same way people ask why such a thing as black history month exists in Britain but not white history month. This is like asking why London has a Chinatown but not an England Town. England and whiteness are so omnipresent they can seem invisible. White history isn't projected as white history because it is simply 'history' – it dominates TV shows and curricula and surrounds us constantly. I wrote in a European language, travelled through European streets and grappled constantly with European history, though it's true that I'm neither an anthropologist nor a historian; I'm a writer and photographer. I'm also a black citizen living in Europe, now, and this journey was an attempt to make sense of that. With my brown skin and my British passport – still a free ticket into mainland Europe at the time of writing – one cold October morning, I set out in search of the Afropeans.

Prologue: Sheffield

I was born black, working class and northern in Margaret Thatcher's Britain.

The area I grew up in was Firth Park in Sheffield, which takes its name from the industrialist Mark Firth, a major player in the steel industry during the Industrial Revolution whose family also part owned the once world-famous cutlery firm Firth Browns, where generations of my family were employed. Firth Park was developed in the 1870s to provide workers and their families with a place to live near the factories they worked in. Britain's colonies had already been used to bolster its armed forces, and after the Second World War, with its human resources depleted and needing to rebuild itself cheaply, Britain opened its doors to colonial subjects for much-needed muscle to plug the gap in the labour market. What the postwar government in Britain didn't count on, however, was that it wouldn't be so easy to uproot these workers once they had served their purpose. The British Empire had conquered much of the world, and colonization was often justified as a means of 'civilizing' the colonized workers, or in other words 'making them British', so not only did the workers feel they had earned their right to stay, some of those first immigrants saw themselves as Brits heading home to the motherland. They'd been taught to speak, act and think English, applying themselves to learning Britain's history and geography while their own folklore, religions and wisdom, born from the landscapes or journeys of their ancestors, were dominated and demoted. When the war was over and normal life slowly resumed, the presence of black and Asian men and women was met with resistance, few bothering to really question why these new communities might be here in the first place. They were here, of course, because Britain had been over there.*

Successive British governments did not properly explain this. Those in Westminster didn't have to deal directly with these new arrivals, didn't have to work with them or foster the kind of goodwill it takes to connect with people from other cultures as neighbours; this bridge was left to the working classes to construct, or, as sometimes happened, refuse to build. More cynically, these new communities were visible scapegoats to be used at will for any societal failings – Britain's power, influence and prosperity were reduced after the Second World War but, instead of looking at the complex socio-economic factors behind this it was easier to blame high unemployment, falling educational standards and a shaken national identity on those people down the road who

* To paraphrase the Sri Lankan novelist Ambalavaner Sivanandan.

looked and spoke a little differently. Many of the older generation of black Northerners, who had to survive in smaller enclaves of otherness than their London counterparts, were, as is true of many first-generation immigrants, generally well behaved, attempting to ingratiate and integrate themselves into their new homeland.

I remember visiting an ex-girlfriend's brother, who was white, at a hairdresser's he worked at in Barnsley. I drew a few curious stares but was then able to sit quietly and wait for him to finish, largely ignored as the only black person in the shop. About half an hour later, the most famous black comedian the North has ever produced, the late Charlie Williams, walked in, spotted me straight away, pointed and, drawing attention to me in a loud voice said, 'Look, it's my cousin!', and everybody burst out laughing. He was offered a chocolate out of an open box on a coffee table and said, 'Go on, then, I will have one, it keeps my colour up.' He was using humour as an apology for our visible difference, feeling he needed to address the elephant in the room before anyone else had a chance to, effectively saying something similar to the South Asian character in Andrea Dunbar's *Rita, Sue and Bob Too*: 'I can't help being a Paki.'

I never felt the need to apologize for my presence. The multicultural make-up of Firth Park where I grew up comprised not only a white working-class community but established Yemeni, Jamaican, Pakistani and Indian communities, and later, more recent economic migrants and political refugees from Syria, Albania, Kosovo and Somalia. My childhood bedroom has, over the years, been like a VIP box for street opera. From it I've watched everything from Diwali and Eid celebrations to reggae parties, joy-riders, gangland shootings, rap battles, Yemeni weddings and, every so often, Prince Naseem Hamed's red Ferrari parking up next door (our neighbour Mohammed was a relative). It was no multicultural 'utopia' in the conventional sense, but it was alive and convivial, entrepreneurial and dynamic, built upon the tolerant atmosphere that comes with sharing a space daily with other people with diverse beliefs and

cultures. I was proud to be from Firth Park because many of the
neighbouring and more homogeneously white areas of lower socio-
economic status that surrounded us were post-industrial carcasses,
harbouring boredom, depression, paranoia and demoralization.
Firth Park was anything but boring. It was rough, but it was full of
culture and community spirit.*

My neighbour Mohammed was more older brother to me than
neighbour and was part of a larger network of people who looked
out for each other. His family would feed me, take me on excursions
across the country and have my back if I ever had trouble with any
of the rough families in the area. I looked up to Mohammed because
he rarely lost his cool and was smart, charming and respected in the
community. In his younger days he was not only a skilful footballer
and a bit of a ladykiller but, most impressively, the local *Street
Fighter* 2 champion, the lone arcade machine to be found in Kenya
Fried Chicken. Mohammed was Yemeni but culturally took part in
that great ideological construct of 'blackness' that had been laid
down in the 70s and 80s and bore fruit in the 90s through hip-hop
culture. It was Mo who introduced me to hip-hop and everything
that came with it, playing me pirated VHS recordings of *Wild Style*,
The Exorcist, *Scarface* and Chinese kung fu B-movies (the source
material every hip-hop album seemed to reference at that time), and
taught me to repeat some of the swear words in those movies in

* Whenever I return to Sheffield, I notice the shifting demographics of Page Hall,
an area neighbouring Firth Park, and my own tolerance of multiculturalism is put
to the test. An area once home to those Pakistani, Yemeni and Jamaican communities I know well now comprises mostly of a group I'm not as culturally familiar
with: Slovakian Romas. The streets are littered, men stand on street corners in
groups, children run around barefoot and are sometimes filthy and broken-down
cars line the streets. But I'm not at all offended by this, and I'm puzzled when white
working-class Sheffielders are. The scene completely mirrors white working-class
life in the 50s – the photographs I take of the area now aren't at all dissimilar to the
black-and-white images you see of the area back then. 'We were dirt poor but we
had a community, everybody knew each other and would help each other out – not
like now,' you hear pensioners lament. Yet it is the very life that is currently being
lived by the Romas that those pensioners respond to with disgust: a living, breathing working-class culture.

Arabic. *Aneek umak ana!* He also taught me how to play chess and shared with me the joys of Arabic cuisine; I was eating kohbs, lahme and aseed when I would have otherwise been living on a diet of Findus crispy pancakes, Mars bars and takeaway chips.

What impressed me most about Mo was the way he stayed true to his Arabic roots but also integrated with the white, working-class community, and without becoming a Charlie Williams-style clown. Many other second-generation ethnic minorities in the area gained the respect of white people through brute force: it wasn't given to them, so they took it, and became feared. But Mo found a happy medium, survived without losing his integrity, celebrated his Yemeni heritage by somehow making it relevant – attractive, even – to white people and expertly commingling multiple cultures into one he could work with. In this, he was much like Prince Naseem, who after a fight would speak in a mixture of Jamaican patois, African-American ebonics and strong working-class Sheffield dialect before praising Allah for his win, as if all these things sitting side by side was the most natural thing. And of course it was. Charlie Williams was something of an anomaly on the streets of Yorkshire in the 40s; Naseem Hamed in the 90s was not.

Compared to some of the white 'trouble families' (as my mother called them), Mohammed's family were a positive influence on me in terms of community solidarity, cultured conversation and emphasis on spirituality and education. There was a jovial, street-culture façade to our interactions, but his home and customs were encoded with knowledge, education and art and added to the collective wisdom in my upbringing when school was failing me. Islam is, after all, a deeply scholarly religion.

The Yemeni and Jamaican communities had managed, some-how, to steal some of Britain back and mould it in their own image by creating art, culture, intellectual thought and, in the end, a life, despite the worst odds. It was the type of living, breathing, street-level multiculturalism that has been exploited, appropriated or studied then either superficially transfigured or cruelly demonized by politicians, academics and theorists from a distorting distance. Tony Blair's New Labour was a step up from Margaret Thatcher, to be sure, but too often in ways that were only symbolic. This local community, however, while miraculously conjuring something akin to an authentic and enriching lifestyle – the very thing it was being denied systematically – could only sustain itself for so long without becoming undone by the external pressures of race, class and geography. That's why I was compelled to search for an energy beyond the love of the local and the aloof distance of the national and global. A liminal, translocal energy that ultimately provided communion with a wider black European diaspora which, over the years, has helped me maintain my balance and transcend the less empowering dynamics of my upbringing. I'd seen how many of my peers ended up suffering from a kind of participation fatigue and how the magic that had appeared under such pressure became strained without additional sustenance.

There was a brutal reminder of this shortly before I set out on my journey around Europe, when I was back living at my mom's temporarily after packing it all in in London. I was woken up by the words: 'I could have got you locked up nuff times, but I didn't. And it's not just 'cause I'm on crack, dickhead.' It was Tina, a Jamaican woman who lived three doors away on our terrace row. I reached for my phone and checked the time – 7.15 – then peeked through the blinds to look at Horninglow Road, a view I know better than any other. The window was coated with morning frost and through it the terraced houses looked almost quaint in a colourway of dawn teal and street-lamp gold. Tina was arguing with a younger girl in her early twenties, a member of a notorious white family, and their fighting continued.

'You lickal pussy 'ole, who do you think you are?' shouted Tina, who was holding a big stick in her hand.

'Tina, you mong, you better gi' me mi bag back, kasme!' snarled the white girl in a harsh Sheffield street slang, a strangely satisfying melange of working-class northern dialect, Jamaican patois, Urdu, among other things. As well as the big stick, Tina was holding a cheap-looking brown imitation-leather bag under her arm. There was a scuffle as the white girl reached for it and Tina swung the stick wildly, missing the girl's face by centimetres. The girl retreated for a moment, but she kept shouting aggressively. Tina goaded her on.

'Come den, you pussy claat!'

The other girl turned and ran away. Then, after a moment's silence, her shrill voice pierced the morning calm again.

'Who's bad nah, then? Who's a bad gyal nah?' She emerged from a nearby garden with a house brick and headed back towards Tina.

'Gimme mi bag back nah or I'll smash this in your fuckin' face,' said the girl.

'Come den, lickal gyal. I fuckin' dare ya, DO IT,' said Tina.

Tina staggered over and punched the girl in the face. A scuffle followed and fists flew. In the skirmish the stick was dropped, Tina somehow ended up with the brick and the white girl with her bag. Then, as if a switch had been thrown, Tina relented. She dropped the brick and walked back into her house without saying a thing. But the young girl kept ranting.

'Watch nah, you pussy! You punched me straight int' face and I din't even feel owt. I'ma come back and bang ya, truss! You fuckin' pussy 'ole! Watch nah! I don't care who you know, I'm bringing man to fuck you up!'

She said this while following Tina to her door, albeit at a safe distance. And then, when it was closed, her hair all ruffled and her face flustered and red, she walked past my house, seeing Mohammed leaning out of the window next door. In a soft, warm voice, she said, 'Sorry about that, Mo'ammid, love, din't mean to wake you up, darlin. She tried teefing mi bag, din't she?' and then stumbled off down the road.

Tina hadn't always been such a mess. I remember when she was young and well turned out and would tease me about my large, unruly Afro, begging me to let her braid it into neat cane-rows. She still asks when she sees me, but now it's her hair, nappy and knotty, needing the attention she offers to mine. The bright-eyed and witty woman I once knew was now a crackhead who'd turned her terrace house into a crack den which armed police regularly raided and where gunshots were frequently heard. Her slow deterioration into dependency was a reminder why it was so important for me to leave this place. There were lots of reminders, in fact: Firth Park was full of Tinas. People I'd grown up with had become predictable statistics and, for a while, each time I visited home a childhood friend was on the front page of the *Sheffield Star*. One murdered a three-year-old child; another lad down the road was stabbed to death; a former football teammate was sent down for twenty-two years for attempted murder, his own father having been murdered in the local park only a few years earlier . . . And I keep hearing of various schoolfriends who have ended up in mental institutions, the trauma and pressure of maintaining themselves as black people on the straight and narrow in a pathologically racist country becoming too much for them. I knew them as kids who liked to play with Transformers or kick a ball in the park. We'd have games of chess in my mom's kitchen or water fights on the road. At around sixteen or seventeen, our lives started to head in different directions. I went to college then got a part-time job as a youth worker, while many of my friends gradually fell by the wayside.

The only discernible difference between us was that my parents had created a fairly stable home – my mom had the support of her white working-class family; my dad, an African-American actor and singer, commanded some respect as an entertainer. Through my dad we got to travel, not out of necessity but for pleasure, because my mom and I visited various places across the country and sometimes abroad to see him acting in a play or a musical.

I'd been given frequent flashes, beyond what I'd seen through a screen, of a world that was so much bigger than Firth Park, so my parameters of success weren't based upon its micropolitics. Like when the so-called 'postcode wars' gripped Sheffield and 'my' area of S5 was at war with nearby S3 and a spate of violent attacks and murders ensued.

Alain de Botton might be a strange person to reference at this point, but he eloquently explored what was happening to those around me in *Status Anxiety* (2004):

> Those without status remain unseen, they are treated brusquely, their complexities are trampled upon and their identities ignored ... the penalty ... lies ... in the challenge that low status poses to a sense of self-respect. Discomfort can be endured without complaint for long periods when it is un-accompanied by humiliation; as shown by the example of soldiers and explorers who have willingly endured privations that far exceeded those of the poorest in their societies, and yet who were sustained through their hardships by an awareness of the esteem they were held in by others.[1]

That was it. I grew up seeing that age is not kind to the bad-boy: in adolescence, an ASBO was almost like having a GCSE in street credentials, and we were all enticed by the attractive mix of danger and excitement that had been connected to young black identity in popular culture. Though his story was so much deeper than this, I know I wasn't the only one who wasted daydream space on visions of being shot like Tupac Shakur. But what happens when adulthood arrives and you're a thirty-year-old who is losing your sixpack, can't read or write and has been diagnosed by behavioural therapists and prison psychologists as a sociopath? What happens when the ghetto glamour is gone?

It's too far to walk to the town centre from Firth Park, really, but I always do, because what I think of as the disparate fragments of my culture lurk in the crevices of the journey. Pleased with my moderately sized backpack, filled with enough clothes and essentials for five months in Europe, I made my way up towards Meadowhall shopping centre, through the 'Flower Estate', where you'll find drug-dealers and joy-riders populating Honeysuckle Road, Sunflower Grove, Lavender Way, Clover Gardens and Primrose Avenue. Sheffield is like that. The prettiest names denote the roughest places. Chaucer School – on Wordsworth Avenue – is one of the worst in the city, and the average lad you'll find in Southey Green has little inclination towards romantic verse. So far was Robert Southey from our reality, growing up, I had no idea that the green was named after a poet until well into adolescence, and that it should be pronounced 'Suthie'; the area is mispronounced locally as 'Southee'.

Firth Park leads on to Wincobank, said to be the site of an Iron Age hill fort dating back to 500BCE, but you would be hard pressed to find any trace of it. Just terrace houses and an off licence with a bright yellow façade that looks home-made. My route from Firth Park to the city centre also leads past the largest listed building in Europe, which makes it sound more grandiose than it is: the building in question is the brutalist Park Hill Flats, which, until being gentrified and privatized, loomed over the city like a monolithic monster and coated everything beneath it in a thick layer of shadow. But Park Hill is an apt landmark: Sheffielders love to hate their city, getting nostalgic when the eyesores they've been complaining about for years are demolished and being offended when anyone from outside the city holds the same Sheffield-equals-shithole view as they do.

This begrudging, surreptitious pride Sheffielders have in their dishevelled urban landscape is rooted in what I believe to be a subconscious acknowledgement of what it offers: a down-to-earth, off-the-grid sense of freedom. Just under 500 kilometres from Westminster, the fading postwar buildings embody a sociable, working-class atmosphere that existed before Primark and Starbucks colonized the high streets, when unions were empowered and working-class culture hadn't been reduced to Kim Kardashian curves and *Love Island* abs. The plans for the city drawn up in the 50s by Sheffield council's city architect John B. Womersley were bold

and socialist in mood.* Over time, I have witnessed the destruction
not only of civic working-class spaces and geographies but of the
very idea of the civic within the minds of the working-class community; aspirations of private comfort have replaced community
spirit and intellectual engagement with ideas that go beyond capitalist convenience. Communities once connected by local industries
and imbued with a sense of pride and craftsmanship have been displaced by anonymous environments of globalization – you can't
build much of a culture around call centres and shopping malls. I'm
speaking here of the working-class north of Sheffield where I was
born and raised, which sits adrift from the leafy enclaves of university professors, students and artists who have come up through the
more prosperous, middle-class south of the city.

As Margaret Thatcher opened Britain up to free trade in the
80s, effectively crushing the industrial foundations of the north of
England, the socioeconomic conditions and urban landscapes of
my part of Sheffield were strikingly similar to those of New York
in the 70s. This, combined with the bootleg copies of the seminal
1983 hip-hop-culture documentary *Wild Style* that were floating
about, turned much of the city into Europe's premier playground
for graffiti artists and music-makers. Council estates became concrete canvases and the tops of tower blocks broadcast pirate-radio
stations. This was the flip side to all the death and violence I experienced growing up: the growth of one of the most important
cultural movements of the late-twentieth century – hip-hop, a movement capable of both waylaying and exacerbating our problems.

Sheffield's reputation as a safe haven for graffiti artists came to
an abrupt end in the mid-90s when a twenty-two-year-old whose
tags seemed to cover every square inch of the city was caught and
sentenced to five years in prison. Simon Sunderland aka Fista (his
tag came from a misspelling of 'first' when he attempted his initial
piece of graffiti) was inspired by hip-hop culture, but it wasn't long

* In 'Ten Years of Housing in Sheffield' (1961) the descriptions of all the projects
are in three languages: English, French and Russian.

before tagging for tagging's sake became an addiction. His work often straddled the fine line between street art and what many saw as pure vandalism; his motivation was somewhere between political protest and adrenal necessity.

'It's a blind society,' he said in an interview shortly before he was caught and imprisoned. 'Every day, everywhere we go, we're bombarded with these big adverts, making money, selling lies . . . The advertisers try to vandalize our minds with images of a materialistic society.' Every so often, a beautiful, full-colour block-lettered Fista 'piece' or 'production' would appear – the type of graffiti that brightens up drab urban landscapes – but what most people remember him for was his 'bombing': quick, economical scrawls of his tag on buses and bus shelters, train tunnels, rolling stock, motorway bridges, factories and anything else he could gain access to. What set him apart from other taggers of the time was that he specifically targeted conspicuous surfaces of the city, so his name embedded its way into your subconscious the way any form of major advertising does. He became a local celebrity who shunned celebrity, a well-known brand that wasn't trying to sell you anything and a mysterious presence that had everybody gossiping. Schoolkids would say Fista was their brother, or cousin, or even claim to be Fista themselves.

The year he was put away, 1996, a whole host of subversive traditions in the West were lost to what, at the time, many thought of as progressive politics and innovations. Social-media seedlings were sprouting up online, there was an economic boom and Tony Blair was about to be elected Prime Minister. In the United States a Telecoms act consolidated radio ownership to a handful of major players, splintering hip-hop into mainstream and underground factions (killing it, basically). Post-war high-rises were being demolished all over Britain and America; Harry Handelsman's Manhattan Loft Corporation set off a wave of East London gentrification; Rudy Giuliani, then mayor of New York, changed New York's social landscape for ever; and Tupac Shakur was murdered, which signalled the end of Death Row Records, perhaps the closest thing the 90s had to the Black Panther Party.*

During this period, Sheffield city centre became a more controlled and corporate environment and people like Fista didn't fit the plan so the government ploughed money into a crack anti-vandalism unit called Grime Busters whose mission was to rid the city of all graffiti, past and present. Instead of trying to nurture the little bit of creative energy that had somehow managed to grow out of the poverty and high unemployment of a post-industrial working class, they vilified its leaders. While the late Jean-Michel Basquiat – who started out as a graffiti artist tagging SAMO in New York City, in a style comparable to Simon Sunderland – was selling paintings for half a million pounds,† Fista was locked up in a grim prison in the north of England as the government erased all traces of his work.

One of the Grime Busters was recorded on local television saying, 'Imagine you left your car in the drive, woke up the next morning and someone had drawn a big eagle on it, and people said, "That's a nice eagle." That's not the point, though, is it? It's your property, and you didn't want it there so it shouldn't be there, should

---

* Tupac Shakur's mother, Afeni, was one of the Panther 21, and was pregnant with Tupac while she was serving time. His godmother, Assata, is still in exile in Cuba because of her activities on behalf of the party, and his godfather, Geronimo Pratt, was a high-ranking senior member – Tupac was, essentially, raised by the Black Panthers. In the 80s Huey Newton was haphazardly attempting to galvanize the criminal underground as a way to take back control of the streets under Ronald Reagan's government, and in many ways Tupac and Suge Knight had similar ideas. At Death Row Records there were corporate CEOs, Bloods and Crips and community workers mixing with an unprecedented group of talent – Dr Dre, Snoop Dogg, Nate Dogg, DeVante Swing and Tupac all in the same building. The goal, it is said, was to turn record-buyers into voters. There is an astonishingly vivid portrait of life at Death Row Records in 'How to Survive Puberty at Twenty-five' by Nina Bhadreshwar, who was born and raised in Barnsley and set up a graffiti magazine in Sheffield with Fista before moving to South Central to work for Death Row Records.

† Now worth easily quadruple that amount. At the time of writing a painting by the artist that was previously owned by David Bowie is up for auction with an estimate of £3.5 million.

it?' But I wonder what the homeowners living on, say, Rutland Road, make of that enormous, gaudy Virgin Media ad outside their house? Did anybody ask them for their permission? How do you go about getting your signs and symbols or adverts officially recognized? Nobody I grew up with knew, except that it involved an amount of money none of us could reasonably hope ever to attain.

For a while it was a game of cat and mouse between the Grime Busters and the graffiti artists. Sheffield taggers made the national press and became either *Daily Mail* villains or underground anti-heroes. Mist1, Crome, Des, SB2 and others joined Fista in the pantheon of the Sheffield graffiti scene to become household names, even if only for fifteen minutes. Graff Cats, like B-Boys and emcees, got old, had families to support and found it hard to sustain a culture that had to be lived, not just toyed with. New anti-graffiti paint was used to cover the walls of the city centre and the Grime Busters' diligence eventually paid off: any graffiti that wasn't immediately rubbed away by their powered jets of water faded over time and wasn't replaced – the speed at which the tags were being destroyed made it pointless. This, along with a general decline in hip-hop as a culture, rather than just a music genre, in younger generations across the West and the threat of serious jail time all but spelled the end of a once-legendary scene.

I choose 'Afropean' as a potentially progressive self-identifier (rather than 'European') because there is something about the nature of Europe that destroys by assimilation, something I learned first hand when I moved to London and became immersed in a UK hip-hop scene run behind the scenes by white private-school kids who turned their noses up at UK grime for not being 'real' – unlike their complex, privately funded lyricism over old-skool beats made out of expensive vintage-vinyl collections.

Every time I return to Sheffield I search the streets, hoping to find a Fista tag, a ghost-trace of the raw, pre-digital Sheffield I remember from childhood. His heavy sentence was intended to send a message out to the rest of the graffiti community, and his tags were more specifically targeted by the Grime Busters than any-one else's. When I eventually found one on a bridge near the abandoned Brightside railway station, the defiant white lettering looked tired and skeletal and, more than anything, defeated. The system had won. Nowadays, graffiti, much like other elements of hip-hop, has been toned down, neutered and commodified. It is commissioned by people who want Banksy-style stencils on the walls of cultural-industry quarters. You're as likely to see it included in those advertising billboards Fista deplored as sprayed on the walls nearby. Except, this time, it is legal, corporate vandalism.

My nostalgia for Fista's graffiti is rooted in its association with the steel city's fringe communities. Like the graff, there was some-thing ephemeral about the black community in Sheffield. It was never as solid or as sure of itself as London's, and everything con-nected with it was underground and clandestine. A friend of a friend would let you in and tell you about the illegal Jamaican blues parties that Docker or Donkeyman was throwing, or the dial for SCR, the pirate-radio station broadcasting out of various Shef-field high-rises which played all the garage, ragga, RnB and hip-hop that was so hard to get hold of before the internet. One of the first major black festivals was a DIY Caribbean street affair in Pitsmoor called Summer Jam, which eventually grew into Music in the Sun, held in Don Valley Bowl – one of the few occasions when all Sheffield's black community would congregate in a single place each year. Though there were a few important long-standing organizations, such as the Non-Stop Foundation, there was a sense that the most successful displays of multicultural Sheffield had sprouted up out of the community organically.

All those organizations are now defunct, but even in their hey-day they struck me as vulnerable and temporary; as soon as the council tried to control them, you knew it spelled death. When the system got involved, put on curfews, vetted the music, sanctioned and colonized the space with corporate sponsors, that sense of pend-ing alienation crept back in. Somebody would be put in charge who wasn't from the community, or at the very least had to answer to somebody who came from outside. As I walk around these stale spaces today, once home to a lost, uncommemorated history, sometimes I like to imagine something similar to the English Heritage blue plaques that honour the former residences of famous and distinguished scholars, artists and explorers. I'd choose to commemorate 'Mr Menace, Sheffield's best emcee' on a row of terrace houses or tell passers-by that 'SCR, Sheffield's pioneering pirate-radio station, was broadcast here' on the low-rise student accommodation where a now-demolished council estate once stood.

Black culture in Sheffield, for me at least, wasn't solely synonymous with black people. My route into the community came not through my father (who, being a 'glamorous' African-American singer, wasn't as much a part of the black British experience), but through a white friend, Leon Hackett, who grew up in Pitsmoor. Living in an area where the majority of residents were from Jamaica, Leon very quickly had to learn all about Jamaican culture to survive, and in many ways identified more with it than with white working-class Sheffield. Part of a large family, he and his brothers spoke perfect patois and a lot of them became emcees and DJs on the scene. Along with Mohammed, it was Leon who first introduced me to hip-hop, which at the time still felt like an underground club that wasn't so easy to be inducted into. We'd freestyle for hours over instrumentals and go through the painstaking process of making mixtapes by recording J Rugged and MC Nige's shows on SCR, using the stop and start buttons on our cassette players.

Leon was another reason I wanted to see the rest of Europe through the eyes of black culture. How else had it influenced and permeated its way into the consciousness of the continent's white population? How much of this reverse colonization could I find? African art had influenced cubism and art deco in France; Jamaicans had created a huge reggae scene and an identification with Rastafarianism in Germany; Stuart Hall had radically altered the way culture was studied in the UK at university level – what instances could I find where assimilation was really working for black communities, and influencing the look and feel of Europe? I knew all too well that this had long been happening, because it represents the genesis of my existence: I'm a Northern soul baby.

Coined by Dave Godin, a music journalist for *Blues and Soul* magazine, 'Northern soul' is a term to describe a musical phenomenon that gripped the working-men's clubs and casinos in industrial cities in the north of England in the 60s and 70s.

'The British obsession with class has, over the years, ensured that white working-class people have experienced a parallel kind of experience to black Americans,' says Godin, attempting to explain the root of this strange union of cultures. I have to disagree with that assessment – you can't compare the Jim Crow laws and violence African-Americans suffered with the hardships in the North or the class struggle in the 1960s – but there was certainly something about the grit and pain in this music born out of oppression that resonated with white working-class communities. My mother's family, like many working-class northerners, had Irish heritage, having escaped the great famine, and it may well be that the memory of displacement of those connected to the Irish Atlantic chimed with the music of the black Atlantic – the diasporic dispersal of people across the Atlantic Ocean. More than anything, though, it was about escapism: to finish a week's graft in the pits or mines or steelworks and lose yourself in a foreign, 'exotic' culture for a few hours on the dance floor was liberating. This was definitely the case for my mother, whose family were among the poorest living in the Burngreave area of Sheffield. The music provided a flash of colour to her life in a grotty industrial city and she met my father at a derelict Victorian house near her home in Pitsmoor that had been turned into a club called The Mojo by the late entrepreneurial lothario Peter Stringfellow.

It was the late 60s when my dad first came to Britain, with a band called The Fantastic Temptations. They toured the North, performing hits like 'My Girl' and 'I Wish It Would Rain', and won a good fanbase, gaining a reputation across the country for their live performances. The only problem was, they weren't the real Temptations but part of a scam by a promoter who was capitalizing on the original band's success. This wasn't an isolated incident – groups were frequently promoted as various, more famous, soul acts from the US – The Platters, The Drifters, The Isley Brothers, and so on – to a soul-hungry crowd of white working-class fans who didn't ask too many questions. If they were good-looking, black, could sing and gave everyone something to dance to, then everyone was happy. Apart from the original recording artists.

Eventually, The Fantastic Temptations were found out and threatened with legal action so they promptly changed their name to The Fantastics and had some success in their own right. My dad recalls meeting the real Temptations in Sheffield and preparing himself for a fist fight, until he realized they weren't angry at all – the fake Temptations had done a good job, helping to promote the band's name in Britain, and this spurred The Fantastics on to a top-ten hit with the song 'Something Old, Something New' in the early 70s.

While Northern soul represented an escape from the tough realities of working-class life in Sheffield, so, too, was it an escape for my dad from the many street gangs in Brooklyn and the prospect of the Vietnam draft. His music was a ticket to a land where his African-Americanness wasn't considered part of a national problem; when the black British community were on the front line fighting with petrol bombs against police in Brixton, my dad was performing in various Andrew Lloyd Webber musicals in the West End. Dad's blackness wasn't directly connected to a colonial empire, or part of a problematic shared history here in Europe. Brits could say to him, 'Aren't those Americans evil? Come in, Richie, love, have a cuppa,' at the same time turning a blind eye to the less glamorous black British community who were *their* problem. Brits, on the whole, and Sheffielders in particular, had found him an attractive, exciting addition to the country because his lineage and cultural distance didn't make them feel uncomfortable or pose too many immediate contradictory questions. Every time my mom's family had a get-together he was the toast of the party, all these white working-class blokes and lasses with tattoos and pints of beer crowding around him. 'That's Richie,' they would say. 'The singer from New York!' I don't consider my white family racist, but Dad couldn't ever be mistaken for one of those wogs from down the road.

It's hard to work out how or if the cultural transactions taking place in Northern soul and other movements like it had any kind of truly transformative effect on how white Europeans saw black people. I recently attended a Northern soul weekender (held at a Pontins resort) with my dad to experience the surreal atmosphere of skinheads who looked like football hooligans dancing their hearts out to black music. The fans knew the music better than the musicians.

Dad knew a kind of fame at these weekenders and, whether he was performing or not, the organizers would always offer him a free chalet, pay for his food and for all his drinks. He told me that the same had happened to friends of his, some fellow African-American musicians who got a call asking them to perform a song they had almost forgotten they had recorded – a song that was huge on the Northern soul circuit but perhaps only recorded as a demo in the States. More than anything, the Northern soul scene was for collectors, and was born of a strange situation in the 60s and 70s, when DJs from the UK would go over to America and buy huge batches of records that hadn't sold. Record companies would let them go for practically nothing, happy to shift the surplus stock from their warehouses. But these young British DJs were also shrewd entrepreneurs – they had identified a market, and it would be years before the labels got savvy to what they were doing: buying stock and reselling it as hard-to-find imports from America to a hungry audience of white people in the north of England and making a fortune in the process. These tracks, often unbeknown to the artists and record labels, would become huge underground club hits. Fast-forward three or four decades and there is still a call for such artists from ageing club-goers now in their fifties and sixties, trying to evoke their heyday. If Northern soul was no great cultural lesson for white Brits, the scene did at least offer a bit of glory in their twilight years to black 'stars' who had previously never really shone. Much like the American armed forces stationed across Europe after the Second World War, it also left behind a generation of mixed-race children living on the continent with a somewhat alternative black European identity.

As I boarded the Midland Main Line bound for London, where my Eurostar awaited, I was searching for a way to protect the knowledge and the secret beauty which I knew lurked among all the mess of my upbringing in Firth Park while also attempting to transcend it. Looking back at all the violence and death and realizing it wasn't necessarily normal made me want to travel in the name of those who couldn't, or didn't – the working-class black community and children of immigrants – in search of a Europe both they and I might recognize as our own. And so it was that I found myself setting off as that rarest of creatures: the black backpacker.

PARIS

A Tour of Black Paris

As the Eurostar pulled into the cavernous entrance of the Gare du Nord at dusk, I sat back for a moment and watched the same commuters I'd seen elegantly sipping their Sauvignon Blancs and *café noirs* just a moment ago lose their grace, awkwardly pushing, struggling with baggage and queuing up to dash out on to the platform. They had families to catch up with, friends to see, business to attend to and parties to schmooze at – the things I was about to opt out of for a few months.

Having no obligations should have been a pleasant feeling, I suppose, and yet, sitting there alone on the Eurostar, rain droplets on the windows disfiguring the platform beyond them and West African cleaners as shadow-like as Ralph Ellison's Invisible Man taking the place of those well-heeled commuters I'd just seen alight, I experienced the kind of trepidation people often have before setting out on a long journey. It suddenly struck me that what lay before me was an empty, disquieting expanse of loneliness and uncertainty. That I'd just entered a geographic landmass in which I would be a foreigner in every capacity. Was there really a cohesive idea of a black Europe I might find some sort of solidarity with? Everything suddenly struck me as an abstraction: who was 'black'? What was 'Europe'?

With a sense of foreboding pulling me back into my seat, I sat for a few minutes until I must have been the last passenger on the train, surrounded by the remnants left behind by my former travelling companions – empty crisp packets, mini bottles of wine rolling on their side and tables stained with coffee rings – and learned the lesson of slowing down in order to tap into a new big-city frequency. Various tempos reveal different realities, and very often Europe's black workforce inhabits the liminal terrain I'd just experienced, as cleaners, taxi drivers, porters, security guards, ticket sellers and nightclub bouncers; they are there and not there. I knew of this world already, of course; I'd been part of it in the past but had never before thought of it as an *invisible* world through which white Europe blithely passes without ever really seeing.

I watched the two Senegalese men joke with one another in creolized French, making the most of the banality of tidying and preparing the carriage for what would likely be another set of mostly white commuters. This job was hardly enviable and struck me as symbolic of a power dynamic between Africans and Europeans that hadn't changed for centuries; whatever European countries like to suggest, black people were still cleaning white people's toilets, changing their bedsheets, guarding their buildings and sweeping their floors. They were also being accused of 'stealing' these jobs (which nobody wanted) while simultaneously managing, somehow, to live as lazy freeloaders. They could be both these things in the imagination, on news bulletins, in the right-leaning press, as long as nobody ever really acknowledged their existence in daily interactions, as long as their lives and humanity and work were all rendered invisible in the flesh.

As soon as I stepped down on to the platform, Paris presented itself as a city occupied by African communities in a way even I had never noticed on previous trips. I suppose, if I had been searching Europe for its pensioners, or its Chinese communities, the continent would appear full of those demographics, too. I knew that, apart from London, Paris had the largest black presence in Europe, but it struck me as overwhelmingly black, from station staff to the commuters passing through and on the Métro, as I voyaged beneath the North African quarter of Barbès-Rochechouart and the West African market hub of Château Rouge on Ligne 4, to my digs on rue Caulaincourt. This was also a city that had its very own tours designed to celebrate this long, rich history, and I'd booked to be on one of them the day after I arrived, curious to see some commerce centred around black tourism.

After a terrible night full of anonymous snores and stinks (my first ever night in a hostel) I overslept and woke up groggy, worried I was going to be too late for the tour. In my email correspondence with the tour leader Ricki Stevenson, however, she wrote, 'We never leave anyone behind so don't worry if you're running on French-people time.' When I finally arrived ten minutes late at our meeting point, Café Brioche Dorée, a somewhat banal French café chain, I felt an eager curiosity about what I'd find. How many people would be taking the black Paris tour? Would they be black or white? What had brought them to it?

In the corner of the room sat a black man and woman, middle-aged and neatly dressed, obviously waiting for somebody. They were distinct from the many black French customers at the café and I knew they were African-American from a mile away; they had the paunch that comes with having more space and home comforts and an unfussy neatness that is evidence of the discipline and organization it takes to achieve a certain amount of economic success in America as a member of its black community.

They were Jimmy and Niecy Brown, and Jimmy pronounced their names as though they were a business. He was miffed that Ricki, our guide, hadn't yet shown up, and wary and defensive of me until he found out that my dad had been born and raised in Brooklyn. When I saw his frostiness thaw a little at the mention of this, I laid on my second-hand African-Americanness thickly, not putting on an accent exactly but softening my 't's a little and saying things like 'So whadda you guys doing so far from "home"?', implying that America was a psychic home we shared. I talked of the cook-outs we have at the Pitts family reunions every year in South Carolina. I was sort of mimicking the way I'd noticed my dad act when he was around other African-Americans in the UK. Watching him, I'd always feel as though he was a member of a secret club that my mom and I didn't have access to. My dad never tried to be overtly English, and still has his Brooklyn accent after four decades living in Sheffield, but something about his character would change when he met a fellow African-American. He was mildly subdued, slightly secretive even, when he presented himself in interactions with Brits, black or white, but would suddenly come alive when speaking to a 'brother'. That was one of the words he'd use, and he'd laugh and clown in a way that made me, with my Yorkshire accent, feel envious and flat.

Jimmy was boasting that he'd already seen half the world but had made this particular trip because he'd always promised Niecy he'd whisk her off to see Paris, a city that occupies a special place in the imagination of many African-Americans. Just then two women walked – or, more accurately – *sauntered* over. Though these women were both American, unlike Jimmy and Niecy they could have passed for French, one wearing a red woollen beret with a woollen jacket, the other in a crocheted hat and a yellow mac. One of these elegant women turned out to be our guide.

Right from the start, I could see that Jimmy was going to give Ricki a hard time. She introduced herself warmly: 'Hi, I'm Ricki Stevenson, and I'm gonna go ahead and guess that you all are my group.' But Jimmy just scowled and said, 'We were starting to think you might not show up.' The woman she was with, also African-American, was called Clemence, worked at a publishing company in New York and was a trainee tea master. Both women were middle-class academics, and their knowledge seemed to clash with Jimmy's, who would go on to dismiss almost all their observations with his own brand of experiential wisdom. He was keen to let us all know he had *lived* and that his education at the school of *life* was where the real knowledge was at.

When we each had to introduce ourselves around the table, I felt culturally flimsy, as though my identity was vague and half formed compared to my American friends', my English accent lacking substance when talking about black identity and theirs

thronged with experience, their intonations carrying more explicitly historical narratives of blackness. We had to say why we were
taking the tour, and I stumbled over my words, incoherently spurt-
ing out that I was thinking of writing a book about black Europe,
which I regretted immediately, but at the mention of this the table
came alive, saying how it was a great idea. Clemence asked if she
could see a manuscript once it had been written (it was the first
time I'd had the notion that my scruffy notebooks might one day
form something called a 'manuscript'), Jimmy said, 'I've got some
stories for your book,' and Ricki mentioned texts for research,
such as *Three Years in Europe* by William Wells Brown (1852).
Wells Brown's astonishing story began in the cotton fields of Ken-
tucky and ended with him giving lectures in Europe and authoring
numerous acclaimed works, including what is widely considered
the first novel by an African-American, *Clotel, or The President's
Daughter* (1853). In his European travel narrative he explained the
mood of self-determination in which this transition was achieved:
'He who escapes slavery at the age of twenty years, without any
education, as did the writer of this letter, must read when others
are asleep, if he would catch up with the rest of the world.'

His journey led to a more dramatic transformation than many
of us living in the twenty-first century can imagine, but those
words resonated with my experience of studying at a British school
and the lack of historical figures I was taught about who looked
like me or shared similar beginnings. My blackness was lived at
home, in the street, at the barber's, through vernacular culture, but
was largely absent in any place of study or officialdom, and it
wasn't until I left school that I began to assemble disparate bits of
information to fill in the blanks of my own black identity and its
relation to history at large by 'reading when others were asleep'.
It's why tours like the one Ricki Stevenson was giving are so
important, and it wasn't a surprise that it was an African-American
woman who had had the chutzpah to set up the first one in the city:
she was used to the support of a unifying economic class of black

people who themselves are used to learning – and expect to learn – about their history wherever they go. To them, the idea of this book of mine, which seemed a vague, preposterous one back in the UK, even to me at the time, was a no-brainer. They were used to being catered for and to supporting work emanating from other members of the black diaspora.

After our introductions, Ricki handed us all a sheet of paper with a list of names of black historical figures, then asked us to put a tick next to all the people we thought might have either lived in Paris or had a strong connection with the city. If I had played the game in earnest, I'd have ticked off maybe a third of the names, but I suspected it was a trick question and that everyone on the list should be ticked. I didn't say so, because I didn't want to spoil Ricki's big reveal – that would be a job for Jimmy.

'You pro'ly just gon' tell us they all been here,' he said.

'And you'd be correct,' replied Ricki, unfazed by the smart alec of the group, and went on to tell us about Alexandre Dumas, who carved out a legendary space in the canon of French literature with world-famous novels such as *The Three Musketeers* (1844) and *The Count of Monte Cristo* (1844–5). Dumas's West African grand-mother, Marie-Cessette, had been an enslaved woman working on a plantation in Haiti in the late 1700s and was ultimately emanci-pated because of her physical beauty – bought for a 'golden price' by Marquis Alexandre Antoine Davy de la Pailleterie, a French nobleman. It's unclear how complicit Marie-Cessette was in the love affair that would ensue with her 'master'. On the one hand, when his finances started to wane, the marquis sold the four chil-dren he had with Marie-Cessette back into slavery, indicating that the power dynamic between white master and black slaves hadn't shifted terribly. On the other hand, he did sell the children to a 'mulatto' colonialist, perhaps in the hope of fairer treatment, and eventually bought back his only son, later sending him to Paris to attend a prestigious military school. This young boy was Thomas Alexandre Dumas, who would go on to become a general in the

French army and the highest-ranking black soldier in Europe's history, and himself had a son who would become one of the most famous French novelists of all time, Alexandre Dumas. Alexandre Dumas's son, also Alexandre, would go on to achieve a lauded place in French society as a playwright and novelist. Jean-Fernand Brierre, the Haitian poet and politician who contributed much to the Negritude movement, was a descendant of Marie-Cessette's sister Rosette. This is the type of grand Afropean lineage you don't often hear about.

As the tour group headed out along the Champs-Élysées, Ricki made not just contemporary blackness visible but lifted the veil of Europe to reveal black histories all over the city. Paris's most famous avenue was no longer a place of high-end boutiques and suggestions of white European greatness but evocative of the 369th infantry regiment, also known as the Harlem Hellfighters (due to being comprised mostly of men of African-American and Puerto Rican descent – who made up the cultural language of Harlem in the early twentieth century). Stationed in France during the First World War, they fought bravely in the trenches, setting a record for the longest deployment of any unit, playing an instrumental role in several key battles and winning the French Croix de Guerre medal for bravery. Despite this acknowledgement, when the war was won, US government officials refused to allow them to join the 1919 Champs-Élysées victory march, a racist PR manoeuvre the Allies would later replicate at the end of the Second World War with regard to black soldiers from the French colonies. The Hellfighters managed to leave a lasting legacy not just through their bravery but also through their music; under the direction of band leader James Reese Europe, they essentially introduced France to jazz and doo wop, an indelible mark no member of the government could erase.

When we arrived at the Arc de Triomphe, Ricki told us how the monument had been turned into a symbol of freedom and a place of pilgrimage by African-American artists and intellectuals who had visited the city, from Frederick Douglass to Booker T. Washington and Countee Coullen, ever since, said Ricki, 'William Wells Brown climbed its stairs in 1849 and described how "you could look out on a city where you are finally free, even from bounty hunters and fugitive slave laws" '. This imagining of Paris still holds weight for many, and I saw it in the eyes of Jimmy when we were on the bus driving towards Richard Wright's former home in the suburb of Neuilly. He was looking wistfully out of the window at the coffee-coloured townhouses and the stylish Parisians filling the streets and found it hard to believe that anybody actually lived in such a place. The whole city was, for Jimmy, a film set, with even its homeless people appearing to him as something oddly picturesque – this wasn't Skid Row in Los Angeles, it was *Les Mis* poverty, Roma women in headscarves begging beneath dramatic Napoleonic fountains and scattering pigeons. He turned to Ricki and asked if she liked it in Paris.

Because everything he'd said so far had seemed loaded, Ricki was unsure where he was going with the question and asked him what he meant.

'Do. You. Like. It. Here?' he repeated pointedly, and Ricki told him that yes, of course she did, and wanted to know why he asked, and suddenly his facial expression became earnest.

'Because I do, too. I could live here, you know. I walk around the streets and it feels as though people don't see me. In a good way, I mean. It's like I ain't black here, I'm just a human being.'

'Well, that's because you're an American, Jimmy,' said Ricki. 'The Afro-French have a very different experience here than you or me. This idea African-Americans have about racism not existing in France is ridiculous because it does, *in abundance*. Even if you look at some of the comparatively successful African-Americans who came and lived in France – Baldwin, Wright, Baker and many others – you'll notice that they all died alone, and often penniless.' Jimmy, though, was too busy admiring the view out of the bus window – he'd barely listened to a thing Ricki had said all day and, more and more, I found it harder to concentrate on the information Ricki was giving me because Jimmy had started to sort of take me under his wing – I would be taking two tours for the price of one: Ricki Stevenson's tour of black Paris, and Jimmy Brown's tour of his own life, a life that at least partly explained the romance of Europe held by black Americans.

Much like my dad and many of the people Ricki mentioned who managed to make a home in Europe, as a young man Jimmy had escaped a violently racist America for a Europe that perhaps exoticized African-Americans but at least wasn't lynching them. He left as a seventeen-year-old with the US Navy's submarine division in the 1960s, hating white people, he said. That's when he found what he called his 'promised land'. And the name of this utopia?

'Scotland. We were stationed in Holy Loch and what I loved about that place was that nobody was pre-judged on race but instead on faith – it wasn't about whether you were black or white, it was about being Protestant or Catholic. That's when I realized it wasn't white people who were my enemies, but *American* whites.'

Jimmy spent two years in Scotland in total and described them as the best years of his life, one experience in particular changing his views. Looking over at Ricki, Clemence and his wife, Niecy, to make sure we were a safe distance from them, he started whispering about a woman called Bey'ey.

'The Scottish girls loved us, but this one girl Bey'ey was my true Scottish romance. I met her at the pub and we hit it off! We went back to her house that night and let's just say we had *a lot* of fun. But it was like I fell asleep in heaven and then woke up in hell. Bey'ey invited me downstairs and her entire family was there sitting at the table, looking up at me. Can you imagine that shit? Four white faces staring at me, a *black* man coming down from the bedroom with Bey'ey – their white family member!'

I kept wondering if I was hearing the name right, and initially presumed Bey'ey was some traditional Scottish name I'd never heard before, but I came to realize her name was Betty and, all these years later, Jimmy was still pronouncing it the way he'd heard it come out of Scottish mouths phonetically.

'I was in absolute shock! Thought I was a dead man and couldn't believe Bey'ey would set me up like that. I was ready to run and get my ass the hell out of there, but the family just looked up at me and welcomed me down for something to eat. I sat there having breakfast with this white family and I could not believe it. Things changed from that point on.'

Every time I think of Jimmy now, I also wonder where Scottish Betty might be and whether her family have any idea of the role they played in shifting the views of a bitter black man and setting him free – not from slavery but from his own crippling prejudice. It reminded me of the potential of working-class solidarity, and how tragically those bonds have been continually undermined by people in power, how the presence of black people has been spun into a threat rather than an opportunity to strengthen working-class culture.

We headed north towards Neuilly, an upmarket district and formerly the home and hangout spot of a number of black intellectuals from the 30s to the 60s, including James Baldwin and his sometime friend, mentor and later rival Richard Wright. Just before entering the district, Ricki stopped us on a bridge overlooking a bypass. 'See that stream of cars down there? That piece of road circles right around central Paris and is known as Le Périphérique. Everything outside the periphery is considered a suburb. We are about to enter one of the nice suburbs of Paris, but the French word for 'suburb' usually has connotations of something much less quaint than in English – as you can see, there is a different world outside that romantic depiction of Paris on postcards.'

Ricki pointed towards a series of spooky white tower blocks standing ominously in the distance, illuminated by a low sun and shimmering in the hazy pollution like an otherworldly apparition. It really was another world. Ricki told us that some say the French word for 'suburb', *banlieue*, comes from the words *banissement* ('banishment') and *lieu* ('place'). *Banlieue*: 'place of banishment'.

In the early nineteenth century Paris was a city rampant with crime and disease so, funded largely by colonial riches from Africa, Napoleon III decided to clear the slums, commissioning city planner Georges-Eugène Haussmann to create a new Paris with better sewage systems and wider streets that could be patrolled and controlled, to replace the shady, revolution-friendly labyrinth the city had become. Aside from the newer streets being easier to police, the poor and unwanted were also driven further out of the centre of Paris because of the higher rents these new, luxurious townhouses commanded. It was the era that gave birth to the Paris the world knows and loves but, today, beyond the periphery, the 'banished ones' still reside, now often immigrants from West and North Africa, as well as Roma travelling communities who are cut off from the centre of the city geographically and imaginatively. Napoleon and Haussmann may have pushed the poor out, but it was another legendary architect, Le Corbusier, who, in contrast to the extravagant Haussmann (and, in many ways, attempting to serve as an antithesis), created a template for the concrete tower blocks that are home to such social unrest today.

With a design principle called Unité d'habitation, Le Corbusier gave birth to a new architectural idea that would spread across France and the rest of the world like wildfire in the postwar years and, in essence, spawn the birth of what we now know as the Projects, or council estates. If you visit the original Unité d'habitation, built between 1947 and 1952 in Marseille, today, a far superior building to the many low-budget high-rise imitations that it inspired (and containing apartments that now sell for hundreds of thousands of euros), it feels more like an impressive sculpture than a pleasing place to dwell, a piece of art you'd appreciate in a gallery but wouldn't necessarily have at home or, in this case, *as* your home. Both Haussmann and Le Corbusier were ahead of their time and appear to have had good intentions, but between them they created a landscape perfect for breeding angst in poor communities. Through his luxurious housing ideals Haussmann first pushed the poor out of the heart of the city, and then, with depressing austerity and modernist experimentation, Le Corbusier pushed them up into the sky, into faceless concrete cages sandwiched on top of one another, later left to fall into decay by the state.

The area of the city Richard Wright and James Baldwin inhabited in the 40s and 50s was Haussmann's Paris, and Neuilly, now among the most expensive districts in the city, was even then unobtainable for most of the Afro-French community. Walking down the main boulevard, through artisanal market stalls selling mouthwatering tapenades, cheeses and saucissons, kicking through autumn leaves which matched the warm, neutral hues of the buildings, then looking up at beautiful iron balconies jutting out from windows with wooden French shutters, it was easy to see what inspired this unashamedly gushing love letter Wright, author of the polemical American classic *Native Son* (1940), wrote about his adoptive home in the 40s:

> Yes, the effect of Paris is deep! Paris does something to one and what it does is good – I love this, my adopted city. Naturally in such an atmosphere there is no race tension or conflict. Men are not prejudged here on the basis of their skin or nationality, and I have never heard a Frenchman tell anybody to 'go back where you came from'. I have encountered among the French no social snobbery: men are accepted as individuals, the more individualistic a man is the more acceptable he is . . . The French are a civilised people and to live among them is a joy. 'sois raisonnable', that is; 'be reasonable' is their motto.[1]

Only a few days later I would find myself wandering around a *banlieue* where Wright's words, the type that still so often inform African-American ideas about Paris, tragically contradicted the modern-day reality for many of its black population. As informative as the tour of black Paris was – and I got the feeling Ricki was tailoring it to this particular group – the focus on stories of expats and the general feeling of African-American exceptionalism began to frustrate me a little.

Clemence had mentioned how difficult it sometimes was to tell the ethnicity of Parisians, and during my time in France I, too, noticed how many 'white' people had a complexion not too unlike my own, with hair of a similar consistency. Ricki laughed and said, 'Girl, when it rains their hair goes frizzy just like ours! But if you look at where France sits in Europe, and its southern shores, you can see why that would be the case. There are strong North African roots here, dating back to the Moorish travellers. Africa has been entering Europe through France for centuries.' This was all well and good, but I wanted to feel more of this Afro-French influence on the tour.

At the church in the place de la Madeleine, Ricki evoked the story of Josephine Baker, whose funeral was held there. 'The only American woman to receive full military honours,' she said proudly. Baker died peacefully in her bed in 1975, surrounded by paper clippings of all her rave reviews, just days after her critically acclaimed retrospective show *Josephine à Bobino*, in honour of her fifty-year career – and also, truth be told, a desperate attempt to escape insolvency. When she started out, Baker's talent as a performer received a lukewarm reception in America; it was when she was invited to perform at the legendary Revue Nègre in Paris – a show born out of the jazz and doo-wop music African-American soldiers brought with them during the First World War – that she became an overnight sensation in France. It was 1925, the year the International Exposition of Modern Decorative and Industrial Arts gave birth to art deco, and Paris was considered the most progressive and modern city in the world. Art deco was influenced by cubism, and it's no secret that cubism was influenced by the African sculptural tradition: modern buildings, paintings and designs were suffused with stylized African motifs and symbolism. This is what 'modern' meant in 1925: a modern society thought of itself as an outward-looking one underpinned by frivolity; steam liners and steam engines came with global travel and exploration; automobiles were fast; and avant-garde art movements like surrealism and edgy nightclubs laughed in the face of anything stuffy or old-fashioned. Racism was stuffy and old-fashioned, and in Paris a love of black culture became the hippest, most subversive way to show you were roaring along with the 20s. Josephine Baker thrived in this atmosphere, as she played up to and mocked old notions of the 'black savage', dressed in leopard-print costume and dancing wildly to bongo drums. The whole point of appreciating Baker was to show you were cultured enough to be in on the irony. On this tour, however, there was little about the Francophone African movement that came after Baker and took this colonial critique to new levels over the next two or three decades.

Baker and her peers brought with them to Paris not just their talents but the seeds of an entire culture that had fuelled their creative fruition: the Harlem Renaissance. This moment in America during the 20s connected and galvanized the first generation of a black diaspora who had been born free and produced groundbreaking work across literature, political theory, art and music. By the 30s the Great Depression had quelled the fires of this powerful black activity in Harlem, and by the 50s Langston Hughes described it as 'a dream deferred', referring to how the crippling poverty in Harlem didn't align with the American dream. But in the imagination of many – and I don't want to get too romantic about this – the Harlem of the 20s embodied a black diaspora dream, which I think became a 'dream dispersed'. The Harlem Renaissance and many of its biggest proponents scattered across the globe, some making ties with the international movement in the USSR, while others moved to Western Europe – more often than not, to Paris. The influence of these black American intellectuals, who themselves had been powered by the worldly, diasporic flavour of the Harlem Renaissance, was merged with the experience of black French thinkers and scholars who'd moved to

Paris from the French colonies for their studies, most notably Aimé Césaire from Martinique, Senegalese poet Léopold Sédar Senghor and Léon Dumas from French Guiana. Together, they fuelled what would become known as the Negritude movement.

These intellectuals weren't directly involved with the Harlem Renaissance but were figuratively and literally Renaissance men; their poetry was influenced by jazz but suffused with politics; Senghor would later become the first president of Senegal, Aimé Césaire became a mayor in Martinique after working for some time as a teacher and Dumas was elected as a Guinean representative in the French National Assembly. They were anti-colonialists and, in a country where the black population is even today somewhat divided along hierarchical cultural lines (those from the Caribbean being perceived as closer to being 'French' than their West African and Maghrebian counterparts), brought black African and black Caribbean communities together by setting up journals, spreading Marxist thought and organizing cultural events across France and Francophone Africa and the Antilles. They disseminated their poetry and politics in a spirit of celebration, provocatively suggesting that if blackness wasn't a construct, and did exist as a race, it existed as the seat of civilization and the height of art and beauty. Negritude used the racial injustices prevalent in European societies to question and demean the West's idea of itself as the most civilized collection of cultures in history; the true sign of being backward and uncultured in an increasingly connected and modern world was, they argued, racism. The European, supposedly 'enlightened civilization' had produced Hitler and the Holocaust, dropped the atomic bomb, massacred millions of Congolese and lynched black men and women – who, really, were the savage animals? The Negritude movement drew attention to some of the horrific massacres enacted in the name of Western civilization in order to challenge the predominant and prevailing imperial narrative of the West as heroes, givers of culture and kindness, and it convinced not just black Africans and Caribbeans but also white Europeans. But as I was about to find out on my tour of black Paris, it hadn't managed to convince everyone.

'Welcome to Little Africa!' said Ricki, as we alighted another bus and finally immersed ourselves in some Afro-French culture rather than an expat American one. 'Little Africa' was Ricki's name for the neighbouring areas of Château Rouge and Barbès-Rochechouart, and we were greeted by a crowded and discombobulating street full of Senegalese, Cameroonian, Algerian, Tunisian and Moroccan market stalls. The Haussmann buildings that cocooned it all were losing their battle to stay Parisian clichés, their façades and interiors reverse-colonized by African aesthetics. Senegalese women bartered for a better price at fruit stalls and old men gossiped on mismatched chairs planted on street corners as Arabic men entered a makeshift mosque. My African-American friends were in a state of shock. 'This is insane,' said Jimmy, about seven or eight times, and then, 'It's like we on 125th,' referring to the street in New York that runs through Harlem.

What struck me most was how out of place they all looked as African-Americans, how frigid and conservative they suddenly appeared. Jimmy kept telling Niecy to watch her bag and Clemence was on edge, as though worried about touching anything and getting dirty. There was a nervous haughtiness about the way they held themselves. I, on the other hand, felt completely relaxed: Château Rouge wasn't so different to Firth Park, where I grew up, or the part of Peckham I lived in in London. Perhaps, as Jimmy suggested, it wasn't so different from areas of America either, but it was more that the image before them – perhaps 90 per cent brown skinned and thoroughly African – didn't square with the images Paris (and the rest of Europe, for that matter) shares with the outside world. America has long had a way of commodifying blackness – indeed, Africans were brought over as commodities in the trans-Atlantic slave trade – but the offshoot of this was that blackness had been etched into the brand stamp of America. The US exports its blackness; Europe does not.

The stores in Château Rouge were fiercely independent, with beautiful DIY signage, fonts painted by hand, very slightly off-kilter, like old Coca-Cola logos on Haitian beach shacks. They sold oddments: outdated electronics, Ghanaian fabrics, mixtapes from Côte d'Ivoire, specific ingredients for African recipes and palates, and intricate haircuts. Château Rouge was brimming with treasure and junk – the backwash of second-hand one-offs from Africa and Europe, antiqued by journeys between the two.

I started taking photographs and was immediately clocked by a Senegalese woman who didn't want hers taken. West African women tended to be the hardest to photograph candidly because they were always on the lookout and very vocal if they caught you. 'No photo! No photo!' she shouted angrily, creating a bit of a scene. This was all fair game, I thought; it is an incredibly rude thing to take a photograph of somebody without asking. I was never bothered when somebody got angry; I just apologized, deleted the photograph and put my camera away. But Clemence and Jimmy took exception to the way the woman shouted at me and opened up a world of bigotry I found fairly shocking. If I ever had any ideas about an unspoken brotherhood among the black diaspora, they were about to be challenged by my American companions.

'I bet that woman is here illegally – or probably doing something illegal,' said Clemence, snootily.

Jimmy, with a look of anger and disgust, added, 'I bet half the people here are illegals – that is where France's problems are, for sure: too many people have clocked on to a good thing and are draining the economy.'

Ricki corrected him: 'Actually, this area has its own economy, and a healthy one at that – money circulates the area twelve times before leaving and it is very self-sufficient.'

But Jimmy began to sound more and more like Donald Trump. As we walked through the crowded streets to a restaurant Ricki had recommended, I could see he was getting himself worked up about the woman who had shouted at me.

'Look at the way they dress – it's because a lot of them are stupid, dressing up all multicoloured and shit. They look like clowns. That's why Africa is so messed up, because they're corrupt and ignorant. And they ugly too! That's why they use all that colour – to hide how ugly they are.'

Racism and prejudice are cages – a prison sentence alienating those who hold these attitudes from the beautiful diversity of the world – and I pity people with those afflictions. But these comments by Jimmy, who had told me he'd experienced the worst kind of racism in America, hugely disappointed me. I had been enjoying his mild irreverence until then, but his outburst made me cool off in our conversations, as he kept on trying to impress me with controversial and contrarian remarks. Perhaps he realized, and a little later, when he'd calmed down, he started to change his tune, and almost as an apology said to me, 'I love the colours here. I think Europe needs more colour.' Then he told me a strange story about how he had worked in Alaska, helping to lay pipes for the Trans-Alaska pipeline system. 'Let me tell you something, son, when I worked on those pipes there were times where I'd spend up to two months without seeing another soul, and that taught me a very valuable lesson about humanity. It taught me that other people's thoughts are like viruses and you become infected with ideas about the world that aren't your own. Spending all that time alone stripped everything away until all I was left with was who I *really* am.'

I didn't know what to do with this information, and was saved by Ricki, who told us we'd reached our last spot on the tour: her favourite Senegalese restaurant.

Ricki had been a soldier. The tour had been a challenging one: Clemence turned her nose up at everything, Niecy didn't seem to understand anything and Jimmy and I spent most of our time back from the group, him talking, me trying to make sure I memorized everything he was saying to write down later. I felt a bit sorry for her at the end of it all; even this big 'Ta da!' at the end of a long day had turned sour. The food, I thought, was excellent, and as we

ate we were serenaded by a man playing his kora (a harp-like West African instrument), but after a few spoonfuls Jimmy said, 'I wanna get out of here,' and Clemence whispered to Niecy, 'I bet the hygiene is poor.'

After the meal we said our goodbyes and exchanged email addresses, promising to stay in touch, and there was suddenly an odd sense of camaraderie, or perhaps acknowledgement, the type you give someone when you know you've just experienced something with them that, for better or worse, you'll remember for a long time. I was glad to have met Jimmy and Niecy Brown, Clemence with her beret, and elegant, knowledgeable Ricki, but I left the tour with no doubt in my mind that, despite my best impressions, and the blood in my veins, I would have to look beyond African America for answers about my situation as a black man in Europe and orientate myself more confidently along an Afropean axis.

An Afropean *Flâneur*

Leaving the tour group at the entrance to the Métro, I took a walk through Château Rouge's shadowy backstreets to my hostel. Perhaps because of the area's name, I noticed more red light than I otherwise would have: warm hues seemed to leak out under doorways, around corners, out of shop windows, reflecting against damp pavements. There were hawkers on the streets, and smells of sizzling meat mingled with a subtle fragrance of side-street trash, rotting leftovers from the market fruit stalls and pools of fishy water from the ice that had been keeping seafood fresh. Shopkeepers, whose opening hours looked as if they were based on customer demand that day, watched bad-quality footage of African TV shows on small, boxy televisions sets. In the darkness it reminded me a little of wandering around the Sierra Leonean capital, Freetown, at night, with that same wild magic, half threatening, half welcoming, an unofficial and off-grid enclave that disrupted Paris's persuasive picture-postcard narrative. And though I was on edge, slightly, I was also somewhat relieved, feeling threatened not out of estrangement but out of recognition – Château Rouge was Firth Park and Peckham, and at night it was wise to keep your wits about you. The opposite attitude is taken by the oblivious hipsters one can find getting pissed and being loud, who enter such places in the same spirit of intrepid colonialism their forebears did, sleeping with natives, getting into trouble and getting out as soon as it gets too real.

It struck me that, however long I ended up staying in Paris, I should base myself in this 'Little Africa' if I was going to become more acquainted with black culture in the city. I looked around for hotels and found four or five hovel-ish places, all run by Algerians, and was turned away at every place – a surprise, because my personal experience had been that Arabs make the world's most gracious hosts. All over France, though, I noticed that Arabic communities, especially Algerians, had been rendered tough- and brutal-looking in a way that cannot be said of many other nations they live in – what was this country doing to them?

Not only was each hotel I visited full but, it appeared, indefinitely so. At one place, with stained curtains and a fraying red carpet with a 70s-looking floral pattern which, judging by its state, was probably from the 70s, I asked the receptionist if they had any rooms. I say 'receptionist'; what I mean is a man wearing a T-shirt and sandals who, with a frown, asked me what I wanted. 'No, full, full,' he said, shooing me away. 'When is the next room available?' I asked, knowing I would never stay there anyway. 'Not for very, very long time,' said the man. Was Château Rouge really in such high demand?

So, remaining at my hostel in Montmartre over the next few days, I was drawn temporarily into the romantic vision of Paris, the official version it wants the world to see, *flâneur*ing through the city and lulled into tourism. Very few paths in central Paris aren't part of some sort of tourist trail, every boulevard leading to a priceless piece of art or a scene from a famous movie. I traced Hemingway's steps in Montparnasse, passing the haunts of Gertrude Stein, F. Scott Fitzgerald, Salvador Dalí, Pablo Picasso and others, and paid eight euros for a coffee in an old drinking 'dive' of theirs called La Closerie des Lilas. The interior of this brasserie was sumptuous, with dark, glossy oak and burgundy seating gleaming under dim lighting, so that it looked as if the place was made out of chocolate and caramel. I'm sure it was more down to earth in the 20s, but Hemingway was a hipster: one of many writers and artists of a certain era who cynically presented themselves as being a broke, struggling artist scraping a living in Paris; it was with great bitterness that I discovered nearly all of them were loaded. It was all lies: if any of it got too much for them, colonizing the picturesque squalor of 20s Paris, they could get their parents to pay for a flight home to upper-middle-class America, or wherever. I'd worked my arse off for ten years solid to afford this trip around Europe, and even then I ended up going pretty heavily in debt to fund it. This later made me wonder if that's why I saw so few fellow young black backpackers on my journey. Every spare penny they acquired was being spent on survival: education, building a home, eating regularly, and so on. Perhaps that's why festivals, camping and other carefree pursuits are usually white, middle-class affairs. To starve as Hemingway described in *A Moveable Feast* (1964) is the highest of luxuries; suffering as experiment, pain for literary purposes, frugality for fun. So many of those scruffy creatives from that time – the great names of the early twentieth century – had talent and skill made possible by free time and frivolity. Creating important art back then and – more importantly – at the same time holding on to your integrity was an expensive pursuit, unless you let it destroy you, like it did so many black artists throughout the years. But fuck it, there I was, broke and brown-skinned and strolling through late-autumn afternoons, trying not to think too much about the future . . . musing, happening upon, writing, wandering, photographing, documenting and experiencing Paris's famous monuments with new eyes: Europe through the gaze of a genuinely broke but unencumbered black traveller, gradually beginning to blur out the suggestive Parisian backdrops and pull focus on the invisible blackness in the foreground.

Wandering the grounds of the Eiffel Tower, for instance, was for me less about a grandiose monument of past glory and more a journey through Paris's struggling immigrant communities: West African men selling Eiffel Tower miniatures and Rasta bands, Indians hawking squidgy toys and low-tech plastic spinning helicopters that were apparently irresistible to any kid who passed by, and disenfranchised Romas begging and holding plaques that claimed they were deaf and mute. In almost all the cities I visited, the Romas have a reputation of being the dregs of Europe. Nobody wanted them around and, on the face of it, it would be easy to come to such a conclusion – criminality appeared to be rife, and the men and women walking around Paris pretending to be deaf and mute were ubiquitous. But systematically speaking, the Romas really were deaf and mute – they had little representation in seats of power and had cultivated an unofficial life estranged from European society in order to survive.* They were persecuted across Eastern Europe after the fall of the Soviet Empire and the subsequent break-up of Czechoslovakia (in the Czech Republic, over a quarter of a million were refused citizenship by the new establishment). This led to high unemployment and displacement, with communities making the most of being able to travel freely when more Eastern European countries joined the single market. Things haven't been much better for the Roma in the West of Europe. Over the last few years dozens of Roma settlements have been demolished and, in 2009, in a scene uncomfortably reminiscent of Nazi convoys of Jewish immigrants, armed police used Paris's tram system to cart Romas off after raiding a settlement near Bobigny station, which is, poignantly, where a memorial stands in honour of the 22,400 Jews taken to concentration camps from there during wartime occupation. France deported tens of thousands of Romany gypsies after former president Nicolas Sarkozy specifically targeted people of Romanian and Bulgarian heritage

---

* At the end of my trip, back in Paris just before getting the train home, two Roma kids, perhaps a brother and a sister, handed me a card that read that they were deaf and mute. As the younger child placed the laminated A4 card in front of me, obscuring the view of my phone, which was resting on a table, his sister swiped it. I didn't realize it was missing until five minutes later, and it contained around 10,000 words worth of notes. It should be noted that when I later spoke to a Roma activist and scholar, she asked, 'How did you know they were Roma?' The simple answer was that I didn't know; I could only assume. The Parisian police told me that they were Roma, and that I would never get my phone back. Before I could ask any more questions they gave me a crime reference number for insurance and shunted me out the door.

who weren't in work, despite those countries being part of the European Union. Some countries were *more* European than others, it seems, and all this was an early sign of the troubles facing a New Europe that was slowly attempting to integrate the East into federalism.

As I made my way across the esplanade a guy with dreads and a beaming smile walked over and asked me where I was from. 'England,' I said. While I was answering he had already begun to tie a bracelet on my arm in an elaborate criss-crossing fashion. 'How much?' I asked. 'For you, brother, not-ting,' and, not taking 'England' for an answer, asked, 'Where are you *really* from?' What this question really means is: 'Why have you got brown skin?' When white people ask it, it always seems loaded, as if to insinuate, to quote Caryl Phillips, 'reduce yourself, stranger'. When somebody with brown skin asks me this question, however, the reverse seems to be true. It suggests, 'You're like me, you're from where I'm from, expand on this, brother.' I told him that my dad is African-American and that a recent DNA test revealed I was from modern-day Togo, Sierra Leone, Gambia, Côte d'Ivoire, Ghana and Senegal. He smiled and said, 'I'm from Ghana and my friend over there is from Salone.' He beckoned his friend over and there were more brother-isms, but I wondered if, as soon as I handed over some cash, I would go from being their brother back to being a random tourist.

'How is life treating you in Paris, brother? I asked the Sierra Leonian.

He said, in an accent that was as African-American as it was West African, 'No good for black man, brother! No jobs – I been here eight months and it's too racist here. Maybe I go to the UK.'

He looked at me to see whether or not I thought it was a good idea, but I had no answers. Britain seemed to me to be reverting back to the 50s with its backwards, misdirected vilification of immigrants. Having just started my journey around Europe, I was already getting the sense that I'd probably be hard pressed to find a spot where the same couldn't be said.

The Ghanaian was nearly finished with the bracelet, which he tied by attaching a piece of string to my little finger to hold the design in place. Then he took out some nail clippers and offered to cut my nails. I declined then asked, 'How much'? 'It's free to you, but if you'd like to offer a donation that is okay.' He was happy with two euros and I was happy with my bracelet, in red, black, green and yellow string, which I like to imagine he chose because they are the colours of Pan-Africanism but which he probably chose as a reference to Bob Marley. It was amazing how many black men I met in Europe, fresh from Africa, who had constructed outward identities that were pastiches of black diaspora cultural icons produced in and adopted by the West . . . variants of Bob Marley, 2Pac, Drake, and so on. It was about survival: they knew full well that some forms of blackness are more acceptable than others, that there is a hierarchy imposed by the white gaze.

Further along, I watched other African men – always men – work in shifts, unravelling a bag and turning it into a mat on which to display their stock. Though various immigrant communities shared the experience of scratching a living in a country and continent that doesn't want them there, they kept themselves to themselves as insular tribes haunting separate sections of monuments. On the surface level, at least, there was little interaction between the West Africans up top when you first approach the Champs de Mars and the Indians down at the base of the tower, yet the unofficial commerce before me operated like a well-rehearsed waltz. Until, that is, something sparked mass panic among the sellers; it was as though the ground was shuddering from an earthquake. That's when I realized the bags that doubled as display mats were ingeniously designed, with pull cords at each corner of the fabric. In seconds the bags enveloped in one fluid movement all they had for sale in a Santa-style sack, and in the blink of an eye all the sellers were making a dash for it.

I asked one of the Indian men what was happening and he pointed down to the Eiffel Tower and said, calmly, 'Police.' When

I looked around I realized that nobody was panicking after all –
this was standard procedure, but the impressive speed at which
everybody dispersed made everything seem frenetic.

There must have been some sort of secret code, because it was
another couple of minutes or so before I saw any police on the
scene. They were chasing a young African man, who was eventually wrestled to the ground violently, and as they handcuffed and
carted him off, I took a few photographs and got caught by a
policeman who chastised me angrily, giving me a look that said I
should probably scarper, along with the hawkers.

The charged atmosphere of Paris continued as I made my way
back through Montparnasse and followed rue de Rivoli on to the
Champs-Élysées, where I noticed a large group of well-dressed
black men and women walking like they were on a mission. I
joined them and asked a striking-looking woman called Shirley,
tall with dark skin, drugged eyelids, a shaved head and perfectly
symmetrical features (I later found out she was a catwalk model
as well as an activist), what was going on.

'What is going on is France thinks they can treat us however
they want, and we've had enough!' she said.

World-famous French perfumier Jean-Paul Guerlain had
appeared on long-running primetime news and culture show *13
Heures* and said, without blinking an eye, 'I worked like a nigger
[on my new fragrance]. I don't know if niggers have always worked
like that, but anyway . . .' To 'work like a nigger', Guerlain later
claimed, was a harmless phrase used commonly by people of his
generation, you know, back in the good old days, when it was okay
to be racist.

When I asked Shirley why he would feel comfortable using this
language on a major TV show, she said that it always happened in
France and that white people had become so accustomed to nobody
raising their voices that the recent rise of discontent from black
communities had come as something of a shock. Shirley was right
about the black community finally standing up to racism, quite

literally: about five hundred black French men and women were standing outside the Guerlain store on the Champs-Élysées, and when I visited the anti-Guerlain Facebook page there were thousands of page likes.

The scenes were far from the unorganized violence of the 2005 French riots. In fact, the demonstration was a fiercely intellectual response: many of the spokespeople for the black community were middle-class black academics, creatives and intellectuals, such as Rokhaya Diallo, a columnist for French station Canal +, who was recently dismissed from a governmental advisory body when members of a right-wing party wrote a letter of complaint. Her crime was essentially being black and female and speaking up for others in her position. Here, though, Rokhaya was in good company. Ananias Léki Dago, part of a wave of incredibly gifted young Francophone African street photographers, was the official demonstration documentarian, and he was joined by Isabelle Boni-Claverie, a Sorbonne graduate and award-winning director of French and Côte d'Ivoire heritage. There were families and students, fashionistas and social workers, in attendance, giving the manifestation an elegant appearance. Here was the more positive interplay of cultures I'd originally been hoping to find: people who were at once French and black and yet represented something that didn't lend itself to hyphenation. They were people for whom 'Afropean' was a new configuration of ideas, connected to Africa and Europe but transcending both. Those second-, third- and fourth-generation faces of new multicultural Europe; sons and daughters of post-colonialism, or perhaps decolonialism. They had been educated by Europe, paid taxes and took part in society yet were also often told to go home, that they didn't belong, didn't look right. I saw them as the coming together of exponentially increasing cultural transactions since the days of conquest and as a clear and coherent culture unifying W. E. B. Du Bois's 'double consciousness', which he described as 'two souls, two thoughts, two unreconciled strivings; two warring ideals in one dark body,

whose dogged strength alone keeps it from being torn asunder'.[1]
The lines between blackness and Europeanness, even at such a
charged event, were being blurred.

This particular demonstration was like seeing the Afropean
struggle up close and personal. Jean-Paul Guerlain represented old
European privilege, as the inheritor of a dynasty started by his
great-grandfather, who sold perfume to Napoleon III in the mid-
nineteenth century. Napoleon III was the man who opened up
France's foreign policy in order to extend the French Empire and
encourage the country's second age of colonial rule. Indeed, the
Paris of the Champs-Élysées and Haussmann boulevards was
made possible only because of the riches brought from the continued expansion of colonialism and slavery from the seventeenth
century through to the nineteenth century, the type that funded
the Industrial Revolution and led to much of Europe's prosperity.

The store was covered in red, white and black banners reading

'Boycott Guerlain', and Renée Clément, who was from the pan-African OÉUA (Organization of the United States of Africa) was shouting through a megaphone at the crowds. Her hair was scraped back and she wore scarlet lipstick, making her look elegant in a severe kind of way, like the boss of a Fortune 500 company. She was surrounded by members of her organization and by many other black activists, all with the same look, and the scene reminded me of a 70s Black Panther rally: the form was important to the function of the words; the group emitted angry but composed and intellectual black power. They were all dressed in black stream-lined clothes, roll necks and leathers, Afros and braids, and the gathering crowd and activists all appeared to know each other. In Europe, I don't think I'd personally ever witnessed a scene so black and organized and beautiful.

I thought of a visit to New York I'd made recently, when I met up with Afro-French soul music group Les Nubians, which comprises sisters Hélène and Célia Faussart. They were born in Paris, moved to Chad as children, then returned to France eight years later, where they made a name for themselves gigging at poetry slams and cafés in Paris and Bordeaux. After the release of their Grammy-nominated debut album *Princesses Nubiennes*, they re-located to Bedford–Stuyvesant in Brooklyn, right around the corner from where my father grew up. When I asked what had inspired the move, Hélène told me, 'We left France because they didn't know what to do with us. They loved to promote "la *black* musique", using the English word, but we said, "No, if you want to say we are making black music, then take ownership, use the French word for "black" and call it "la musique noire". But they really didn't like that. France hates to recognize race, yet they were okay to call us black in another language.' In Brooklyn, they had found a creative community of black artists and musicians, or a borough that Teju Cole often describes as 'one of the world's great African cities' – Talib Kweli and Erykah Badu were their neighbours – and there they could sustain their black French identities in a way that was denied to them in France. And that is what Europe's black diaspora needs more than ever: connection and collaboration to create a climate than can sustain plurality and produce a louder voice when facing racism. It was the power I was feeling on the Champs-Élysées that day.

It was a sunny Saturday on Paris's most famous stretch of road and the demonstration had caused Guerlain to close its flagship store. This wasn't the first demonstration either, and it wouldn't be the last. There wasn't any notice on the store to explain why it wasn't open, but what could they say? *Our master perfumer called black people niggers and it looks like there might be some around today, so we're closed. Business will resume when everyone's forgotten what was said.* But nobody did forget and, thanks to the continued protests and pressure by the 'Boycott Guerlain' groups, Jean-Paul Guerlain, the last family master perfumer still connected to the business, was taken to court for his actions, resulting in the brand's parent company severing all ties.

The crowd outside Guerlain grew larger and louder and carried banners that read, 'I don't work like a nigger either,' and I noticed a group of tall, imposing black men moving through the signs, dressed in black and with the aura of an entourage of security guards. Leading them was a guy who had the presence of a heavyweight boxer, Rex Kazadi, a former gang member from the *banlieues* who'd turned a corner and was now taking part in politics. This group of men oversaw the proceedings with a certain amount of detachment, then wandered off up the Champs-Élysées like they were on some kind of mission. They walked so purposefully I decided to follow them and, when I finally caught up, I asked Rex where they were going. He shot me a stare and said, 'Revolution is not about talking, it's about action.'

We entered an expensive-looking shopping mall near L'Opéra and headed straight over to the Guerlain counter. There were perhaps ten men, all over six feet tall, and they circled the kiosk with their backs to it, staring sternly out at the petit-bourgeois

consumers. It was clear nobody would be shopping at Guerlain today. I was also dressed in black, and for a while I didn't know if I was part of this rogue demonstration or not. Before leaving I managed to get Rex's number and, after a few texts back and forth, he said he would meet me in Clichy-sous-Bois, one of France's most notorious *banlieues*.

Four Days in Clichy-sous-Bois

Clichy-sous-Bois is only fifteen kilometres from the centre of Paris, but getting there is inefficient and disorienting – in the time it took me to reach this eastern Parisian suburb I could almost have made it back to Britain. The area isn't served by any motorways, A-roads, trains or Métros, and the hour-and-a-half commute seemed designed to discourage the journey. In fact, besides Rex Kazadi, everyone I spoke to discouraged the journey. As I set off into what was, in my imagination, some dark urban wilderness, I reminded myself that I, too, was from a place with high immigration and a bad reputation on the outskirts of town and had often felt that my neck of the woods had been misrepresented. 'Neck of the woods' is an apt expression, *sous-bois* meaning 'under the woods', and I was keen to see what stories were hidden beneath the shrub of sensational headlines.

In order to prepare myself for the *banlieues* I read a book that was first published in 1990 and written by a man who had once owned an underground leftist publishing house responsible for the first edition of Frantz Fanon's *The Wretched of the Earth*. It was François Maspero's *Roissy Express*, in which the writer, along with photographer Anaïk Frantz, journeyed into the no-man's-land of Paris's suburbs and eloquently depicted the tensions bubbling in the *banlieues*, prophesying that the margins of French society were about to explode, as they did on a number of devastating occasions throughout the 90s and 00s. Describing this mood was no easy task, and Maspero's words clearly didn't come easily – at times, you get the sense that both writer and photographer were losing the will to live. The words 'Nothing to report' often made the final manuscript; 'falling behind with notes' was another admission. The *banlieues* were turning two creative intellectuals into unproductive loiterers, but at least they could leave, reassess, edit.

In the end, the suburbs they traversed weren't presented as something shocking; on the contrary, they appeared frighteningly banal:

> The squalor is disappearing and unemployment is rising: each generation has its own forms of poverty, which maybe only the next generation will really know how to comprehend. Exterior poverty, poverty for outside exhibition from the golden age of the picturesque – thank you, Robert Doisneau . . . is now only the fate of dropouts, tramps and drifters . . . [but] how do you photograph all the poverty behind the smooth walls, the silent walls – the poverty of depression and fear, of all the strains of everyday life, of so much loneliness?[1]

A contrast to 'official' Paris was evident even in the section of the Gare du Nord that serves the suburbs, located in a conjoining station known as Magenta. The line E platform was cramped with the shiny brown faces of perspiring commuters, drenched in a bizarrely dim lighting and with air that was thick and close, creating an agitated, overcrowded atmosphere. After wrestling my way on to the train, a group of young black teenage girls who were being loud and silly became more so when an old white woman – one of only a handful of white people who'd boarded the train – chastised them for their unruly behaviour. I didn't know then that these were the demographics that made up much of the suburbs: the young and black shunted with the elderly and white, all of them poor and with common interests but distanced from each other by culture and politics.

It didn't take long for the Haussmann utopia to morph into high-rise dystopia, the frilly Paris of our collective imagination quickly giving way to epic expanses of concrete tower blocks, all of various shapes but a uniformly grubby off-white in colour, jutting out like tobacco-stained teeth. Line E only reached as far as Le Raincy, which I thought would be a prelude of the horrors to come, but when I exited the station to find a bus to take me the rest of the way I felt a weird tinge of anticlimax. Le Raincy's modest tree-lined streets weren't what I expected, and had appeared much worse when I'd looked at them through the scratched windows of the train from a distance. There were neat walkways serving cafés only slightly too bland to be quaint, and it all felt more like what the word 'suburb' in England often conjures up in the imagination: uniformity and whiteness. Of course, not all Paris's suburbs are ghettos, and Clichy was still another seven kilometres away.

I didn't have a clue where I was going and instinctively latched myself on to a moving sway of brown faces, which led me to the right bus stop. I got on the 601 – one of only two buses that served Clichy – and realized I didn't even know where to get off, just that my bed for the next four nights would be in a twenty-five-euro hotel which on its website described itself unpromisingly as 'ultra-economical'. Hotel Formula One, the only hotel or B'n'B in Clichy-sous-Bois, was located on the boulevard Émile Zola, an interesting choice for a street name there because few novelists of France's Second Empire wrote of the era with more clarity than Zola, who, through his works of fiction, was critical of the corruption present during Napoleon III's reign. In *La Curée* (*The Kill*), first published in 1872 (the year before Napoleon's death and the year after the Second Empire fell in the Franco-Prussian War), through one of his protagonists, the unscrupulous reality magnate Saccard, he explains how civilians of nineteenth-century Paris weren't forced out of the centre of the city merely by the government but also by ruthless landlords intent on making a killing from the transformation.

> The mechanisms of expropriation, of the powerful system that for fifteen years turned Paris upside-down, creating fortunes and bringing ruin, are of the simplest. As soon as a new boulevard is decided upon, the surveyors draw up the plan in separate sections and establish a valuation of the buildings. As a rule, in the case of houses let as apartments, they add up the total amount of the rents after making enquiries, and are thus able to determine the approximate value.[2]

Landlords and investors with networks of knowledge would work this system by pushing up rent threefold when they caught wind of the new developments, and threatened eviction to those tenants who refused. Any who did object would be kicked out and replaced by a new fake tenant who would temporarily pay very little and sign anything they were asked to. The new houses would then be valued in accordance with the supposed rent being paid and could be sold on for three or four times more than they were worth, proving that gentrification isn't only a twenty-first-century phenomenon.

In that way, the new Paris of Haussmann was won, and those who could afford it inhabited the now much safer centre of the city, while the poor were pushed further and further out, creating the marooned, neglected communities found on the outskirts today. This is strikingly similar to the current rampant displacement of the working classes in London, as buildings such as the Heygate Estate in Elephant and Castle and Robin Hood Gardens in the Isle of Dogs are demolished and age-old communities torn apart to be replaced by new-builds bought up by foreign investment, sometimes by way of money laundering. A quota of the original residents are promised local rehousing, but building work is staggered until an offer of something random, often on the other side of town, is reluctantly accepted out of desperation and necessity. Gentrification as ethnic and class cleansing.

The 601 bus, like so many servants of public transport in Paris, had windows etched with graffiti from top to bottom, and through the lattice of glass carvings the unremarkable tree-lined terraces and semi-detached suburban homes morphed suddenly and dramatically into monochrome housing estates. As a teenager, I had always assumed films such as *La Haine* (1995) and *District 13* (2004) were France's attempts at keeping up with America in the ghetto stakes – a posturing vision of France for the hip-hop generation. But of course I was mistaken: it was the other way around – French hip-hop was so pertinent and popular because, like UK grime emanating out of the wastelands of East London in the early oos, it transmitted a hidden reality, inspired by and hatched together from the crumbs of crumbling socioeconomic environments. DJ Kool Herc essentially created hip-hop in 70s crack-ridden New York with a broken record player which kept skipping and playing the same portion of a record over and over again. The very foundations of hip-hop are rooted in the cultivation of creativity within strict constraints, and the traditionally inflexible musical rules – a 4/4 beat at around 96bpm often with no live instruments or formal musical training, just a sample of music replaying over and over – mimic the constraints of the black experience in a poor area where a life has to be made without local amenities, jobs, healthcare or hope. Lyricists spat themselves free, weaving intricate, multisyllabic rhyme schemes and evocative stories, often imbued with revenge fantasies (rappers aren't really killing cops; it's the other way round) within a musical prison.

Clichy-sous-Bois, which I had discernibly now entered, was easily as run-down as anything in South Central or Queens, perhaps even more so. The landscape was a mutation, buildings stretched and elongated into tall, concrete zombies, dead behind the eyes with rotting crevices stitched together with patches of rusting sheets of metal, wearing graffiti like tattoos and scarred from old surface wounds that hadn't been repaired. There were darkened cavities all over them, some with burn marks where windows once were, broken glass covered the streets and there was garbage where children's play areas should have been standing. In *Roissy Express*, somebody tells Maspero, 'Don't confuse the people who live here with those hideous façades,'[3] but as dusk began to settle and hooded figures wandered around as though they, too, were zombies, I couldn't tell whether they had sculpted these buildings into their own likeness or the buildings had informed their behaviour. The truth is that what I saw before me seemed a grim cycle of hopelessness.

Under the fading light Clichy resembled Chernobyl and, in places, Aleppo – a deserted half-town falling to pieces. There really had been a kind of war going on, ever since two Clichy kids were chased to their deaths by the police in 2005. Zyed Benna, seventeen, and his friend Bouna Traoré, fifteen, were near a factory that had been broken into. When the police arrived on the scene the two boys panicked and, along with a group of friends, ran into an electrical plant, where they were electrocuted to death. The news spread like wildfire among immigrant and some white communities, and so did the violence, and soon whole areas were being torched, more often than not by young black and Arab men, eventually leading to a state of national emergency being declared by then French president Nicolas Sarkozy. During this period almost 9,000 vehicles were destroyed across nearly 300 towns causing 200 million euros worth of damage. News outlets at the time focused on whether or not the two boys had indeed been chased to their death by police or if it was some terrible self-imposed accident, and the French president called for a heavy-handed 'zero tolerance' policy towards the rioters, who he labelled as 'scum' – but all this of course missed the point. It was simply one senseless tragedy too many over the years, produced by gross mistrust and neglect by the French state. This was also only one battle in a war very specifically between young people – namely, the children of immigrants – and a country they were born in but were being rejected by. At the time of writing, forty per cent of the inhabitants in Clichy-sous-Bois are under twenty years old, and unemployment in the area is at 32 per cent, three times the national average.

As soon as the bus entered Clichy, which really did resemble a battleground, I realized this wasn't going to be anything like Firth Park or Pitsmoor in Sheffield, or even Broadwater Farm or Thamesmead in London. There were no direct comparisons to be made with any estate I had ever known in Britain. Clichy was a completely different beast. In the north of England there are deprived council estates on the outskirts of the city, with poor links to the centre, and in London there are what former British Prime Minister David Cameron labelled 'sink estates' – crime-riddled inner-city high-rises – but nothing as dramatically destitute as this. What made Clichy particularly depressing was the idea that the area still, technically, fell under the name of the world's most romantic city. The discrepancy between the exported vision of Paris and what I was witnessing in the *banlieue* made me think of that bizarre condition known as Paris Syndrome, a psychological disorder which supposedly induces anxiety and dizziness, among other things, in some tourists from the Far East when they visit a Paris that doesn't measure up to the idealized versions seen in movies and coffee-table books.

I made my way to the front of the bus and asked the driver where boulevard Émile Zola was, and he pointed vaguely backwards towards four o'clock, so I pressed the bell and alighted at the next available stop. On my left was a huge estate being torn down; on my right, two giant dilapidated tower blocks that probably needed to be torn down. Many of the window frames didn't have glass in them and the only reason I knew the dwellings were still inhabited was that I could make out various African fabrics – from kente cloth to North African tapestries – hung out to dry, draped over the balconies. I started to dread just what that 'ultra-economical' my hotel was advertised as actually meant in a place like Clichy.

After convincing the hotel porter through an intercom that I had a reservation, I was buzzed through a steel fence as though entering a prison compound and walked through a courtyard containing a building that resembled a low-rise postmodern office block: a weird bit of 80s corporate commerce shoehorned into the destitution. Hotel Formula One was a sad, cheap place but, there among the darkened high-rises, it felt like entering a sanctuary. A middle-aged Moroccan man with grey skin and bags under his apathetic eyes checked me in and, looking for a bit of reassurance, I asked him if Clichy was safe, thinking he'd laugh me off, but he didn't, just gave me a concerned half-smile, told me to be careful and handed me my room key.

My room was a sparse oblong of space containing a plastic chair and a weirdly shaped bunk that was a double bed on the bottom and a single bed on top. Everything was asylum white and I was hit by a strong whiff of suicide. I put down my bags, peeked out of the lone window, which had steel bars over it, and looked out on to an empty car park lit by a lone streetlight, and thought to myself, *What is a hotel doing here?* and then *What am I doing here?* I would get answers to both questions, but in that moment I had the feeling that I could easily fade into oblivion in that room. The truth is that I'd been feeling lonely for a few months leading up to my trip, had split up with my long-term girlfriend and was back living at my mom's. London had started to feel pretentious and I felt out of sorts among the hipsters, posh prams, paraben-free organic shampoos and extortionate rents. I also felt disconnected from some of my old schoolfriends back in Sheffield, whose growing casual racism and monotonous, unhealthy lifestyles I couldn't stomach any more. I'd wanted to encounter the black diaspora in Europe for years, but in the end it was the loneliness that pushed me. I felt I wasn't black enough for my old black friends, not white enough for my old white friends, not working class enough for my old area in Sheffield but not middle class enough to survive cliquey London. I suppose I really set out in search of a tribe that might feel like home. I'd been able to run away from all these thoughts in lovely central Paris by strolling the boulevards, making voluminous notes in quaint cafés and relentless picture-taking. But there was something about that anonymous room and Clichy that confronted me with my depression.

I spent the evening reading more of Maspero's *Roissy Express*, which told a familiar story:

> The problem with the estates, says Akim, is that they don't let go of you easily: they're shut in on themselves, they offer a territory, a form of security. There are kids growing up on [the] estate who have never really searched for other horizons. Even Paris exists only for the odd excursion. The gang ends up taking the place of a second family, of society, and everything takes second place to the role, status and prestige the youngsters can obtain within it: the most important thing is not to lose face in the eyes of the other members. It's tough living on the estate, but it's tough getting out too.[4]

Over the next few days, I wandered Clichy aimlessly, getting chased off one estate after an ill-advised attempt at speaking to a group of young men I'd seen liaising with an orange BMW, and aware that only a few days in a place like this could turn Clichy into a cliché. For the most part I felt what Maspero had felt: Clichy was in turn unsettling and yet incredibly dull, with no one wanting to speak to me and *nothing to report*. One evening I comforted myself by partaking in some globalization, stumbling randomly upon the golden arches of a McDonald's drive-through shimmering like a beacon of radiant goodness in the night-time. It was a new one, full of bright light and colour and glass, which seemed like rare commodities in Clichy. The building was the second most impressive in the entire area, after the one across the road – a police station which was by far the most modern, expensive-looking building for miles. It made me wonder what the police did with themselves, because I hadn't seen any wandering the streets or engaging with members of the community during my many hours of walking.

Inside the McDonald's was perhaps the only sense of community I really felt in Clichy-sous-Bois, and it was being used more like a youth centre: teenage girls gossiping, weary-looking parents feeding their babies cheap cheeseburgers and kids playing in the dedicated children's area. The low-key cheeriness inside this drive-through, so missing in the immediate space outside it, saddened me; what a desperate state of affairs that McDonald's was being so heavily used as one of the few local amenities. As I guiltily scoffed down my Filet O Fish meal under the garish lighting of this drive-through next to a roundabout, I got a text from Rex Kazadi telling me he wouldn't be able to meet, as planned.

On my penultimate morning in Clichy, something was different. I had my machine coffee and stale-bread Hotel Formula One breakfast and set off for another aimless stroll. As soon as I stepped foot outside I heard the melancholy arpeggios of a piano, sampled in a hip-hop track, booming out through the austere off-white tower blocks in the distance. It was a spooky soundtrack because the theme so suited the visuals of the place, and it almost sounded as though the bricks and mortar of the estates themselves were weeping.

The deep timbre of the emcee's voice reverberated through the streets and I followed it until I reached a large crowd of people gathered outside the town hall, where the atmosphere was mournful and tense. The music had been emanating from a large speaker next to a small memorial commemorating Bouna and Zyed, the two teenagers who had lost their lives, and was a track made in their memory. Looking at the date engraved on the stone I suddenly realized they had died on today's date, 27 October, back in 2005, which is why Rex had suggested Clichy would provide answers about the *banlieues*. The whole community was out to hear the town mayor talk about that tragic day and how France might be able to avoid such an occurrence happening again.

I was interested to see if anything had changed because, despite an ambitious urban renewal plan, on the face of it, it hadn't seemed so. Apart from the distraught families of the two boys, who were in floods of tears and placing flowers on the stone memorial, everybody surrounding the mayor was white. This crowd didn't comprise locals, they were journalists, photographers, camera people, politicians, community workers and activists. For the first time, not being French in France gave me an advantage and an insight into the country's cultural divide. As the reporters were all clamouring, eager to get an interesting story and head back to their homes and offices in the arrondissements of Paris, I made my way through the crowd and noticed a sea of brown faces fifty or so metres away on a raised mound of grass. It was as if these young people, many of whom were in their twenties, undoubtedly peers of the teenage boys who had died, were invisible. Even here, in their own backyard, on a day that should have been all about them and not a group of middle-class white reporters passing by, they were being completely ignored.

They stared intently at the proceedings, waiting for someone to say or do something meaningful, but it never came. The mayor and MPs who took to the mic were trying to produce stirring speeches, but they were superficial, designed to tick boxes for the camera crews, not the angry estate kids watching from a distance. How the reporters interpreted the words, and the people who watched those interpretations at home, was all that mattered; after all, those were the people who were employed, paid taxes, voted and engaged with newspapers. Even though I couldn't keep abreast of all that was being said, I understood the generic rehearsed political intonations and cadences devoid of true empathy.

I watched the politicians talk for a good hour, occasionally getting a scant round of applause from the white people at the front, but the young black and Arab men and women looked on, with their arms folded, staring down the notable speakers with resentful gazes. Then, when the show was over, the white people in suits and with recording equipment packed up and disbanded. There was no interaction, no eye contact, no personal greetings or shaking of hands, no recognition at all of those young people standing on the hill who'd been reduced to victims or villains by the French press and needed to be reached.

Not having understood all that was being said left me with the same impression as these youths. The mayor quoted figures, spoke of how much money had been spent and how it had been invested in whatever, but I didn't get wrapped up in the spin and poetry and eloquent turns of phrases. I saw it for what it was: a glib gesture to make the rest of France feel better about the *banlieues*, without confronting the real issues of racism and gross inequality at the heart of the country's problems.

As the crowds dispersed there was a sense of anticlimax in the air. Tears had been shed, flowers laid, speeches made, then everything went back to the way it was, and the young residents who had briefly made themselves present disappeared into the shadows of Clichy-sous-Bois again. The day was once more populated mostly by pensioners and children.

Rex came through for me in the end, suggesting I call one of his contacts, who agreed to meet me at a run-down youth club nearby to discuss what had just happened at the memorial. A self-described 'black French militant', Almamy Kanouté introduced

himself with an outstretched hand that was twice the size of mine, and I immediately recognized him as one of the big guys I'd seen with Rex at the anti-Guerlain protest. He was a tall, well-built Malian man with very dark skin and a large, neatly shaped beard, and his tone was solemn and thoughtful. Trained as a social worker, Almamy was also a political activist and had recently started to get a name for himself as a spokesman for the *banlieues* and as an independent politician with the ultimate goal of 'merging Paris with its suburbs'.

I asked him a straightforward question to begin with – 'What is it like to be black in France?' – to which he frowned and looked down at the floor, as if searching for an answer.

'There is a large black community, as you know, but it isn't like England or America. There is no collective black identity here; West Africans stick together and it's the same with the Caribbeans and those from the Maghreb, so there is no political presence or economic power, and the French government wants to keep it that way. They want to keep us divided so there is no unifying voice, and no power. They are afraid of a black lobby.'

'What about CRAN?' I asked. The Representative Council of Black Associations of France was an organization I'd heard of that had been set up in 2005 almost immediately after the riots and grew further out of a seminar entitled 'Blacks in France: Anatomy of an Invisible Group' held earlier that year, which accurately described the tensions leading up to the riots.

'But the government run CRAN,' said Almamy, 'and as long as this government are pulling the strings we have no chance.'

I asked what the alternative was.

'The problem facing the youth of France, especially here in Clichy, is one of culture. Let's say you have a second-generation black French boy whose parents are from Mali. In Mali we get taught that it is rude to look an adult in the eye, then at school in France, a kid will be told off by his teacher for not looking them in the eye. From a young age there is a conflict going on inside the child's mind.'

Blackness in France was invisible partly because of the black community's attempt to adhere to part of Article 1 of the 1958 French constitution, which reads, 'France shall be an indivisible, secular, democratic and social Republic. It shall ensure the equality of all citizens before the law, without distinction of origin, race or religion. It shall respect all beliefs. It shall be organized on a decentralized basis.' It seemed to me that, on an administrative level, France's black community had been made politically invisible by France's refusal to accept the notion of race but, on a street level, they were all too visible, and subjected to the same discrimination as anywhere else. Almamy agreed.

'That is exactly the problem! France dreams of being a Republic, but it is not. There is only one culture that is considered French and that is white culture. This is why the second-generation black community in France are an angrier generation; they were taught to believe they're French, but in reality the government only sees them as foreigners. When black people in France are truly considered French, that is when France will be the country it claims to be.'

I mentioned Ricki Stevenson's tour of black Paris, and how a lot of African-Americans used to have, and still do to some extent, ideas of Paris being the racial utopia Richard Wright spoke of. Almamy had a wry smile on his face.

'You know what is funny? I am actually looking to America as a blueprint! We need a civil rights movement. In America, everyone is proud to be an American, but within that it is accepted that you have Latinos, Asians, African-Americans, and so on. Even in times of trouble Americans fight for the right to be counted. These various communities have economic power, which is what it all boils down to in the end.'

I thought back to the tour. Ricki had given an example of racism to do with her black French friend being stopped by police and the police talking down to her disrespectfully, using the casual *tu* instead of *vous*, which in France is how you'd address a child, never an adult you didn't know. But Jimmy had laughed this off. Black men were routinely being *murdered* by police where he was from. And in civil-rights-era America, where people were getting lynched, there was little choice *but* to fight. I told this to Almamy.

'I know that, sometimes, especially a few years ago before the riots, people perceived France as a racially tolerant country, and that is because it is so subtle here. You can't touch it. It is a hypocritical system that says everyone is the same, everybody is equal, but the reality is very different. You can't measure the dirty stares, the racist comments and the alienation. You can't even measure things that should be measurable because it is illegal to keep statistics on race, so it's nearly impossible to get reliable statistics on equal opportunities or employment prejudice or rates of income with regard to racial background. And look around you – these black people are not doing so well in France, are they!?'

Former president François Hollande made plans to omit the word 'race' from the section of the constitution I mentioned above and, under a law recently voted in by the National Assembly, France will not recognize the existence of any distinct race or races. From a distance this seems a gallant gesture – after all, race is an artificial construct that has frequently been used to the detriment of people with brown skin. But judging by the troubles I saw during my time in France, it will only make issues of institutional and societal racism even more difficult to track, tackle and make sense of. I asked Almamy how he thought the situation might be improved.

'Black people don't have any economic power in France and that is why they do not count. The Chinese own, the Indians own, but Blacks don't own anything, they are only the customers, the consumers. As a black community we have to come together under a united voice – meet, collaborate, discuss, take charge and be persistent! We have to look at the States and perhaps get the help and input of African-Americans. I am certainly inspired by the role the Black Panthers played in the civil-rights movement, and intend to use them as a framework and reference point for organizing communities here.'

The obsession with America that black activists have in Europe concerned me. Most main strands focus on the insertion of black people into a neo-liberal system, but this brand of capitalism was constructed on the very subjugation of black communities. Capitalism, as they say, is by nature racist; it reduced African-Americans to commodities, and so, too, African-American culture, swallowing radical traditions into an American Dream – Martin Luther King speeches used to promote mobile phones, images of civil-rights protests used to sell cans of Cola. The Black Panthers were perhaps the most interesting point of reference because they understood and embraced socialism and attempted to connect with international movements across the world, even arranging meetings with white workers from the Midwest. Almamy knew all too well about the pitfalls of capitalism and told me that as soon as an employer finds out a potential employee is from somewhere like Clichy-sous-Bois they are not interested in hiring them, and that the government were playing a dangerous game by leaving people to rot at the edge of society.

'They colonized, they welcomed people to the "motherland" to work hard and build this nation, but they neglected the transition. They failed to understand that these people may want and need to progress at some point, or feel entitled to a piece of the pie they provided ingredients for and helped to bake. They thought generation upon generation would be happy to play the role of labourers, but now the sons and daughters of those people want a better life for themselves. When they're not heard or seen they have to find ways to make themselves visible, and it appears violence is the only way for them to do that. As Martin Luther King once said, "A riot is the voice of the unheard."'

Almamy looked at me resignedly when he said this, tired but determined. As I was leaving the youth club I thought of one last question. I wanted to know what he thought of the memorial: had anything changed since 2005?

'No,' he said stoically, and then, 'In fact, things have got worse since then in Clichy-sous-Bois. But let me tell you this: 2005 was only a warning. There was a warning twenty years ago, too, but these weren't organized. This is nothing compared to what will happen, because despite all the burning and violence France still didn't get the message, didn't look at itself but instead pointed the finger at the rioters. What happened in 2005 wasn't a riot, it was a revolt! This generation of young black kids look around and see the older generation who worked hard and who knew a different life, were used to colonization and were grateful to France. The younger kids look at them and say, "Despite all their hard work, they still have nothing!"' It will get to a point where France has no choice *but* to listen.'

As I look back at what Almamy said, shortly before the Bataclan bombings, it sends a shiver up my spine. On Facebook, all I saw were French flags on people's profile pictures, and more zero-tolerance proclamations made by the government. Nobody asked how these *French* citizens, born and raised in the *banlieues*, had come to be suicidal murderers *within France*.

I couldn't wait to leave Clichy-sous-Bois and – more to the point – Paris. Back at Hotel Formula One, after packing up to leave for Belgium, I lay in the darkness, my room lit only by the incandescent glow of the car park leaking through the curtains, and heard, in a strong Mancunian accent:

'Chelsea, shut up, will you – you're going on that bottom bunk whether you like it or not!'

Had I lost my mind? The voices continued . . .

'Mum, Kieran's laughing at me!'

'I don't care! Just go to sleep now. You two have been a nightmare all day long!'

I opened my door and poked my head out into the corridor to see what was going on. A man and woman were standing outside a room, and when the mum saw me she said, 'Sorry, love, we didn't wake you up, did we?'

I told her that she hadn't, that it was just strange to hear English accents. We had a brief 'Brits abroad' moment and I asked them what they were doing in Clichy-sous-Bois. They told me they were heading for Disneyland Paris, had set off a bit late, were running out of petrol and so decided to stop somewhere inexpensive for the night en route. Of course! Disneyland is in the *banlieues*, too. Later, when I looked on Google Maps, I saw that it was only a thirty-minute drive away.

They said they were leaving first thing, so I told them to be careful and not to go out at night. The father looked at me and said, nonchalantly, 'Why? Is it not a very nice area?'

BRUSSELS

Matongé

'Recently voted Europe's most boring capital,' it said of Brussels in my Interrail city guide. After Clichy, this news only eased me further into my seat on a TGV speeding out of Paris in a thundering downpour, though I knew 'boring' was exactly how Brussels wanted to be thought of. It guiltily insists, 'Nothing to see here! That way for chocolates, this way for beer,' not mentioning one of the most brutal massacres that has taken place in the last two centuries, and an extended period of exploitation that, among other things, enabled Belgium to use the best ingredients for its chocolate at low cost, making it world famous. The country has long been trying to wash Congolese blood off its hands.

The only other passengers in a peaceful train carriage were an attractive Congolese woman and her cute, precocious daughter, who was reminding the mother to get their tickets ready for the conductor. As we pulled out of the Gare du Nord they waved through the window at a handsome young man I presumed to be the child's father. He stood on the platform and, as he disappeared from view, it felt as though Paris was spitting us out and swallowing him up. Who knows why they had left without him – they looked happy enough – but it got me thinking of how rarely I'd seen a black family together in public, as a unit, going somewhere to have fun, playing in the park, wandering around a museum or even just walking leisurely down the street together. Not just in Paris, but back in the UK and, as I would see on my journey, throughout Europe. It was becoming evident to me that the continent had a way of keeping black families busy, fragmented and poor. As for young African men, I often saw them wandering alone or loitering as groups, especially at big train stations, and when the TGV pulled into Bruxelles-Midi, they were there again.

These young men were in that age range during which their more successful (often white) peers leave secondary school and then graduate from university. In the UK, which is home to perhaps the most famous black academics in all of Europe, there are at the time of writing only fifty black professors out of over 14,000 professorships (black British professors, if you're reading, don't ever board the same plane together). The African students I spoke to were either the most diligent, or drop-outs, due to the pressures of prejudice, finances and family honour; you either studied with inhuman discipline or yielded and disappeared for ever out of shame. In the UK, many young black men, one of the most under-achieving groups at school, have constructed a safety net for themselves because they understand, if only subconsciously, the impossible societal pressures facing them. Adolph Cameron, head of the Jamaican Teachers' Association, has stated – and this was certainly my experience growing up – that many black male teen-agers have forged a protective culture in which academic success is seen as undermining their masculinity.

In the cultural heart of the African community in Brussels, an area nicknamed 'Matongé' after a market in Kinshasa, something slightly different was going on. A recent study revealed that an estimated one in four young black men possesses a masters degree, and yet in Belgium young black men are also the most likely to be unemployed. Matongé is currently experiencing gentrification, and now Cureghem, a working-class district just west of the central station, is where many non-white communities are starting to settle. Perhaps that's why there were so many young Africans and Arabs in tight-fitting leather jackets hanging out among chaotic and confused crowds of travellers; gap-year backpackers lay on their bags waiting for details of new connections after a series of cancellations due to bad weather. These white kids were around the same age as the black and Arab men, but the nature of their presence couldn't have been more different. They were, quite literally, *going places*. I was a backpacker, too, of course, but my circumstances were somewhere between the all-white middle-class gap-yearers and the poor and entirely browned-skinned loiterers. It was about to be reaffirmed to me that I didn't quite belong to either group.

I still hadn't booked any accommodation, so found a bench and tried to use a wifi signal I'd caught. I saw one of the gap-yearers using his Macbook Pro and asked if he knew what the password was. His name was Cristian, and he was sitting next to a friend from America he'd just made called Francis. Francis was a psychology major who had just finished six months travelling around Europe and was waiting to get a connection to the airport to fly back to the States. He disliked Paris, he said, because of the atmosphere, despite finding it physically beautiful. He loved Berlin for the opposite reasons. Cristian had been studying international politics at Maastricht University and, when I asked him what he

wanted to do after graduation, he told me, 'You know on the news when they say, "And now, it's over to our man in Brussels?" Well, I want to be that man.' He'd taken a gap year that had turned into two, ended up enrolling in a new course on his travels and never wanted to return to England. 'There is nothing left in England for an Englishman. All my friends from international school went back to their countries – Denmark, Germany, various places across Asia – to enrol in university degrees that were heavily subsidized. The thought of paying nine grand a year killed me. England has no future – even the Scots don't want anything to do with us.'

My God, I kept thinking as I talked to them. I was pushing thirty and still winging it; they had both just turned twenty and were about to enter into assuredly professional positions. What, in Cristian's life, made him tenacious enough at twenty-one to think that the role of Belgian correspondent was a viable option open to *him*? Probably that every Belgian correspondent he'd ever seen on TV looked and talked just like he did. In a recent article by Belgian-Nigerian writer Chika Unigwe for the blog 'Africa's a Country', she states that, to her knowledge, there were no black newscasters and few black journalists in the country. Her children were never taught by a black teacher and she never even saw a black bank clerk. Education only makes sense if you can see where hard work might lead, a future you can imagine yourself taking part in.

While we were talking about books – Cristian was reading Daniel Kahneman's *Thinking, Fast and Slow*; Francis was reading a book by a physician I'd never heard of – I started to notice strange behaviour among the crowds. A young Moroccan man with huge eyes and dilated pupils which looked almost as if they had been painted on kept staring at me. There were a lot of weird movements, people criss-crossing us back and forth, sly glances and subtle nods. The Moroccan kid with the strange eyes then sat next to me and I let him know that I had clocked him. Cristian said, 'There are a lot of crazies at this station,' and put his Mac away, but Francis, the future psychologist, took exception to this and said, 'Those "crazies" are the ones who are probably all right. It's the "normal" people you have to watch out for.'

Another, older, Moroccan man, who was sitting on the other side of the back-to-back benches I was sitting on, next to Francis and Cristian, tapped me to point out a piece of paper that was stuck on the back of my jacket. I thanked him and peeled it off. For another ten minutes or so I continued to chat to Cristian and Francis, keeping an eye on the Moroccan guy sitting next to me, who disappeared after a while. Then, as I was about to say good-bye and head to the hostel I'd just booked, two huge security guards dressed in red appeared out of the crowds and wandered over to me with stern faces. They asked where I was from, and for me to show them my passport. When I presented it they wanted to know why I was in Belgium, and the taller of the two guards said, 'We are here for people's safety, yes? We have a camera looking right at you, so we can see everything.' I imagined they presumed I was trying to steal Cristian's laptop and became enraged. Cristian was indignant at the suggestion, too, and it was only when he spoke up in my defence that the guards scarpered. For a moment I felt that I was one of the young international jet-setters, chatting about the future and what books we were reading and politics, then suddenly I was brought back down to earth, different, a black threat to their white safety.

A few minutes later the guards appeared again and said to me. 'You, come with us.' They sat me on a bench a few metres away, then grabbed hold of the older Moroccan man who was sitting behind me. Another guard emerged with the younger Moroccan with the strange eyes. They sat me down with these two fellow brown-skinned strangers, three big, white security guards looking over us, and I started to panic. What did they think I had done? One of the smaller guards looked me straight in the eye and pointed to the two Moroccans next to me. 'We have now looked at the CCTV footage. These two men, they tried to steal from you.

Check your belongings, please.' I checked all my things, and everything was intact. It was explained to me that the two men were in cahoots and I'd been targeted because of the deep pockets of my jacket. The older man had planted the sticker on my back to act as a decoy, so when he told me about it and I turned to peel it off, the younger guy could try to reach into my pocket. It seemed obvious now but, at the time, despite having seen how strangely the young guy was acting, I felt completely aware and in control of the situation. Their attempted thievery was a well-rehearsed waltz.

The two men blithely protested their innocence, and one of the guards said to me, 'We see something on the camera that is not right and we watch. They work in teams. Don't worry, the police will take them away.' I gave my details and a statement, and Cristian and Francis gave theirs, too, as witnesses. Initially, I had wanted to elbow the young Moroccan kid in the face when the guards told me what he had been up to. He knew I had seen him, and had still pursued me, but when Cristian, the future Belgian correspondent, called the two Moroccans 'absolute scum', all I could think was that, even if the men had taken all our things, they were more victims than we were. Yes, we are all accountable for our actions, but some of us are nudged towards more desperate situations than others. Francis was about to fly back to middle-class America, Cristian was heading back to higher education in the Netherlands, both had free tickets into white privilege after their studies. I, too, knew I had privilege as an English speaker and British passport holder with a European name. The young Moroccan man would be spending the night in jail. What was his future? Even if he'd managed to get away with our expensive goods, what kind of existence was it to spend your days wandering a train station looking to steal other people's belongings? It was a path to nowhere. As I left the station, I was feeling a little unsettled but was grateful to be heading to the epicentre of an idea that over the years had provided me with an empowering, imaginative 'somewhere'. To an Afropea conjured by an artist who has fearlessly and eloquently grappled with Belgium's colonial history in her work and life, Belgian-Congolese vocalist Marie Daulne, the tour de force behind the musical project Zap Mama and the first person to use the term 'Afropean' to describe their creativity.

Daulne is the daughter of a Congolese woman of Bantu heritage and a white Belgian expatriate who was murdered by Simba rebels the year she was born, during the Congo crisis of the early 60s. Over 100,000 people were massacred in a four-year uprising that saw the Congo finally win independence from Belgium, only to become engulfed in inter-tribal rivalries resurrected from the period before colonial rule. In a struggle for territory, numerous political leaders were assassinated, including one of the bright hopes of Central Africa's future and the Congo's first democratically elected president, Patrice Lumumba. Lumumba's murder was an attempt by the West to destabilize the country and insert its own power behind the scenes, a story we'll hear all about in Moscow and Marseille.

Finding themselves at the centre of a political storm, Marie and her siblings, along with their mother, first found refuge in a small Pygmy village, where they were shielded from gunfire because of ancient superstitions surrounding pygmies. The Daulnes were later airlifted out of the country in a dramatic rescue mission by Belgian paratroopers, then flown to Belgium and repatriated; Marie's father had held a Belgian passport.

The Pygmy village had contained what Erykah Badu called, when she contacted Daulne to collaborate, 'the sound from the forest', a kind of ancestral yodel that Marie has since incorporated into the cross-cultural blend of her music. 'Afropean' was a term that rose out of the debris of Daulne's tumultuous entrance into the Western world, and one that she could use to describe her cultural allegiance to something new, something not overly invested in any one kind of ethnic nationalism. With this new cultural trajectory, a duality could be celebrated that peered optimistically forward and embraced plurality. It was a place where cultures came together rather than being ripped apart, and where a conscious choice was made to use the power of these two histories in a positive, creative way, rather than dwelling on past tragedies. Daulne's art wasn't about forgetting, more about weaving the cultures into her being in a way that would prevent self-combustion. As Marie herself says: 'At school I was the only black or mixed-race girl and, though we were all Europeans, I wasn't able to explain what was happening deep inside me. I was between two worlds, probably searching for my black roots, which my mother wanted to cut off . . . [but school-friends] used to ask me if people lived in trees where I was from. [Then] when I arrived in Zaire I was so surprised to find the people singing, "Mundeleo, mundeleo, the white girl is here." Now I'm white. The work I do with Zap Mama brings two cultures together. Neither one dominates, and that's how it should be. I take what I have as a European and what I have as an African.'

Although Daulne has always been the brainchild behind the project, Zap Mama originally started out as an a cappella, polyphonic vocal quintet signed by Talking Heads singer David Byrne to his groundbreaking record label Luaka Bop. Over the years the sound of the group has changed to reflect the places it has toured and has incorporated trans-Atlantic influences such as neo-soul, hip-hop and jazz as well as Afrobeat and classical music. With the change of sound, Marie Daulne essentially turned Zap Mama into a solo project, but I love Marie for how unapologetic her music still is for being multicultural, how she has managed to take the chants of Central Africa's Pygmy tribes and merge them with European and American sensibilities in a coherent way, as if the different cultures were parts of the same puzzle. She demonstrated that an individual could have myriad influences yet still cultivate authenticity and challenge the status quo.

Daulne and Byrne first used 'Afropean' to describe the identity behind the band's music in 1991. Byrne came across the group while on a European tour with the Talking Heads and mentioned seeing a 'new continent' emerging, one in which a kind of 'reverse colonization' was taking place. 'Afropean' was used as a 'subtle manifesto', making visible what had already existed, and not as history but as something happening *right now*. This is an issue even stalwarts of black European visual arts often struggle with: moving beyond protest movements, vintage Afros and tribal imagery without entirely leaving them for dust. As Byrne stated in an interview, 'We don't do [album] covers that look . . . like academic records of obscure material of interest only to musicologists and a few weird fringe types,' and that is precisely what 'Afropean' as a mood meant to me, and what Marie Daulne manages to transmit through her art. It said that this was happening now and it was not exotic but a part of contemporary European life. Some people at the Zap Mama gig didn't seem to have got the memo, though.

When I arrived at Ancienne Belgique, a legendary venue for live music in Brussels and the place Zap Mama were first spotted and signed in the early 90s, I was confronted with an interpretation of the 'Afropean' I wasn't necessarily prepared for. There were a lot of dreads, mainly flowing from the heads of white women, some of whom had their locks wrapped up in colourful African fabric. They looked like anthropology lecturers who were living the dream – having sex with their subjects – and they clutched the arms of their indifferent black boyfriends with pride. When the combination was the other way around, there was also a certain dynamic: black women with short white men, all of whom seemed to be wearing flat caps or trilbies. They had a kind of preciseness about them that made me imagine they owned collections of limited-edition Nike trainers and paid thousands for rare funk albums on vinyl. Were black women part of their collection, too? Both the white men and the white women looked as if they'd dragged their partners along, and it seemed to me they were still trying to live that optimistic future the World Music boom of the early 90s had promised, despite the fact that things hadn't quite turned out that way in the new millennium. This was the future as depicted in sci-fi movies of the time such as *Blade*, *The Matrix* and *The Fifth Element*, which, despite their best attempts at depicting a dystopian vision, all painted a somewhat cosy picture of the future. It resembled a World Music festival in Cornwall – piercings, dreads, uncleanliness and liberalism ... with a splash of glow-in-the-dark tribal make-up.

When Marie Daulne arrived on stage my cynicism petered out; she looked like a year 3000 version of Billie Holiday and a huge screen behind her transmitted pan-African imagery and black-and-white geometric shapes and symbols such as you see on Malian tapestries. Her male dancers were topless and sported Motown Afros and the Afrobeat rhythms of a track called 'African Diamond' kicked in, the recorded version featuring the drumming of Fela Kuti's legendary Marseille-based beat maker Tony Allen. It might be argued that this was still a form of appropriation, but she'd charged it with black excellence and independence.

The set shifted across the black diaspora. With 'African Sunset's polyphony we were with the Pygmies in Central Africa, then, after more Afrobeat, the set shifted into the sweaty funk of James Brown, before Marie partially de-robed to whisk us off to Negritude-era Paris. As she lit a faux-cigarette held in an art deco holder, she performed a sultry version of a song she had originally collaborated on with the actor Vincent Cassel. Then came the transcendence of 'Bandy Bandy', her epic collaboration with Erykah Badu, a black Atlantic anthem, and when I looked back at the crowd I felt a bit sheepish about how judgemental I'd been. The audience looked like a live-action interpretation of Ernie Barnes's 'Sugar Shack' artwork that was used for Marvin Gaye's *I Want You* album, sweaty skin in all shades mingling and lost in a state of Afropea; class, race and status didn't matter here, in this magical atmosphere Marie had called into existence.

When I set out on my trip I had hoped to find Afropea in the physical geography of Europe, but after watching Marie Daulne perform and how it made the crowd behave I realized that the dream of an Afropean utopia had to be found first in the realm of ideas. And that is why music is so powerful; it zaps information in abstract ways, suggests a way of being, a lifestyle or, as David Byrne put it, a 'subtle manifesto'. We need opportunities in which we can encounter one another. There were young and old, black and white, and everything in between, all of them influenced by Africa and Europe, and they had congregated at Marie's calling. Her *raison d'être* was to sing her culture into existence by working within African traditions that had almost been lost to colonialism, and to translate and transmit them in tandem with her adoptive European culture, refusing to allow hegemony to creep in. It wasn't about being mixed race – Marie's Zairean mother raised her and, like a lot of first-generation African parents, wanted her daughter's culture and accent to be completely European so that she could integrate into society. I know Andys who are really Ayos, Gurgits who are Ginas, Philips who were once Femis, all now in their twenties and thirties, for that very reason. Unable to speak her mother's tongue of Swahili, Marie had to Africanize herself in a European atmosphere, one that she also had cultural bonds with.

Marie's Afropean world wasn't an entirely metaphysical one, though. Growing up in Matongé, her ideas of Afropea were no doubt partially rooted in this north-western suburb of the city. After making my way through the sweaty spectators in the foyer after the gig, I headed out for an evening stroll to see if I could sense Zap Mama's world in Matongé. The cool late-October breeze blew refreshingly against my damp skin as I wandered the streets under dim golden street lamps. I knew I'd reached Matongé when, on the side of a run-down building, a huge mural appeared entitled *Porte de Namur, Porte de l'amour* – a piece commissioned by the Belgian government and painted by Congolese artist Cheri Samba. The fresco depicts an Afro-European market scene, with black women kissing white men, and vice versa, hair being braided, old men of various ethnicity chatting over a cup of coffee (among them a self-portrait of the artist), as well as numerous cultural transactions taking place within the European uniformity of Belgium's buildings. Though Samba had omitted certain drab details in his painting, such as the McDonald's on the corner, when I walked along the street the atmosphere of the painting was there. Jazz clubs shared boulevards with Afro hair salons, braiding and weaving still going on at that late hour. For a Black community, these are more than just places to get your hair styled, they are community centres, places to gossip, argue over football and politics, and play new music. There was under-the-counter commerce: pirate DVDs, underground mixtapes and clothes that had fallen off the back of a lorry were traded – a bridge that allowed poor people to buy luxuries they'd otherwise find it hard to afford.

Along with the salons and clubs in Matongé there were thrift stores, art galleries and African restaurants, all seemingly serving more than one use. There was a cosy tattiness about the streets, and I strolled around in the shadows with my camera, using the amber glow spilling out of bars and cafés to light my subjects' faces. On the chaussée de Wavre I noticed an old black man sitting looking out of the window and wearing a panama hat which covered his eyes. I took my time to properly frame my photograph, which is when I realized the old man looking out of the window was in fact a sculpture and the building he was sitting in was an African art gallery called Galerie Lumières d'Afrique. I was beckoned in by the owner, Grégoire de Perlinghi, and he laughed when he saw my face. 'You thought he was real, didn't you? Mate, it's why we have him sitting there. He draws everyone's attention to my gallery!'

When Grégoire spoke English it was obvious that he had either a British parent or had lived in England for some time and had picked up bad habits, dropping his 't's and using phrases like 'taking the piss'. It turned out he'd spent seven years living in Liverpool with a girlfriend and, when he talked, I could now hear a subtly Scouse accent mixed in with his local accent. I asked him how business was.

'Not bad, mate. Belgians have always been fascinated by

Africa – the music, the people, the art – but a lot of the time I get these posh people coming in looking around and asking for something "naive" or "primitive". It takes the piss! These people buy African art because it's in fashion but, for me, it's important that the pieces go to good homes. To people who are made happy by looking at good art. What I try to sell are pieces by contemporary artists who want to show a newer, more up-to-date image of Africa.'

Looking around at the walls of the gallery, I could see what he meant. There wasn't a hint of the colonial; not a stick-man 'savage' drawing in sight – in the same way that you wouldn't go to a contemporary European gallery and see images in the style of the cave drawings at Lascaux in France. There was some brilliant work by a young artist from Nantes of Cameroonian and French descent with the striking name of Johan Baggio. His paintings seem to mix Jean-Michel Basquiat's abstractionism with elements of realism, producing some entirely original and complex work. Grégoire was keen to show me the work of a Belgian-Congolese artist called Mufuki Mukuna, who had just launched a new exhibition at the gallery. His work was moody, and in it I saw the jazz of Matongés ambience, with smudges of greys and browns that echoed the buildings of Brussels. The relationship between an artist's heritage and their art is an interesting one. Was I seeing Afro-Europe in Mufuki's work just because I knew where he was from? How important was his ethnicity? How important was *my* ethnicity in reading his work? I had always hoped that the secretive Bristol street artist Banksy would turn out to be a Middle Eastern Muslim woman, because it would utterly disrupt and alter the perception of the famously subversive stencils and the reaction of the audience. I mentioned my thoughts to Grégoire and he suggested I ask the artist himself. Mufuki lived nearby, and we arranged a meeting at the gallery for the next day.

When Mufuki walked through the door he was exactly who I expected him to be from seeing his paintings: he was dressed in modest clothing in earthy colours, a cotton scarf draped poetically around his neck, loose-fitting chinos, a beige linen jacket, spectacles perched low at the end of his nose. He looked both creative and studious, bohemian and Belgian, and radiated a kind, quiet, thoughtful intelligence.

Mufuki was trained in Belgium at the Royal Academy of Fine Arts and sees his art as Belgian in style but personal in content.

'Growing up in Brussels, I felt as though I was kind of in my own bubble, a world of silence. I never really felt at ease around black people or white people. There weren't many mixed-race kids around when I grew up, so I felt like a minority everywhere I went, but sometimes I wonder if this sense of isolation was really due to being mixed race or because of my relationship with art.' He looked at me and smiled. 'You know what artists are like! Did my isolation among races drive me towards creativity, or was it the other way round?'

I felt a similar way. Despite having worked in TV and having a reputation among friends and family of being outgoing, I have always felt like an introvert in disguise, masking my awkward social skills by talking a lot and playing the clown. I was naturally drawn to writing as a child because I felt I could express myself better in words on a page than in a social setting. When I started to enter the literary community it was a relief because there were others who were similar, but were we born like that, or was it the experience of feeling that we never fit in that made us that way? I told Mufuki I was sure growing up feeling that I was between cultures had made me more sensitive to notions of identity and belonging than I would have been had I not been born with the gift of exile. Mufuki agreed. 'I definitely believe that my mixed heritage has provided me with an opportunity to closely observe people and, perhaps, to understand the struggles on both sides. As someone living in Europe, I have had a unique insight into the life of an immigrant, fresh out of Africa, more than I otherwise would have.'

That said, I wondered how he felt about his work being represented by a gallery that was dedicated to 'African art'.

'It's problematic, and sometimes I feel pushed into a little pigeon hole. The world is full of clichés and "African art" is one of them. It's a completely meaningless term because Africa is a continent, not a country.'

But surely, I asked, there were certain themes that link art from Africa together . . . a certain response to climate and colonization, to historical trades between territories. I felt that I could, for the most part, recognize art that came from Europe, South America or Asia.

'Yes, but think of "African art", what it might be like, and then remember that Algeria is the largest country on the continent. And the big problem is that the type of "African art" most people buy is always the same: It is all "contemporary" because, apparently, it hasn't changed in hundreds of years.'

And what about art from the African diaspora? Were there any unifying responses to the experience? Was there, for instance, a Matongé style?

'Not really. Even within Congolese communities, those from the Democratic Republic of Congo stick together and have their own identity, different to those from the French Congo. The Rwandese will stick to their own cafés and the Senegalese to theirs, and I don't really feel a part of any of it. For me, it isn't important where people are from, it is what they are like as individuals, and when I think of that it makes me wonder if not being part of a community isn't all bad. It has allowed me space for self-reflection and self-analysis – made me face my own human identity rather than needing to identify with the construct of something larger. When you are part of a big group you have the tendency to alienate anyone who is different, but I've learned to embrace individuality, and I think that has to do with not fitting in anywhere myself.'

As Mufuki was saying these words, I, sitting there in a little African art gallery with Grégoire, a white Belgian man with a slight Liverpudlian accent and an interest in Africa, and Mufuki, a Belgian-Congolese artist struggling with identity, felt as though I had found members of my own tribe. An inclusive tribe of people who, like Zap Mama, had found themselves as cultural nomads connected by the very notion of not being part of any group connected to class, race or nation. I mentioned Zap Mama and 'Afropean'.

'I like this word!' Mufuki said. 'Maybe that's what I am: An Afropean! My hope is, of course, that people see me simply as an artist, and then, if they look a little further, an artist with two nationalities. There is a famous Korean conductor who once said, "First, I'm a human, next an artist, then I'm from Korea," and that resonated with me. So let's say that first I'm a human, next an artist, and finally an Afropean, in that order.'*

* Our talk would later inspire a piece of art. Mufuki's painting *Afropean Identity* is now available for purchase from Galerie Lumières d'Afrique.

Shortly after saying my goodbyes to Grégoire and Mufuki I escaped into a restaurant called Soleil d'Afrique. The name suited the place, which, with its orange walls and candle-lit interior shining behind an awning, had the hue of a setting savannah sun. It was painted with palm trees and felt like a little African oasis there in Belgium, at the start of a particularly chilly European winter. It was approaching midnight, All Hallows' Eve, and Halloween had passed without a ghoulish figure in sight. I ordered the special, an ice-cold Kinshasa beer and a bowl of hot yassa stew, to warm me up and watched the crowd. Two young white men and a black man were laughing over a beer and a group of Congolese men were playfully arguing about something or other – football, perhaps. A black man and a mixed-race woman with short hair shared dinner, a young black woman sat alone reading a book. This was it, I thought. This was Afropea.

Tervuren Uncensored

Before setting off on my journey through Europe, I'd told myself I would avoid getting too caught up in the web of the continent's history. So much of black Europe had been written out of it, and what *had* been written often only made me angry. It would have been easy to spend five months in Europe's past, at art galleries, libraries and museums housed in old buildings, reading apologetic footnotes or being annoyed by their absence. So many landmarks have been turned into trinkets: you visit a place, get presented with a cartoon version of its history – beheadings, battles and curiosities – buy some chocolates and return to your unrelated life in the present. But I was about to be reminded that Europe's history isn't at all dead, it is still living and breathing and deeply embedded in its society's hierarchies and atmospheres, lurking just out of sight, haunting its systems. To quote something I heard the scholar Michelle Wright say at a conference in this city, 'The past is not behind us, it's all around us in changed form.'

During my time in central Brussels I often watched the last of the autumn leaves bristling and swirling upon cobbled squares, the whole city looking autumnal by nature: by day it was all browns, creamy greys and ashy greens; by night, burnt oranges, muted reds and golden sepia. Boring? For some, maybe, but I found it pleasant in a slightly faded sort of way. I could have happily wandered around obliviously, not thinking too much about the ghosts of colonialism, but one thing led to another . . .

It all started at a shop dedicated to the world's most famous Belgian, Tintin, in the rue de la Colline. I'd been a fan of the jet-set Belgian reporter since I was a child and watched the cartoons on

British TV in the 90s, BBC2 and Channel 4 on Sundays being my first taste of anthropology. As well as *The Adventures of Tintin*, Trans World Sport would run specials about African goalkeepers and obscure sports related to stories across the globe, ranging from kabaddi in India to the socialist politics of German football side FC St Pauli. Then there was *Football Italia*, its bilingual presenter James Richardson sitting in various cafés in picturesque Italian towns reading football news and that of political scandals surrounding the race for the Scudetto. Afternoon TV was full of Westerns from the 40s and 50s, which were so convincing in their negative depictions of Native Americans that when we played cowboys and Indians in the school playground, even though I knew I had some Native American heritage on my father's side, we always thought of the cowboys as the good guys.

Tintin was a good guy, wandering the globe teaching morals and bringing justice to the weak and vulnerable. A perfect opportunity, I didn't realize back then, for colonial propaganda. At the flagship store, which feels as much like a showroom as a toy shop, you can see how Hergé's creation, though designed for children, remains collectable for adults. The characters are elegantly realized and have transcended mere comic-book hero and entered cultural-icon status, but it turns out that not all the characters were created equally.

One of the comics I'd never heard of before, *Tintin in the Congo*, was stacked high on a shelf and partially covered in a red band, and when I pulled it down I understood why it was so discreetly placed out of the way. The text on the red band of the English version read: 'An essential volume for collectors – *Tintin in the Congo* was first published in book form in French in 1931. This brand-new translation by Leslie Lonsdale-Cooper and Michael Turner, the original Tintin translators, includes a fascinating forward describing the publication history of Tintin's African adventure, placing it in its historical context.' The text on the red band continued with a quote from the forward: 'In his portrayal of the Belgian Congo, the young Hergé reflects the colonial attitudes of the time ... he depicted the African people according to the bourgeois, paternalistic stereotypes of the period – an interpretation that some of today's readers may find offensive.'

When I removed the red band I *was* offended straight away. Tintin, looking as human as ever, and Snowy, dog-like as ever, are driving past a giraffe which looked just like a giraffe through the African savannah with a jet-black, gremlin-like creature with mindless goggle eyes and a mouth that covered the whole bottom half of his face. That'll be one of the Congolese, then.

Michael Farr, in his biography of the author, *The Adventures of Hergé, Creator of Tintin*, describes the racist *Tintin in the Congo* in the following way: 'Tintin was a hero, even in Francophone Africa, where, oblivious of modern perceptions of "political correctness", the flawed but entertaining "Tintin in the Congo" (1931) quickly became a favourite adventure.'

Why put 'political correctness' in quotes? To suggest the book offended only over-sensitive do-gooders? Decolonization, especially of one's own mind, is important for the very reason that black communities were brainwashed to the point where they had such little self-worth they would see nothing wrong with the kind of racist, colonial depictions so evident in *Tintin in the Congo*. Coming to terms with the ways the European superiority complex has found its way into your psyche is tricky because it has been transferred through a thousand intimate moments, planted in the fertile, innocent and happy memories of a childhood. The dislodging can prove a painful process, your foundations suddenly disintegrating beneath your feet. Those early, peaceful hours on a weekend morning when I would watch or read and enjoy Tintin and other colonial cartoons such as *Around the World with Willy Fog* and *The Mysterious Cities of Gold* were sacred. I would lie alone on the carpet with a glass of Sunny Delight, the only person awake in the whole house, watching TV as dust particles drifted through beams of morning sun breaking through the venetian blinds of our living room. It hurts to re-evaluate such gentle remembrances, which is no doubt why many don't. And this is true on both sides of the fence – the injustices of colonialism messed up the subconscious of the colonizers and the colonized – very few really want to face and grapple with its legacy.

To see what kind of young white men the Belgian colonial system was trying to produce, we need only look at the story of *Tintin in the Congo*. During his time in the country Tintin hires a 'boy' and proceeds to wander around Kinshasa curtly bossing the locals around. After seeing a bunch of lazing Congolese mooching around a broken train, he says, 'Come on, you lazy bunch, lend a hand,' then breaks up a barbaric fight between two village men arguing over a hat by ripping it in half: 'White man very fair, him give half hat to each one,' says one of the men. This foreign stranger cockily strolls into town and immediately designates himself organizer, leader and infrastructure provider, subjugating the Congolese to the rank of second-class citizens in their own country.

The Congolese liberation movement is represented as an evil golly-like creature who notices that 'White man getting too strong, soon black man not listen to me, their witch doctor!' The witch doctor dresses up as an Aniota, described as follows:

> Aniotas . . . is secret society. They organised to fight white men. When Aniota ordered to kill chief friendly to white man, him put on special costume and mask looking like leopard. On fingers, put steel claws like leopard . . . then Aniota go to kill black chief and leave marks of leopard jaw all on ground so everyone believe leopard is killer!

When his plan is foiled by Tintin he submits with the plea, 'Me your slave, merciful white man!'

Along the way we meet Papa Sebastian, who runs a mission and asks Tintin to teach maths to little black kids: 'Who can tell me what two plus two is? . . . No one? There it is, two plus two? Two plus two equals? Come on, can somebody answer!?'

After our 'hero' returns home all that's left for the Congolese is to comment on this amazing man: 'Them say in Europe all young white men is like Tintin,' and 'Me never before see boula matari, all powerful, like Tintin!' and, finally, a young African mother says to her mischievous child, 'If you not good, you never be like Tintin.' There was no mention, of course, of any of the great African kingdoms that were torn apart by white men from Belgium in one of history's most *unfair* regimes of all time. Like most of our historical evidence about colonialism's devastating impact on Africa (its history told only by those in power), Hergé's story is riddled with such arrogance and violence, depicts a situation so vulgar, that no matter how the story is framed it can't hide the hideousness it so desperately tries to conceal or spin. During his time in the Congo Tintin shoots a crocodile in its mouth, massacres an entire herd of antelope, kills and skins a monkey to wear as a disguise, blasts a python's head off, chokes a boa constrictor to death with its own tail, soccer-kicks a leopard, eats an endangered giant tortoise, catapults a rock in the face of a buffalo and kills an elephant for its tusks. That was, after all, the real reason white Belgian men like Tintin were in the Congo in the first place: for its ivory, and also for its rubber.

Though it wasn't designed for such purposes, as a document, the story now mostly serves to show Belgian colonialism for the despicable thing it was, but instead of the apologist introduction, full of suggestions of Realpolitik, it should have been handed over to a Congolese writer to craft a new introduction and reinterpret the work, making the ugliness of the colonial propaganda even more explicit. It wasn't until 1970, ten years after the liberation of the Congo, that Hergé renounced the story, and though he claimed he wrote it as an impressionable youth in 1930, that isn't entirely correct because he re-drew and reprinted it again in 1946, which was the version I was reading. Due to popular demand, it was published in English in 1991 and survives on the shelves of the Tintin store, which, judging by the clientele in the store that day, still appeals to children.

Racism and poaching aside, *Tintin in the Congo*, the second Tintin story ever written, simply isn't very good. It's Hergé learning his trade, honing his craft and fleshing out the characters, so it's easy, as an adult in the twenty-first century, not to take it seriously. The first time I read it I laughed out loud, but as time has passed I've thought about all the similar stories that pierced my childhood and continue to be transmitted to young people in more subtle and refined forms. The Tarzan films, *Pocahontas*, *Dances with Wolves*, *Avatar*, *Game of Thrones* ... they all depict white characters with special nuance and black characters as props or objects in need of being saved. That, or stories which 'make legends out of massacres', to paraphrase James Baldwin.

After the Tintin store I nipped back to Galerie Lumières d'Afrique to pick up a poster of Cheri Samba's Matongé mural which I'd bought and left on my previous visit and mentioned *Tintin in the Congo* to Grégoire.

'Mate, that's nothing!' he said in his Scouse/Belgian accent. 'Have you been to our famous Africa museum yet? It takes the piss – Hergé got all his ideas for the story from that place.' He told me that Tervuren, the 'Royal Museum for Central Africa', was festering away on the outskirts of the city, full of relics from the years when Belgium ruled the Congo, and hadn't been updated for years. It was so old and colonial that it had been labelled 'a museum of a museum' and supposedly held sinister secrets, with rumours rife that a whole host of horrific artefacts had been hidden from view, from Native American mummies to stuffed African tribesmen and women. Grégoire said, 'God only knows what they've got down in the basement – only about 5 per cent of their collection is on display. They're going to start renovating it, too, soon, so if I were you I'd go now before they brush it all under the carpet.' And so I did.

Tram 44 is a skinny single-carriage train on a line built specifically to serve the museum and felt like a time-travelling machine.

Montgomery station, where I boarded, was very 70s, with flickering fluorescent lights that needed to be repaired and gaudy orange underground trains. The tramline was built in the 60s and passed through beautiful examples of twentieth-century architecture, from mid-century modernism to interwar art deco and turn-of-the-century art nouveau. By the time the tram arrived at its final destination, it felt as though I could've been in 1897, the year the museum was built for King Leopold II's world fair.

It was something to do with the time of day – those moody midweek afternoon hours when all the children, teenagers and employed adults (all the noisemakers) are at work or school and so there is a strange atmosphere in the air, the type you felt when you pulled a sickie at school. As I was in my twenties, these were the hours capitalism tried to deny me, but slipping through the net as an off-season traveller heading for the Brussels suburbs felt like entering a twilight zone. The weather was grey, rainy and windy, the mood melancholy, and I watched elderly men and women with drawn faces sit solemnly in rain macs. The tram plunged into an area of forestry, on a single track sandwiched between rain-sodden autumn trees either side of avenue de Tervuren, and through them I could make out huge detached homes, lush parks and swanky apartments in the famous and frilly Belgian art nouveau style. By the time the tram arrived at the end of the track, I was the only passenger left to alight. I passed a closed pub and two abandoned train carriages, and a sign that read 'Spoorloos', the Flemish word for 'traceless'. Beyond, brooding quietly in the rain and emptiness, was the monumental Royal Museum for Central Africa.

For all its grandeur, the building appeared deserted. Not in disrepair exactly, but dusty and disused, and as I approached the main entrance around the back I was sure the place was closed – perhaps indefinitely so. Before trying the doors I surveyed its grounds, typical of the type of blood-money country estates you find in European countries with a history of colonialism, all manicured lawns and ornate fountains, weeping willows and lush, though meticulously organized, greenery stretching out over acres. As someone with enslaved people in my ancestry, I've always found such complete classical European beauty more than a little unsettling. In the dynamic of world power, this was at the top of the food chain, and every time I visited a place like this I couldn't help but look at it and wonder whose blood had to be shed, which kind of people exploited, in order that a place of such pristine beauty could exist and be maintained.

And it wasn't just the grounds and the echoey silence that gave the place an eerie feel: if ever there was a case for a building being haunted, it would surely be this one. I tried the huge, heavy oak doors that were three times my height and, to my surprise, with some force they creaked open. Inside, an old woman with a sullen face sat at reception and a lone black security guard stood in the corner of the cavernous foyer, lit only by the pale daylight leaking in through the windows. The building had been designed to make use of natural light, and this gave the place an ethereal feel, church-like, with a cool, diffuse lustre unable to adequately fend off the proliferation of shadows. Apart from this odd couple of staff members, there wasn't a soul around, so I asked the receptionist if the place was open, and she answered my question in that continental European way, saying, 'Of course,' even if something isn't particularly evident. Grégoire had been right – the museum was about to close its doors for the first time since it was officially opened to the public in 1910, for major renovation work, and as an offshoot of this was offering the chance to go behind the scenes, head down into its cellars and get one last glimpse of the building in its colonial state.

As well as the dim, shadowy corridors, their walls covered in frowning masks, stolen artefacts, statues of stoic Belgian men, their mean-spiritedness immortalized in the furrows of stern frowns, and the dusty cadavers of long-dead wild African beasts turned into taxidermy, the sheer volume of the interior gave the space an unsettling feel. Its vast emptiness felt inhuman in scale and, having only the echo of my own footsteps as company, it didn't take much for the imagination to populate it with the in-human, with ghosts and malevolent energies. 'If you take a good look around the place, you will see a building in dire need of res-toration,' said the comically posh English voice acting as my audio guide. 'Its infrastructure hasn't been adapted to meet modern-day museum requirements and the permanent exhibition is looking rather dated, as well as still bearing the stamp of its colonial past. All in all, it's high time to retell the story of Africa.'

The problem with this, of course, is that the story of Africa will again be largely retold by white Europeans, with a leaning towards the scientific and the anthropological and still under the banner of Belgian royalty. There was a contemporary photo essay on display – the usual patronizing bullshit about Africa by a white photographer obsessed with two-dimensional vibrancy – of the vacant smiles and colourful suffering of black people. With every photograph, I could hear the photographer righteously thinking, *Look at these poor Congolese. They don't have anything but still manage to smile. We, the West, can learn from their simple lives.* This is partly the reason I was travelling in Europe in the winter: so that any photographs taken would be the polar opposite of the tropical tripe that so often gets shoehorned in with black culture. I didn't want only street festivals and carnivals, I wanted work commutes and the banal humanity of everyday life, which is closer to the reality of the black experience in Europe; we do more than just dance, sing and grin.

In another contemporary photo essay by Jean-Dominique Burton (yes, another middle-aged white man) entitled 'Matongé Matongé', which mirrors the images of Matongé market in the Democratic Republic of Congo with the Matongé of Brussels, the Belgian photographer writes about the latter being 'an insipid hors d'œuvre. Yes, the colours were there, but with a hint of damped down sadness, a Belgian greyness enveloping its inhabitants like the asphalt of Ixelles streets overlaying the crust.' These Belgian

Africans, it seems, just weren't damn colourful enough for him. Later he reveals where the problems with his own depictions lay . . . ' "Congo" – the word has resonated in me since my early childhood, like the muffled beat of the Tam Tam with all its mysteries and its shares of clichés peddled by the tales of colonialists in search of adventure, my only reference being the Royal Museum for Central Africa in Tervuren.' Whether he knew it or not, that view was what he was projecting on to contemporary Congolese communities, documenting only black figures that worked as types.

There were some older photos from the colonial days, which came with apologies – 'Most of the photographs displayed in the gallery are from the museum's collection. They were taken by Europeans and were often used within the context of Colonial propaganda' – but I found them less offensive because they at least knew they found the black body exotic, were honest about otherizing. They were taken during the Congo Free State era between 1885 and 1908, by various photographers who approached their human subjects in the same way they would approach a wild animal: close-ups of tribal scars, phrenological head shots for scientific study. But this approach, in black and white and certainly reductive, contained more objective information than the patronizing contemporary work: all poor African kids face-mugging for the expensive DSLR of a white man, hoping for some loose change.

The faces of the black men and women in the colonial photographs looked quietly haunted and had a strange dignity, considering the circumstances. King Leopold II's reign in the Congo was one of the most brutal and exploitative in the history of colonialism; during it more than 10 million Congolese were murdered, with many more maimed. Like many European countries during the era, King Leopold initially justified Belgium's expeditions to Africa as being philanthropic in nature: a bid to civilize savages, *Tintin in the Congo*-style. But he was really there for the country's ivory and, particularly, its rubber, a resource in high demand back in a Europe in the midst of the industrial age. (Think of America in the Middle East in the twenty-first century.)

There was an original agreement between Belgian officials and various tribesmen on display, whereby the signatory agreed to receive

> ... one piece of cloth per month to each of the undersigned chiefs, besides present of cloth in hand, [for which] they promise to freely of their own accord, for themselves and their heirs and successors for ever ... give up to the said Association the sovereignty and all sovereign and governing rights to all their territories ... All roads and waterways running through this country, the right of collecting tolls on the same, and all game, fishing, mining and forest rights, are to be the absolute property of the said Association.

The signature of the Congolese chief was basically a smudge – of course, the Africans didn't realize what they were being forced to sign, but it wasn't for their eyes, it was for the eyes of other global powers, to transform cruelty into an internationally recognized institution.

Just like King Leopold, Hergé, the writer of *Tintin in the Congo*, never set foot in the country, but unlike King Leopold, he was working out of ignorance – an ignorance encouraged by the powerful colonial propaganda of the very building I was standing in. Like the photographer Jean-Dominique Burton, it was obvious that Hergé got his 'facts' from this museum when I saw a statue of an 'Aniota' – the murderous African witch doctor in the leopard costume – which was depicted in exactly the same pose as the drawing in the comic. Stories of this secret society caught fire in the imaginations of children, but the Aniota issue was blown way out of proportion, along with cannibalism and other forms of 'savagery', to justify the need for Belgian civilization, a civilization that necessitated the torturing, pillaging and hanging of Africans.

It was time to visit the cellars, which hadn't been open to the public before. As I descended the long, slim, creaking mahogany staircase, it was evident I'd be walking into a kind of decrepit freak show straight away. The walls were lined with glass cabinets filled with suspended animation: jars with rotting handwritten labels full of perfectly preserved pickled snakes, frogs and other deformed creatures I couldn't quite make out. It smelled of old death – must, flesh, oily fur and chemicals – which wasn't surprising, I suppose: if the museum was full of anything, it was old death.

The first room I entered featured a collection of dismembered heads of African animals over a hundred years old: bison, buffalo, leopards, lions and even giraffes, their long necks jutting out, as though they had smashed their heads through the walls. Another room was full of skins that were the complete exterior of the animal, so intact they could be placed around an artificial skeleton for future displays. In another room lay the remains of a shipwreck, once thought to be that of Henry Morton Stanley's *Lady Alice*, the boat he used on his first trans-Africa expedition, during which he found the coveted source of the River Congo. The remains later proved not to be those of the *Lady Alice*. Half of the stuff Stanley claimed had happened in his famous travel book turned out to be untrue. There is no doubt, though, that in colonial terms he was the most successful explorer of Africa in history. As detailed in Adam Hochschild's brilliant *King Leopold's Ghost*, Stanley was born into poverty in England and travelled to America to make his name as a journalist, before making his famous search for Dr Livingstone, which inspired Joseph Conrad's *Heart of Darkness* and, by virtue of that, countless other works of fiction. He was also King Leopold's right-hand man in opening up and controlling the Central Africa region and, according to fellow explorer Sir Richard Francis Burton, known for 'shooting negroes as though they were monkeys'.[1]

Beyond the shipwreck were white moulds of African heads and bodies made in 1911 by Belgian sculptor Arsène Matton, which were to be used to make statues for physical anthropology. They had been recently discovered in the cellars, along with some notes from the artist, who commented on how difficult it was to get people to cooperate with his project. They'd run away from him because of 'fear of the unknown', or because they didn't want to appear naked, and it made me wonder how many other bare-assed images of Africans had been forced upon them and, in turn, the rest of the world.

Near the sculptures was a sign with the title 'Human Remains'. It read: 'One of the biggest myths doing the rounds about the museum is that it contains stuffed Africans. This story is completely untrue. There are, however, two mummies.' These bodies were of unknowns, and numerous rumours circulated about who they could have been. I started to get frustrated by some of the vagaries of the museum signage. They were saying so much, and yet saying nothing at all. For instance, I saw no mention anywhere of the 267 non-stuffed, living, breathing Africans brought from the Congo for the museum's launch at the world fair of 1897. They had been shown in a re-created African village in the grounds of Tervuren, with a sign reading 'Do not feed the blacks, they have already been fed.'[2] This was one of a proliferation of 'human zoos' across Europe during the colonial era. Forced to wear their African dress in the colder climate of Brussels, many caught European illnesses and perished, and the fate of the surviving tribesmen and women is uncertain.

There were more sullen artefacts – an entire room of elephant skulls, one giant male skull with its tusk intact as a central showpiece, surrounded by smaller skulls whose tusks had been long lost to the ivory trade. There was another room dedicated to antelope antlers, more tiny carcasses preserved in bottles of spirit, and I decided I'd seen enough and headed back upstairs to hand in my audio guide. A multicultural group of schoolchildren had just arrived with their teacher, and I wondered what kind of questions they would ask, and how the newly renovated museum, set to reopen in 2018, would attempt to answer them.

There was a book of comments near the exit, and I was about to write my own thoughts on the museum when I noticed the last comment by an anonymous visitor, which read: 'The beauty of the artefacts cleverly veils the truth behind the manner in which they were sought . . . murder . . . exploitation.' I decided to let the anonymous voice have the final word.

A Meeting with Caryl Phillips

In the epilogue of *King Leopold's Ghost*, Adam Hochschild writes:

> My greatest frustration lay in how hard it was to portray indi-
> vidual Africans as fully-fledged actors in this story. Historians
> often find such difficulties, since the written record from the col-
> onizers, the rich and powerful, is always more plentiful than it is
> from the colonized, the poor and the powerless ... if we are to
> enter deep into the personal lives of individual Congolese in this
> period, it may have to be done in fiction, as novelists like Chinua
> Achebe have done for the colonial era elsewhere in Africa.[1]

Through his writing, the author Caryl Phillips is, more than anyone else, the person who has helped counteract the damage done by
my childhood readings of stuff like the Tintin stories and *The Heart
of Darkness*; his sane, nuanced but restrained prose supplants the stupid, ugly, two-dimensional black characters often presented for
beautiful, living, breathing, thoughtful ones. His literary novels are the
perfect antithesis of colonial propaganda and, as I continue to explore
my Afro-European identity in relation to the continent I call home, his
non-fiction has been a priceless map of under-explored territory.

His first published piece of non-fiction, *The European Tribe*
(1987), is one of the few direct precursors to this book. The difference is that Caryl wandered as a young black man in his twenties
through white Europe, before the work of his generation had
helped the continent even entertain the idea that there were black
people taking an active part in its societies. The work is quietly
subversive, playing with the notion of an approach white
people often assume when travelling in Africa: as an outsider

observing a strange tribe practising odd rituals. He normalized the black gaze, becoming an invisible eye, and instead otherized Europeans as something strange and exotic with a nudge and a wink.

I'd sent an email to Caryl's literary agent when I found out he'd be in Belgium around the same time as me, hoping to connect with a literary hero, the same way he himself had once reached out to James Baldwin on his own European sojourn in the 80s, and he generously agreed to meet up with me in the café of Liège's elegant Crowne Plaza hotel.

When he emerged out of the lift, dressed in the only outfit I've ever seen him in since (head to toe in non-committal black), he greeted me quietly but warmly, with eyes that looked slightly jet-lagged. Either that or he'd been up all night writing, the non-space of a hotel room being Caryl's favourite place to work. We both ordered a black coffee, and Caryl asked about the nature of my travels. I told him that it had parallels with *The European Tribe*, except it flipped the journey on its head. That my book was aimed more robustly towards being black in *black* Europe.

'Well, things have changed a bit since I travelled,' he said, with the slightly nasal, wry voice and pithy intelligence I've come to associate him with. He wasn't just talking about the fall of the Berlin Wall, the geopolitical restructuring of large sections of Eastern Europe and the fall of Communism, of September 11th or the mass migrations to Western Europe from Syria, Sudan, Somalia, Eritrea, Poland, Albania, Kosovo, Ethiopia and Afghanistan, but also of the predominance and exposure of black European sport and music stars, scholars, academics and TV personalities.* As Caryl has put it, 'It's not just the new ways one can travel these

---

* Before setting out on my journey, I approached a publisher with the idea for this book and they replied, 'It's already been done,' mentioning *The European Tribe*, a book that had been written around the time I was born. This frequently happens to young creatives setting out to tackle the idea of blackness – I've had first-hand experience of it in TV, literature and radio – commissioners make narrow room for one or two ideas every so often, with various angles on the same theme unthinkable.

days, or the new boundaries on the European map, the major change is visibility. Back then I lost count of the times I walked into a pub, restaurant or museum and had the heads of bewildered Europeans turn and look at me. It's possible to think about nationality in a new way. [Afro-Italian footballer] Balotelli forces the debate about identity in Italy, and most other European countries now have non-white footballers, which wasn't the case in the early 80s. It would be difficult to look at the continent today and find a place without some consciousness of non-white communities, and that simply wasn't true when I wrote *The European Tribe*.'[2]

But Caryl did question how much had really changed in the way Europe has dealt with its black communities in the last thirty years and he has, despite various offers, refused to write a follow-up because, depressed as the notion made him, he felt he would come to exactly the same conclusions today. When you read his summary in *The European Tribe*, it's hard to argue with him:

Europe, at this late hour, is trying to forge a new unity through trade, despite the divisions at the heart of the European consciousness, as squabbling tribes stare at each other across national boundaries. Politically in a state of panic, economically no longer dominant, Europe seems now to be left with only the role of moral leader to play.

But before she can become a moral leader she must go to confession. She must not be too proud to admit that she is in the same position as much of the Third World in terms of an increasingly paranoid allegiance and dependency on one camp or the other. And she must acknowledge that the continued toleration of racism in her belly threatens to consume any chance of a positive moral initiative. She still looks askance at 'strangers' as they alone reinforce a sense of self. Ultimately, the one certainty for Europe is that she knows a 'nigger' when she sees one: she should – they were a figment of her imagination, a product of her creative mind.[3]

This last statement echoes the sentiments of his friend James Baldwin, who once said, 'I didn't invent him. White people invented him ... I've always known that I am not a nigger ... he's unnecessary to me, so he must be necessary to you.'

The European Tribe caused a bit of a furore when it was published and, growing tired of Europe's – and especially Britain's – rigid sense of itself, Caryl left for America in the early 90s and hasn't looked back. Like Europe did for Wright and Baldwin, Caryl told me that America allowed him the chance to focus on his craft rather than pigeonholing him as a professional at being black.

'You find that as soon as you open your mouth and speak with an English accent, you are embraced by white America in a way that African-Americans aren't. You're "different" because there is no shared history for them to feel uneasy about. In Britain, as a young black writer, I was constantly being asked to be a social commentator. I didn't want to keep having to explain how I felt when black kids in Brixton were murdered, I wanted to focus on being a good writer.'

This should not be mistaken for apathy; on the contrary, when I mentioned being incensed at the depiction of black people in *Tintin in the Congo*, Caryl revealed exactly what his methodology was when he told me, 'Don't get angry, just refocus on your work to make a change ... you're an artist with far more penetrative weapons at your disposal. And as you work, just remember: no well-behaved black man ever changed anything.' Caryl mentioned a story about a white friend during his time at Oxford who had asked him to meet her father. He held racist views and she felt that Caryl's articulate intelligence might help her father see sense. 'Initially, I was a bit put out by the request, thinking, *That's not my job*. But the more I thought about it, the more I realized that, actually, perhaps that *is* my job.'

Sitting there dressed in black, expounding thoughtfully on the dilemma of blackness, Caryl struck me as that rarely celebrated type of black success story. There was no 'get rich or die trying' ethos, no super-capitalist brand-endorsing mega-celebrity or hyper-sexualized fashion-icon status, he didn't do social media and rarely appeared on television. He represented understated, almost stealthy influence. Caryl was a black kid from a council estate in the north of England who was being read across the world, taught about in higher education and was himself teaching and influencing the minds of the super-privileged at one of the world's best universities, currently serving as a professor of English at Yale. And he made this all too rare journey with hard work and focus on his craft, any anger or disenchantment found not in a Twitter rant but in subtle and well-considered arguments in beautifully written prose, in *deep work* that allows us to enter into the minds of those often written out of history. It isn't the only way to make a change, but it certainly is a path that isn't promoted nearly enough to and among black communities in the West. I mentioned my experience at Bruxelles-Midi to Caryl, and how it brought up memories of being embarrassed at the thought of academic success at school, that being black was incompatible with being a boffin, but he played down his own achievements and said, 'Well, I did go to Oxford, but you're presuming I got good grades . . .' and then graciously invited me to have dinner later that evening, after his talk, with a group of scholars and friends who would help me understand how a once-prominent black British intelligentsia had until recently disappeared from the mainstream.

That's where I met the Jamaican-born dub poet Linton Kwesi Johnson, a long-time friend of Caryl's and perhaps the most coherent voice of a Brixtonized black Britain that neither I nor Caryl ever really belonged to. Linton might be said to represent the nucleus of black British identity, at the heart of the UK equivalent of what Ta-Nehisi Coates, when describing the centre of black thought at New York's predominantly black Howard University, called 'The Mecca'. Over a candle-lit table at an elegant Moroccan restaurant in the heart of Liège, slightly tipsy from a Belgian gin called Peket, Linton recalled the first time he heard of this strange writer from up north. 'He must have been about nineteen or twenty, and he used to send me these letters, saying he admired my work and wanted to meet up, and I thought, *Who's this lickal Oxford bwoy?* And, to tell you the truth, I ignored them, but over the years we have become firm friends.'

For Caryl (or Caz, as Linton and other close friends and colleagues around the table call him), then a young man reading English at Oxford, reaching out to Linton must have been an attempt to connect the cultural dots of an increasingly complex identity. Where could a black kid from the north of England, now moving into a new social class through an elite education, find a scene or collective that could empower his work?

Watching these two old friends – two of my literary idols – talk, I thought of how observing a conversation between people who are simply keeping it real with one another produces an abundance of knowledge. As I listened to their old stories through lively, teasing banter and their thoughts on black British literature, Caryl and Linton struck me as individuals who had taken hugely different paths and ended up at the same destination: a place of wisdom and integrity. Their friendship personified what the construct of black Britain should be at its core: a unifying search for truth and identity against the backdrop of colonial hegemony and misinformation, the creation or unveiling of a history that has been disfigured by the place you call home. As Stuart Hall famously proclaimed, he wasn't truly Jamaican until he left Jamaica and moved to Britain.

Perhaps the biggest topic of discussion around the table was the black British canon and the importance of mentors in order to allow us to stand on the shoulders of giants. Linton said that he owed a lot to Samuel Selvon, the Jamaican writer responsible for *The Lonely Londoners* (1956), perhaps the most illuminating novel about the experience of the Windrush generation in postwar

Britain. Sam had shown Linton 'great kindness' and encouragement, embracing the Jamaican vernacular as a valid form of prose.
Caryl mentioned having recently met up with the St Lucian Nobel
laureate Derek Walcott at his home on the island. 'A difficult man,
but that's why we love him. His eyes teared up as I left and there
was the sense that it might be the last time we'd see each other.'
When Caryl mentioned Derek, I noticed Linton go a little quiet.
'He thinks Derek doesn't like him,' smiled Caryl. It seemed Linton
had felt Walcott never took him seriously as a poet, which Caryl
thought was both amusing and completely inaccurate. 'Derek
loves you, and I really don't understand why you think he has
something against you.' Deflecting the issue somewhat, Linton
looked at me and said, 'In the English-speaking Caribbean we
have two schools of poetry; Walcott is more colonial – a guy who
has mastered the English language – and then there's [Kamau]
Brathwaite, who is more lyrical, and uses slang. The two poets
divide people.'

Hearing Caryl's and Linton's differing journeys towards the
writing scene as they were growing up, it struck me that there had
been a sense of community that was missing among my generation.* Young black British writers, and black presenters and actors,
deal with each other with a certain amount of apprehension.
Rather than the intellectual pursuits and friendly competition that
produced excellence and camaraderie in the 70s and 80s, the type
of connection I see among my peers is often of the unhealthy var-
iety, with more visibility but less collaboration. Perhaps it's because
we don't have the established channels and outlets we once had in
Britain. If I'm not *the* black creative in my field, then someone else
will be, and there won't be enough room for the both of us. This,

* Gary Younge once told me that he felt part of a surge of black thought in the
mainstream, mentioning that Chris Ofili had won the Turner Prize in 1998,
Younge's own debut non-fiction book *No Place Like Home* was published in 1999
and Zadie Smith's *White Teeth* came out in 2000. Younge recalled Ofili saying to
him, 'I remember looking behind us, searching for the next generation coming up,
and they weren't there.'

thankfully, is slowly changing, as writers and artists such as Cecile Emeke, Akala, Afua Hirsch and Reni-Eddo Lodge cut out the middle men by hammering out a space online, forcing the establishment to take notice after building up their own audience, or forging networks through technologies such as WhatsApp. But only recently a friend of mine was told by a producer at a major broadcaster that his audition hadn't been successful because they 'already had their black presenter'. There are two unhelpful ideas floating around that have created this situation. One is that we black Brits aren't black at all; we're British and should get over it. The other is that when jobs come up we're suddenly all too black. 'We aren't looking for another black presenter.' But . . . I thought I was just British?

I expressed this frustration and Caryl said that a lot of creative and artistic unity in the 80s came through organizations like the Black Theatre Co-operative and the Keskidee Centre, Britain's first (now defunct) fine arts centre for the black community, which would commission its own projects, and the left-wing black literature and feminist scene that produced such things as the Theatre of Black Women, through which authors and playwrights like Bernardine Evaristo, Patricia St Hilaire and Paulette Randall came to prominence. Some of this movement was funded by the Greater London Council, dismantled by Margaret Thatcher in 1986. Later, blackness was seen by many as a limiting prism through which to work as a writer and artist.

Caryl said, 'There was a feeling at the time that all the work had been done, and black Britain had integrated so fully into society that it was now simply "Britain", which of course wasn't true.' There was also the issue of the commodification of blackness. In an excellent 2004 conversation between Kodwo Eshun and John Akomfrah about the Black Audio Film Collective, which I cherish as being one of the most inspirational and foremost examples of black British collective excellence, Eshun paraphrases the art critic Kobena Mercer: '[We now live in] an era of multicultural normalization, in which diversity is increasingly administered as a social and cultural norm in postmodernity. Mercer went on to say that contemporary artists no longer feel responsible for constructing Afrodiasporic presence as an object of knowledge in the marketplace of multicultural commodity fetishism.' This chimes with something French anthropologist and essayist Marc Augé wrote:

> Before they are even formulated, calls for pluralism, for diversity, for recasting, for the redefinition of criteria, for openness to other cultures, are absorbed, proclaimed, trivialised and staged by the system, meaning in concrete terms by the media, the fixed and moving image, the political and other authorities. The difficulty facing art, in the broadest sense of the word, has always been to distance itself from a society that it has to embody, nonetheless, if it wants to be understood . . . it has to be expressive and reflexive if it wants to show us anything we do not see daily on TV or in the supermarket.[4]

As blackness in Britain was commodified and neutered by a country that in the 90s was convincing itself of being a 'post-racial' society, and that blackness had won and made itself invisible, blackness had to find a different form to move forward. Now, in light of the recent spike in nationalism, and the evidence that Britain, and the rest of the West for that matter, clearly isn't post-racial, it seems that it is time to reclaim blackness for collective change.

Organizations such as the Keskidee Centre and Race Today gave people like Caryl his first sense of a black community, which was perhaps not as empowered in 60s and 70s Leeds, and Linton a hub of black literary and intellectual excellence, when the rest of society saw people like him as a social 'problem'. When I complained about the lack of such centres of black excellence in existence today, Linton set me straight.

'We went through hard times with the British Black Panthers so that the next generation could thrive. You kids don't realize how good you've got it, compared to what we had to go through. It's like Chinua [Achebe] once said, "We wrote about politics so you can write about daffodils." '

It's true (for the time being, and of course with notable high-profile exceptions such as the killings of Stephen Lawrence and Mark Duggan) that my generation in Britain hasn't had to resort to the kind of desperate organized protest movements like the British Black Panthers in order to defend ourselves against skinhead gangs and overt, violent racism from police, like Linton's. But there is a certain disjuncture between all those writers who came of age and collaborated in the 80s and young black Britons today. It's as though all this great knowledge work was done and then not passed down to the next generation as coherently as it should have been. How many twenty-somethings could name a Linton Kwesi Johnson poem? How many have read a Caryl Phillips novel? Know who Kobena Mercer is? Could reference Bernardine Evaristo's activism in the 80s? I'd read my way through Toni Morrison, Ralph Ellison, Richard Wright, James Baldwin and Alice Walker way before I'd read anything Caryl had written. Yet Caryl's work was much more pertinent to my life as a black kid growing up in 90s Britain than civil-rights-era writing from across the Atlantic. Why was so much important black British writing languishing on the dusty shelves of specialist bookstores, or confined to the dark recesses of cultural studies (where I eventually found *The European Tribe*)? Why is so much of the Black Audio Film Collective's work out of print and difficult to obtain?

I posed these rhetorical questions to Caryl, and he shot me a characteristically bemused smile that was in fact full of understanding. 'Just a moment – you found a book I wrote thirty years ago in a bookstore . . . ? What is there to complain about?' Many bookshops didn't even have a cultural studies section to house such a book when Caryl was crafting his skills as a young reader and writer.

The drinks in Liège flowed through the night, the atmosphere tipsy and convivial. My memories of the rest of the evening are scant. I remember that, when I left, Liège was covered in a blanket of snow, with a sky full of huge snowflakes. I stumbled out into it, realizing I'd had too much Peket. I'd told an embarrassing joke that had silenced the whole table, which included top-tier academics from around Europe and America. I'd unwittingly dissed Caryl for his books not being popular enough and suggested that the efforts of Linton's politically engaged generation had failed black Britain. But I staggered out of that restaurant a different man, feeling that there were powerful people in my own image who not only wanted to help me but understood exactly what I was trying to say, and how I might go about saying it more eloquently, because they had made a similar journey.

I had no idea it would happen then, but you are holding this book because Caryl introduced me to Linton, who introduced me to his partner Sharmilla, who introduced me to my literary agent, Suresh, who sold my book to Penguin. Caryl Phillips, or Caz, as I, too, now call him, was the first real author from the older generation I'd ever connected with, and continues to act as a mentor, helping me navigate my way through this treacherous terrain of class and race in literary high society. African-American academic and philosopher Cornel West has mentioned how, despite imagery that seems to suggest the contrary, empowered black intellectual and political traditions are fragile things, with a long history of being crushed and constantly in danger of being lost. Yet these legacies continue to survive somehow, and it's each generation's responsibility to keep dusting them off and to contribute another chapter. It would be in Amsterdam that I'd meet a group of people providing the ideal template on how to do just that.

AMSTERDAM

Fight the Power

As I'd seen in Brussels, darkness deforms a city and calls in certain characters, especially around train stations. Even day dwellers are different by night – drunker, freer, wilder – and drizzly Amsterdam greeted me as a cliché of itself, which is to say it resembled a free-for-all freak show. It was a kind of sinister version of William Klein's *Broadway by Light*, all disorientation and distortion, neon-lit signs, rainy reflections, everything moving and flashing against a shiny night-black canvas as British bruisers on stag-dos staggered around with surreal faces. As always, the most obnoxious behaviour I witnessed on the continent was being enacted by British men.

The route to my hostel took me past bondage stores selling huge spiked dildos in electric colours, reductive images of Bob Marley being used to advertise the sale of Moroccan 'zero zero' hash brownies and a gay-underwear boutique with some boxer shorts that had the words 'Good boys go to heaven, bad boys go to Amsterdam' printed on the crotch. As I passed through the stoned, swaying, male-heavy masses and drug pedlars who offered a shopping list in super-fast time – 'Charlie, weed, mushroom, speed . . . !?' – with obese tattooed men in football shirts bathed in the crimson lights of prostitutes' windows, it struck me that parts of Amsterdam at night really were a kind of hell.

Because I'd left booking until the last minute, the only place I could find within my budget was a place called Shelter City, 'a Christian hostel in the heart of the red-light district', which on arrival subjected me to some awful live Jason Mraz-style acoustic music with a Christian twist. My sanctuary would be The Devil, or De Duivel, a legendary hip-hop spot nearby, where I would contemplate the sacred texts of Mobb Deep and Nasir Jones every night. One evening, the barman-cum-DJ informed me that Public Enemy were performing that very night and some tickets were still available. I ran straight over to the venue, Paradiso, bought my ticket and, as I entered, Public Enemy were already on stage performing to drunk middle-aged white men and women splashing plastic pints of Heineken on to my trainers. There was a lot of Dad dancing and Black Power fists thrown out willy-nilly, in the way Ibiza ravers make chemical-induced shapes with their hands to house music. The pissed crowd shouted, 'I'm black and I'm proud!' and 'Fight the power!', which of course is fine for people of all colours to shout, but nobody here was fighting any power. If anything, being a 95 per cent Western, white, male, management-aged audience, *they were* the power! In the middle of the show Flavor Flav, who has appeared on everything from *Celebrity Big Brother* to *Celebrity Wife Swap* this century, thanked the crowd for supporting his reality-TV show, *Flavor of Love*, adding, with that part self-justifying, part self-loathing slogan all sell-outs embrace, 'Hey, man, we all gotta pay our bills,' to which the hammered, incoherent audience cheered rapturously. Even Chuck D had recently and somewhat demeaningly parodied himself in a Will Ferrell movie as a spoof black militant called Malcolm Y. The experience left me traumatized; mumble rap was one thing, but seeing Public Enemy in such a state made me realize that, in the twenty-first century, US hip-hop culture is no longer a place where important social issues and political ideas are being worked out in public. Was it even a culture any more? Thankfully, I'd find the spirit of black resistance that hip-hop once boldly embodied and transmitted alive and well elsewhere in the Dutch capital.

*

By day, central Amsterdam wears an entirely different face and is one of the world's most pleasant cities. Parts of the city evoked the Brooklyn neighbourhood my father grew up in, something to do with the autumnal hue of the streets, which, like New York, were most beautiful when littered with leaves, and the rows of elongated terraces of reddish brick buildings lining the boulevards like brownstones. New York was once a Dutch trading post called Nieuw Amsterdam and, though physical remnants of the Netherlands' influence are now scant, there are a few Dutch architectural cues, most notably the stoop found on brownstones, *stoep* being a Dutch word for a feature used to elevate the entrance of a home in case of flooding, a frequent threat in this low-lying country. Many of the place names that conjure up black heritage in contemporary New York have Dutch heritage: Brooklyn is from Breukelen, a town on the outskirts of Utrecht; Harlem comes from the town of Haarlem near Amsterdam; Bedford–Stuyvesant is partly named after Peter Stuyvesant, the last director general of the 'New Netherland'

colony. The Bronx comes from Jonas Bronck, a Dutch farmer; Coney Island is old Dutch: Conyne Eylandt; Rikers Island is named after Dutch settler Abraham Rycken; and another of New York's five boroughs, Staten Island, comes from Staten Eylandt, after state generals who governed what was then known as the United Provinces of the Netherlands. Located in the east of the city is Lange Eylandt, or Long Island, where Public Enemy formed.

That areas of America are named after people and parts of Europe isn't especially surprising, but I did come up with a paper-thin theory about why Dutch hip-hop sounds so natural and pleasing to the ear (Zwolle's Opgezwolle are possibly the dopest crew ever to emerge out of Europe) – because Wu Tang, Biggie, Jay-Z, KRS-One, and so on, had partly developed the language and flow of rap with rhyme schemes that frequently orchestrated themselves around Dutch words and intonations (Biggie rhyming 'Stuyvesart' with 'livest one', and so on). Here in Amsterdam, though, I discovered a richer, deeper, more profound connection between New York and Amsterdam, with a legacy that has begun to be resurrected by young members of the city's Afro-Surinamese community.

A short, peaceful walk to the east of the red-light district sits Hugo Olijfveld House, a large reddish-brown building that backs on to a sleepy section of Amsterdam's Lozings canal, and as I approached I was once again reminded of New York – specifically the boys' high school that my father attended in Brooklyn – and indeed the premises had once been the site of a school. It was taken over in 1973, just before Surinamese independence, by Suriname's oldest association, Ons Suriname, and given its current name in honour of one of its revolutionary board members. This quiet, relatively unassuming building housed an independent black energy in Amsterdam with roots dating back to the early twentieth century, had played a role in the Surinamese independence movement, international Marxist politics and even the Harlem Renaissance, and was about to open up another critical chapter in its proud if somewhat concealed history.

The Surinamese community make up the Netherlands' largest ethnic minority, but there are many Surinamese ethnicities. Afro-Surinamese are the descendants of black men and women brought over to Suriname from West Africa by Dutch slave ships; Indian and Chinese communities came later, to fill the cheap-labour market shortage after the abolition of slavery; while the maroons have a rich and distinct history connected to those who escaped and fought against slavery before abolition and formed their own culture, communities and settlements, sometimes mixing with the indigenous population who had been displaced in their own land by the Dutch. That's not to say that Surinamese culture doesn't have a certain coherence; as well as the history of social interactions, commerce, language, culture and hybrid religions built out of all of the above, one thing all the Surinamese men and women I spoke to in Amsterdam seem to have to deal with is Dutch historical amnesia about why they are in the Netherlands, on the part of a white majority that refuses to acknowledge the existence of Dutch racism, or the history of its slavery and colonialism.

I was greeted at the door of Ons Suriname by Ivette Forster, a filmmaker and television presenter and one of the most recognizable Dutch-Surinamese newscasters, who operates out of one of many creative spaces in the building. She led me up an unglamorous stairway with brickwork walls covered thickly in years of layers of paint, and the lustre of their glossy patina opened up on to a landing of large windows flooding narrow corridors with golden daylight, illuminating original artworks that ranged from black portraiture to black abstraction, across generations of artists, and I got that familiar, magical and all too rare feeling of entering a truly independent black organization space. It had been born out of community and necessity and gradually given form by tight budgets and volunteers, with an atmosphere that was part community club, part grassroots organization, part DIY creative space. All this was far away from what the more ubiquitous, corporate projection of blackness offers, with the type of soulless sheen you might see in a mainstream European gallery once every blue moon, the type where you now see Jean-Michel Basquiat paintings hanging. No, this was the type of place where Basquiat would have *created* the paintings, in a building that was rooted and atmospheric, organic and authentic, which is to say that it had been largely left alone to forge its own identity off-grid and had the sort of subtle stubbornness and calculated reticence needed to survive as something black and European.

I was introduced to Delano Veira, one of the senior members of staff in charge of running the building, and was initially met with a brief and cautious half-smile, before he disappeared and I began speaking with some of the younger occupants of the building, Mitchell Esajas and Jessica de Abreu, two members of Amsterdam's New Urban Collective. Both in their late twenties and of Surinamese heritage, they were a little more forthcoming because they knew of the work I'd been doing with Afropean.com, and though Mitchell had to leave to organize an exhibition under a tight deadline, after giving me a tour of the building, Jessica sat down with me for hours.

Jessica's mother was Afro-Surinamese and her father was born in British Guyana and is of Portuguese descent. She is a brown-skinned female activist, three things which, when combined, white media love to portray as either steely, cool and aloof or as hysterical figures with a chip on their shoulder; as Grace Jones once said about the way society, informed by media, perceives powerful black women: 'A man putting his foot down is in control. He's strong. A woman putting her foot down is out of control. She's weak.'[1] In a patriarchal society women had more hurdles, to be sure, but the truth is that my generation of black activism is often governed by sober and warm black women; they are behind everything from Black Lives Matter in America to Enpad (European Network for People of African Descent) operating out of Germany, to the demos I'd seen in Paris; they are the people who usually hire me for black-related events in London, and among them are various top-tier academics, scholars and writers. As a straight black male who grew up in the 90s, when to call something or someone 'gay' was an attempt to undermine it or them, I'm grateful for a new zeitgeist of intersectional black thought that is often led by feminism and queerness; to be black and strong is no longer reduced to notions of hyper-masculinity, and I found Jessica the personification of this female energy that was moving and shaking the black European community behind the scenes. I did have to check myself for the worst kind of masculine pride, though. Surrounded by old photographs, books and letters (research material for the upcoming exhibition), Jessica asked if I had heard of Hermina and Otto Huiswoud in a way that I perceived was suggesting I should have. As sometimes happens to the hungry writer, especially one feeling the weight of representation on their back, I felt this confused build-up of ego and shame and expectation and wanted to say, *Oh, The Huiswouds? Naturally!*' and wing my way through the conversation to justify the time Jessica was giving to me. But watching Caryl Phillips elegantly answer questions at his talk in Belgium had left an impression on me. Most of his answers had been insightful and veraciously articulate, but one of the most surprisingly impressive responses he gave came when somebody asked a convoluted academic question about the meaning of one of the characters in his novels and he said, simply and honestly, 'I don't know.' It was an example of how conscious incompetence is more powerful than competent ignorance. Thankfully, I overcame the urge to lie and confessed to Jessica, albeit begrudgingly, that I didn't know who Hermina or Otto Huiswoud were.

'Don't worry, we didn't know much about them either,' she said, sensing, I think, that I'd been on the verge of lying, and continued: 'which is incredible, because they are important internationally but especially to the Dutch Surinamese community. What we're working on at the moment – and why Mitchell has had to go – is an exhibition to honour their life, because it is an amazing story that really is missing from too many history books. That is why we wanted to set up the Black Archives in the first place, as a place of study and personal research, and also as a place of resistance, especially to the notion that black people's history is only defined by slavery. The archives are about understanding our history in terms of our own religions, cultures and resistance movements.'

Jessica and Mitchell discovered the story of the Huiswouds after forming the New Urban Collective, a network of Afro-Dutch students and young professionals set up when many realized that obtaining a higher education or even having a decent career wouldn't necessarily insulate them from racism, which, despite being somewhat subtle in the Netherlands, operates deeply at an institutional level. Jessica was born and raised in Amsterdam, referred to herself as black Dutch and, though possessing a traditional education in the human sciences as a cultural, social and business anthropologist, found that her options were limited.

'Higher education can feel inaccessible for people of colour, especially black people in the Netherlands, so we were small in number and began to feel marginalized. The New Urban Collective started simply as a space to feel safe at the university, not only in our bodies but also in our thoughts. We organized meetings every two months to talk openly about the things Dutch society claims don't exist, but we know do, such as racism and inequality. There are all these layers and it doesn't matter how hard you work, you will always be seen as a problem if you're a black person in the Netherlands. I'm studying for my third masters, which is quite privileged but, as I like to say, I have a middle-class education and a working-class bank account.'

As the New Urban Collective grew and connected, there was a realization that many of those all too few black Dutch success stories networking at the universities were certainly rich in one way: they had *cultural* capital as inheritors of the powerful but hidden knowledge of a previous generation. The decision was made to share that powerful black Dutch history among a wider group, bridging a common void between educated middle-class black communities and those who feel they don't belong in the academy, a goal that has ultimately taken shape in the Black Archives. Jessica, who exuded what she was attempting to promote, was simultaneously down to earth and intellectual, and told me how the unveiling of all this history began.

'When we spoke we realized that many of us were actually descended from activists and academics. Two of our members, Thiemo and Miguel Heilbron, are the sons of Waldo Heilbron, who was an important sociologist at the University of Amsterdam and did critical research on the history of colonialism and Dutch slavery. He had this plethora of books at home, so when he passed away in 2009 his sons thought it would be a good idea to make them accessible to the public. Half of those books went to the International Institute of Social History, and they approached the New Urban Collective with the other half.'

After acquiring this collection of books, the New Urban Collective found themselves in another fortuitous situation. They'd been running on a shoestring budget in a small room in the rapidly gentrifying area of Amsterdam North, with Waldo Heilbron's books gathering dust on twelve-euro bookshelves from Ikea, and were increasingly struggling to afford the rent. One of the members, Quinsy Gario, who has received national attention for his work challenging the racist Dutch folk character Black Pete (a golliwog, essentially), was attempting to connect with the ageing Ons Suriname association to help them engage younger members of the community and diversify the space. The New Urban Collective became part of that diversification and were offered an office to operate out of.

As we sat and talked in this modern, organized work space, which felt a little fresher and more contemporary than the rest of the building, Jessica showed me some photographs of how it used to look – dusty and full of boxes of books stacked in a seemingly haphazard way, clearly undisturbed for years. They came to a deal with Delano, who runs the building: if they organized the books, they could have the room and incorporate the books into the

Waldo Heilbron collection they already had. That was how the Black Archives began.

'As we were organizing it all we realized that in all these boxes was this whole history – this long tradition of resistance that we as a collective did not know. A history contained in books, letters and archives from the lives of these two activists Hermina and Otto Huiswoud. As we began to build the collection and people heard about it, we started to receive donations from other places in a similar fashion – sons and daughters of black intellectuals who wanted to contribute their parents' collections, and it really grew from there.'

Looking around at the archives, I could see it was small but established, welcoming but with an air of officialdom – a great work and study space powered by an inspiring atmosphere that I could see myself in. It must be how so many white kids who pass through Europe's private schools feel; as though they're taking part in some sort of grand lineage of intellectual endeavour, born from a history they can own and into a future they can shape. At the Black Archives there were books by black Dutch scholars such as Gloria Wekker and Philomena Essed, magnum opus texts like C. L. R. James's *The Black Jacobins* (1938), W. E. B. Du Bois's *The Souls of Black Folk* (1903), Paul Gilroy's *The Black Atlantic* (1993), Frantz Fanon's *The Wretched of the Earth* (1963), plays and poetry from the Negritude Movement and the Harlem Renaissance, classic works of decolonial literature like Chinua Achebe's *Things Fall Apart* (1958) and Wole Soyinka's *Death and the King's Horseman* (1975), and many of them were first editions, with some containing personal notes from the author. There were faded 30s photographs of Otto Huiswoud with African-American poet Langston Hughes in Uzbekistan (with warm handwritten words from Hughes to Hermina Huiswoud on the reverse) and Jamaican poet Claude McKay in Moscow, and old texts I'd never heard of that had been gathered over decades of black intellectual detective work, organization, travel and resistance, acquired and pieced together to advance black communities under the worst odds, filling in the blanks left by Western amnesia or oppression. They were all the physical relics of hidden but remarkable stories written out of national European discourses and curriculums, framed around the lives of two people responsible for the very building I was standing in. Those stories began in the Caribbean, were marinated in New York and ended up in the Netherlands, and were now being resurrected to begin a new journey long after the lives of the protagonists had ended.

Hermina Dumont, or Hermie, as she was known throughout most of her life, was born in British Guyana to a relatively middle-class black family, but after the death of her father when she was young, Hermina and her mother were forced to scratch out a modest living running a small hotel in the former British Guyana capital New Amsterdam for a few years, and later lost everything when a raging blaze turned their business into cinders.

The fire may have been a piece of tragic bad luck, but when they caught the ship to New York in the bitterly cold winter of 1919 the Dumonts were not alone in their migration to the Big Apple, joined as they were by many members of the black diaspora fleeing the various after-effects of slavery, which, after all, had only officially ended with the previous generation. Rural hardship and poverty, segregation, official or otherwise, gross inequality, violence, provocation, deeply restrictive and ingrained structural racism and high unemployment; these were the conditions for the vast majority of the world's black populations across the West at that time. Like many of their travel companions, the Dumonts found a home in the north of the United States – Harlem, New York, to be exact, which was then a burgeoning black neighbourhood being established by those who had fled the poverty-stricken segregated Southern states in a mass exodus in the years after the American Civil War for the international, marginally more progressive industrial cities of the north.

The societal fabric of Harlem operated in much the same way as many localized immigrant areas operate today; a trailblazing family member or acquaintance set up a base and a network in an undesirable neighbourhood, as close as possible to somewhere unskilled labour was needed, which was sustained by older, more established immigrant communities who had themselves fled poverty and persecution, often made up of black, Jewish and Irish people, and offered a point of access for other friends and family members from back home. The shared struggles formed a certain conviviality among these groups, if not always solidarity. For the Dumonts the trailblazer was Hermina's auntie, who had managed to make a home for herself in New York ahead of their arrival, and in Harlem Hermina found odd jobs in the best type of work a determined, intelligent black woman at that time could hope for, which was mainly secretarial. Applying her aptitudes to these seemingly menial roles would help Hermina develop important organizational skills and an attention to detail she would use on a much larger, more political scale later in life. And it would be there in the lively, communal, cosmopolitan atmosphere of 20s Harlem – a life lived out on the *stoep* – that Hermina would meet the love of her life, her longtime husband and partner-in-arms, Otto Huiswoud.

Otto was the son of a father born into slavery in Suriname – then Dutch Guiana – who had been emancipated when he was eleven years old when Dutch slavery ended three decades after it did in Britain, in 1863. Despite what right-wing racist rhetoric loves to suggest, the abolition of slavery wasn't a magical wand that created an egalitarian society overnight. Indeed, it still hasn't created one. When slavery was abolished in the Netherlands, for instance, as in many other areas bound by the Atlantic, authorities were more sympathetic to slave owners than the slaves themselves. In the Dutch colonies enslaved people were forced to keep working for next to nothing for another ten years, essentially to prove that they deserved their freedom, and during this 'trial period' the state gave financial compensation to the plantation *owners* for their 'loss of property', with no reparation for those enslaved.

It's easy to see why many of the first generation of black thinkers after the abolition of slavery worked so steadfastly for what was often called something along the lines of 'the future of the Negro Race', 'the solving of the Negro problem' or 'the Negro question', and why Harlem became a hotbed of potential answers.

Unlike Hermina's, Otto's journey to New York was atypical and had come nearly ten years earlier, in January 1910. In Suriname he'd been apprenticed as a printer, a job which, through the very physical and rare encounter with books for a black teenager, helped to develop in Otto an early interest in literature. However, like so many young black men in the early twentieth century, he succumbed to the lure of the ocean, that vast expanse which seemed to exist outside the oppressive laws of the nation state and its frequent inequalities, and he found work as a seaman, working on a banana boat headed for Amsterdam. The captain of this particular ship, who had seemed so reasonable during enrolment, turned out to be a drunken tyrant at sea, and his behaviour towards the staff became so abhorrent that, when the ship made a brief stop-off in New York, Otto, along with two other deckhands, also young black Surinamese men, skipped ship, freezing and broke, barely speaking a word of English and without any travel documents.

Armed with only a birth certificate, a letter of recommendation from his parish priest, a suitcase full of tropical clothing, a barely passable amount of English and his wits, Otto, like many superheroes of first-generation immigration, somehow constructed a life for himself out of these scant ingredients. The three men, asking around for jobs using Otto's broken English, fell in with a mixed-race couple, a black man and his white Irish wife, who had a place over a saloon bar and fed them hot stew and cold beer, offered them a room to stay for the night and even a connection to possible employment. This was working-class solidarity in action nearly a decade before Lenin installed it as an international political movement. Otto used the skills he'd learned back in Suriname to work for a Jewish printer, a job he started the day after he arrived, thanks to an introduction from his host. This fortunate start in a city with a reputation for welcoming immigrants quickly gave way to the sombre reality of structural racial discrimination – when Otto lost his job because his boss went out of business, he couldn't become an accredited printer himself, due to the National Printers Union's refusal to induct black people.

If New York at large was certainly no picnic, the atmosphere of prejudice and inequality was mitigated somewhat by a collective consciousness at street level in a scene that would become known as the Harlem Renaissance, that nucleus of black diaspora excellence located in the northern Manhattan area during the 20s which would reverberate throughout the twentieth century. The era has been reduced by mainstream media to gaudy dancing and jazz music, but the true beauty of the Harlem Renaissance lay in the fact that it was a social space for culture creation, connecting the first generation of born-free black creatives and intellectuals from around the world who were attempting to reconstruct, empower and uplift the black community. It included many names we'll hear more about throughout this book; political thinkers such as Marcus Garvey and W. E. B. Du Bois, poets and writers like Claude McKay, Langston Hughes, Countee Cullen, Zora Neale Hurston, Alain Locke, musicians like Fats Waller, Louis Armstrong and Duke Ellington, dancers and artists such as Josephine Baker, Lois Mailou Jones and Aaron Douglas. It was a complete movement, scored, illustrated and scribed into history, and as Otto Huiswoud's transformation from broke, uneducated teenager to major player in the American communist party would show, it was a crucible of radical black thought, a meeting of the minds that helped cultivate an atmosphere of intelligence and resistance as well as high-level art and literature: a magnet and a mecca for the new generation of the black diaspora.

A major force behind the politicization of Harlem was the so-called 'father of Harlem radicalism', Hubert Henry Harrison, one of many soap-box speakers spreading a brand of black socialism throughout the working-class streets. While the over-regulation and gentrification of metropolises in the twenty-first century make spontaneous, communal meetings increasingly difficult, historically, people have migrated to big cities not only for employment opportunities but because they're places of difference, places where one's soul might be ignited, one's mind broadened and challenged, where every day unexpected opportunities emerge, a place where one becomes *cultured*. This is exactly what happened to Otto – he fell under the spell of Harrison quite by chance, listening to Harlem's riveting orators simply to practise his English and get free entertainment of an evening.

After Otto met and married Hermina in this dynamic, gregarious black enclave of New York, the Huiswouds were inducted into the Harlem melange by Harrison and became a fixture on the social scene, with frequent lunches, debates, dinners and soirées in the company of luminaries such as Langston Hughes and Claude McKay, Richard B. Moore and many others. Within this group of friends, you had former residents of places such as Suriname, Jamaica, Missouri, Sainte-Croix and Barbados, with mother tongues of American English, British English, patois, Creole, Dutch and Danish. The Harlem Renaissance, then, was fuelled by movement and multicultural collaboration, which in turn made it the nexus of formally displaced and subjugated peoples. It became an African diaspora city, built on the foundations of African-Americans who'd travelled north and men and women from all over the Caribbean bringing various languages, cultures, educations, tales of resistance, folk stories and ideas that had survived European colonialism with them. This connected to the socialist mood being spread in Europe at a time when the Russian Revolution appeared to herald a new world order that might power up black communities fighting against Western imperialism. The Cold War is often thought of as beginning after the Second World War, but the seeds of it were being planted much earlier, and black communities already at this time found themselves in the middle of the transnational ideological tug of war between East and West.

Otto Huiswoud ultimately became the first black founding member of the American communist party and played an important part in the political foundation of Harlem, before spreading socialism across the globe; during his time he met with Frantz Fanon in Algeria, debated Marcus Garvey in Jamaica, organized with Kwame Nkrumah in Ghana and even met with Lenin in Moscow. His extraordinary travels and work rate throughout the 20s and 30s was slowed down by ill health, and on doctor's orders he returned to the warmer climate of Suriname in 1941, but there was to be no homecoming celebration and his health issues were only exacerbated. Upon his arrival he was met by authorities tipped off by a suspicious American government about his political activity and thrown in jail for a year, set free only when the Soviet Union allied with the US against Hitler a year into the Second World War. When the war was finally over, Otto couldn't return to America, where Hermina was still living, because of the anti-communist sentiment that now pervaded the country, so, in deteriorating health, he used his Dutch passport to migrate to Amsterdam.* Otto arrived in 1947 and, after a painful period of time apart, Hermina joined him two years later, travelling in from New York. The reunion was emotional but the celebration was brief, the Huiswouds getting back to work almost immediately, and together they took control of the Ons Suriname association in 1951 and politicized it, turning their headquarters from a place of dancing and music into one of resistance, fighting for Surinamese independence, which, though he contributed to it, Otto never lived to see – he died of liver failure in 1961.

Internal differences within the communist party, which Otto

---

* In a spooky recollection of growing up in Amsterdam, Gloria Wekker recounts how, like many pre-independence migrants from Suriname, she was raised in an old Jewish quarter. It was only as she grew older that she understood why there were so many houses available.

found himself on the wrong side of, and the whitening of communist hero iconography have meant that Otto's story has been left out of numerous key texts about the founding of both the American communist party and the history of communism in general. There was frequently an absence of black actors in the myth-making of the socialist Left, but Joyce Moore Turner's search for the missing narratives of people like Otto and her father Richard B. Moore in an excellent book entitled *Caribbean Crusaders and the Harlem Renaissance*, led her to an interesting discovery:

> Communist Party Comrades who worked with Huiswoud, Moore, and Briggs might have had short memories when they wrote their memoirs, but the three veterans were never forgotten by the Federal Bureau of Investigation. Records of their activities occur far more frequently in government archives than in biographies and histories. Beginning in 1920, surveillance was part of their lives. For decades agents followed them, conducted inquiries and investigations, tapped their telephones, and opened their mail.[2]

If Otto's story is often missing in left-wing history books, Hermina is completely absent, but it is her quiet, methodical organizational and documentarian skills that we can thank for the passing down of the Huiswoud legacy to the Black Archives in Amsterdam. Her memories, memoirs and artefacts were the basis for much of Joyce Moore Turner's account of the Huiswouds' lives and the Harlem Renaissance. Hermina is the reason her and Otto's book collection and archives survived and fell into the right hands, and it is the records she kept (Otto, perhaps for valid reasons, had no archives of his own making during his life) that form the Hermina Huiswoud papers which have been preserved by the Tamiment Library at New York University. She was also key to making sure that Ons Suriname survived as an organization into the twenty-first century, because she outlived her husband by thirty-six years.

When Joyce Moore Turner – who had known Hermina and

Otto as a child through their friendship with her father back in Harlem – began attempting to write the book about their life in the 90s, however, even she stumbled upon some obstacles that could have meant the knowledge Hermina had would die with her, as she explains:

> While conducting research we located her in Amsterdam and sought to visit her. Her initial response was not encouraging. She wrote, 'if you insist you are welcome to "drop over"', and disclaimed having information that we requested. The visit, however, quickly transformed into a warm encounter . . . a close relationship developed, and I visited her every year. Her reserve – and perhaps a trace of caution practiced during the surveillance of her communist years – was apparent on the first visit when she cautioned us not to talk in the apartment and escorted us to Vondelpark.[3]

As we know from the government archives Turner uncovered, Hermina had good reason to be a little paranoid about discussing her past activities, and she refused to have any conversations taped, even by someone so closely connected to her political history. But there may well have been another reason for Hermina's reticence: the world she had fought so hard for appeared, leading up to and at the time of her death, to have fallen into oblivion or been completely neutered. In 1998 she could have easily felt herself to have taken part in the wrong side of history, or at the very least in a political project that had been utterly discredited by society at large.

'She had lived long enough to witness the fall of the Soviet Union,' Turner writes:

> The vision of a more equitable society had been grossly miscarried by Stalin, and the Cold War had created more instruments of war than a satisfying life of peace. She summed up her despair in a few words: 'After seventy years the people of Russia are still suffering. This is not how we thought it would turn

out ...' The apparent demise of socialism, which she had embraced for sixty-five years, seemed to herald her own demise.[4]

When Hermina Huiswoud died in the late 90s, before September 11th, the invasion of Iraq and the global financial collapse, many world leaders bought into the idea that Western liberal democracy had not only rid the world of communism for good, but also that it was going to solve all the world's major problems into the new millennium. In 1992 Francis Fukuyama wrote his famously persuasive but now almost amusingly anachronistic 'The End of History?', based on an infamous 1989 essay in which he suggested that the fall of the USSR was the final stage of a new world order that marked 'the end point of mankind's ideological evolution and the universalisation of Western liberal democracy as the final form of human government'.[5] This accompanied a broader war on the imagination of any worldview that didn't chime with a belief in Western capitalism as the only sensible route forward, and politicians began to speak less about their dreams for a more equal society and more about their business acumen.

I asked Jessica how she attempted to connect to the fragile history of black radicalism and the information that sometimes gets lost between one generation and the next.

'Well, I think this happens in a lot of black communities. I hear it from African-American friends a lot, that there is this gap between, say, the civil-rights generation and the Black Lives Matter movement. I think the older generation sometimes raise an eyebrow, as if to say, *Don't act like you're doing something new.* They feel that their work is being forgotten and we are somehow erasing or overriding it. We have had this with some of the things we've done; older people can feel disempowered and disconnected, and they feel that they can't contribute anything to the new movement. With Delano and Ons Suriname we were lucky that it just happened in a very organic way. Delano invited us here and we enjoyed work that felt like literally unboxing and archiving our history. That is when a connection happens, you need to want to know more about the history that has never been taught to you, and seek out those who lived through it and encourage them to share their memories. What motivates this is when you realize that history is connected to who you are in a very real way, that knowing history is gonna help you know more about yourself and understand why you are so marginalized, socioeconomically, culturally and politically. It gives you the tools to unpack the present and perhaps change the future. So we always just had this intergenerational flavour and when we opened up this story about the Huiswouds it created a link. People came to us from all generations and they were saying, "Oh my god" . . . It brought back so many memories for them, and they were glad we were interested. They really wanted to speak about it, more so than write about it, which is why our task is to do oral history as well as written. None of this was planned, but at least going forward we now know how intergenerational collaboration might be organized.'

The cracks that were papered over in the 90s and 00s are now starting to become painfully evident again, which is bittersweet for black communities, because it has been something of an inspiration for the political re-engagement of a new generation. Black British scholar Kehinde Andrews has claimed that in many ways Trump is a better US president for black people than Obama, and others believe that Brexit Britain is better for immigrant communities than Blair's Britain, because their position is clearer. The so-called 'race card' black communities are chastised for playing no longer resembles the joker to any fair-minded person. The latent racism in Western society that we all knew was always there during the 'post-racial' moment of the late-twentieth and early-twenty-first centuries is being brought to the surface, and this helps to politicize, galvanize and mobilize those who are the targets: being called a nigger does more to motivate and educate, does more to elucidate the position of the victim than the perpetrator. It gives onus and impetus to start organizing in the way Jessica is.

'One thing that we found in the archives is a bunch of old photographs of demonstrations and other political events that had gone on, and we realized that the people in those pictures were the moms and dads of the people in the New Urban Collective, and were involved in various movements. You can see their faces in the crowds, yet many never told their daughters or sons or siblings, probably because they wanted to protect their children from the same things, and perhaps also because they felt that life really was easier for us. My mom, for instance, actually played a role in the resistance with the stuff going on with the Surinamese community in the Bijlmer. Even when she'd see me going out getting involved with recent demonstrations and being arrested, she never told me about her own political history. So now when I'm going through all this drama I actively look for some sort of precedent, and find the people involved to tell me more about it rather than waiting for them to tell me.'

Jessica grew up in the Bijlmer, which, historically, is perhaps the Netherlands' most well-known (or 'notorious', if you read Dutch newspapers) Surinamese area, orientated around the Bijlmermeer housing project, a typically vast, borderline-bonkers estate concocted in the 60s and inaugurated in 1970. From a bird's-eye view the buildings closely resemble the Park Hill housing estate in my home town of Sheffield, and indeed the project was partly inspired by it, shaped into huge honeycomb-like sections over 900 hectares of former farmland to house more than 100,000 inhabitants in over 35,000 dwellings. It was originally built as a futuristic, utopian vision for a growing white middle-class population, with interconnected parks, leisure facilities, canals, schools, playgrounds and intricate networks of traffic streams; car access was separated from kilometres of pedestrianized walkways while *The Jetsons*-style space-age flyovers shuttled trains overhead. When you look at the original plans of Bijlmermeer, free of concrete rot and years of underfunding, they are impressive, laid out in topographical drawings by the accurate pencil of a draughtsman.

But for various reasons, including bureaucratic amendments to the designer's original plans, high rent premiums and the popularity of smaller new towns around Amsterdam built on a more human scale, the Bijlmer grossly exceeded the demand of its target demographic and was left semi-deserted for years. This under-population of the new Bijlmer estate coincided with the years leading up to and succeeding Surinamese independence in 1975, as the immigration of Surinamese people to the Netherlands intensified because of political and socioeconomic uncertainty, and Jessica explained how this created the current – if under threat – identity of modern-day Bijlmer.

'The stream of Surinamese people came to the Netherlands and they didn't have housing because of a Dutch law that forbade more than one Surinamese family living in a single block of housing. But in the Bijlmer, because it was so underpopulated and underused, the Surinamese community squatted and occupied the surplus of flats in the estate, and provided access to housing for other friends and family members that the authorities refused to address. So that's why it's a black neighbourhood, because Surinamese people couldn't find any houses and the government wouldn't give them any. My mom was one of those first people who squatted in Bijlmermeer and said it was quite an organized set-up. The community operated an open-door policy, and if you wanted a place they gave you a choice of various apartments that had been abandoned by the rest of Dutch society. My mom is still there, actually, and has been for thirty-five years. When you google "Bijlmer" all you see is this idea of black criminality, but it was a thriving community built by a disenfranchised people in an unloved part of the city.'

In the 70s and 80s Bijlmer became known as an immigrant area but was largely forgotten about and left to its own devices. However, in the 90s, its reputation reached an all-time low following a catastrophe of colossal proportions that drew global attention to the housing estate and the invisible people living in it.

When, on 4 October 1992, El Al cargo flight 1862 careered into a corner section of the Groeneveen and Klein-Kruitberg flats in the Biljmermeer estate, killing all four people onboard the aircraft and a clearly large but uncertain number of residents, there was initially an outpouring of public sympathy. What the national press focused upon was the enormity of the situation, the heroics of the emergency services and some conspiracy theories about what type of cargo the plane had been carrying, but it eventually became evident that the death toll was hard to calculate because many of the residents in the flats were undocumented 'illegal' immigrants. The Dutch government's first response was encouraging – it offered a one-off amnesty to any resident affected by the crash; they could come forward for help and support regardless of their legal status, to report missing relatives and be given official papers. But other immigrants desperate to be documented, though not directly affected by the crash, started exploiting the offer, and this, along with the enormity of the tragedy, finally brought a taboo and obscured subject into the open: the Netherlands' colonial history. When you look at the newspaper headlines of the time, leaders such as '200 Feared Dead' and 'Confusion about Missing' slowly turned into 'Asylum for Illegal Immigrants after Disaster', and when the victims did indeed turn out to appear to be mostly black and 'illegal', their victim status began to be reframed as villainy. Instead of compassion, the crash ended up sparking a wave of resentment and intensified the perception of Biljmer as a black ghetto.

I'd spent a few rainswept days in Biljmermeer before meeting Jessica and noticed immediately on my approach how different it was to Clichy-sous-Bois in Paris, which was like a rotting leaf that had fallen from the tree of the city. Biljmer, though very much shunted out on the hinterlands, had direct access into the city centre and when I was there I witnessed a diverse community sustaining itself; yes, the inhabitants were mainly Surinamese but, like in many Caribbean cultures, Surinamese heritage and sense of itself is not monolithic, and the markets and restaurants reflected this. There were excellent Chinese-Surinamese restaurants sitting comfortably beside Afro-Surinamese hairdressers', Indian-run market stalls and cosmetics stores and, memorably, indigenous Surinamese sorcerers.

On that first train, shuttling me under a granite-coloured storm cloud and over a labyrinth of asphalt, I noticed something Jessica later mentioned; even from up there on the overhead tracks it was obvious that the sprawl of Bijlmer was becoming gentrified. Construction on the Amsterdam Arena commenced shortly after the crash in 1993 and it was officially opened in 1996, home to huge megastar concerts and the Netherlands' biggest football club, AFC Ajax. This brought with it the usual signs of globalization, such as a new shopping centre packed with an H&M, a Vodafone and a McDonald's, and I thought to myself, *For a black community, this might have been a bigger disaster than the plane crash.* Alighting the train in the pouring rain, I moved swiftly beyond this corporate vision that was creeping up on the lives of residents like a malignant tumour and found a smaller square of independent Surinamese commerce clinging on. I entered an Afro cosmetics store to buy some cocoa butter and wait for the storm to die down, then wandered over to a market stall called Esewara Enterprises which sold woven silks and small, mysteriously dark bottles. A man called Gino wore a traditional outfit that seemed to match his own ethnicity – he had Indian and African features – and he stood arranging the bottles labelled in Dutch and English with titles like 'money oil' and 'love potion'. A black Surinamese man rushed up, exchanged some laughter with the stall owner and then, without a request, was served with an amber-coloured liqueur in an old Brugal Dominican rum bottle. The man sat beside me, giggled, then raised up his shot glass and said, looking at me, 'Is good,' and then downed it in one, a wave of contentment immediately washing over his face. Gino saw me looking and said, 'I make them myself, they are brewed in casks made of very special wood I collect from Africa and Suriname. When you take is like . . . like you know when you take car every six months?' 'Ah, an MOT?' I said, and he smiled. 'Yes, is like MOT for people. It make you better, maybe you have once a week and you feel great – your body work better, is good for pancreatic cancer.' Gino looked over at the man sitting next to me, then turned with a wry smile and added, 'Is also good for aphrodisiac, but you're a young man so you don't need to worry about that!' The man looked at me with a beaming smile again and said, 'It makes you repaired,' before moving on to another stall and saying something in Dutch that I imagined was 'Okay, Gino, same time next week.'

Gino poured a glass of the libido-enhancing formula, which contained something called mang batra, a sort of natural Surinamese Viagra, and instructed me to sip it in order to savour the flavour – it tasted like a strong, spiced whisky – and then down it in one, which I did, and with the alcohol burning my throat I imagined that it probably worked the libido in the same way strong, spiced whisky does. Gino said that the recipes were hundreds of years old, passed down through his ancestors and perfected through generations, and this was just one of many 'enterprises' – he also made his own natural hernia creams, sold beads to ward off bad spirits, and numerous fabrics and textiles.

Perhaps some of this seems like hocus-pocus, but Gino's practice was indeed part of an ancient tradition that had been vital in keeping traditional stories and a sense of culture and history alive among indigenous and black populations – a type of spiritual archive encoded against the eradication of wisdom contained within West African traditions and folklores, which had been crushed by slavery, Christianity and colonialism, under which former slaves were forced to convert.* This tradition belonged to a religion specific to Suriname called Winti, which translates as 'wind' and is a mixture of spirituality brought over from West Africa by enslaved people via indigenous Surinamese beliefs using magic, herbal remedies and rituals to promote balance between humans, as well as communion with the visible and invisible natural forces on earth. These powers take the form of supernatural beings – or Wintis – ancestral spirits situated within the four pantheons of Earth, Water, Forest and Sky. As a dresiman – a healer who works with herbs – Gino was closely associated with the gods of the Earth pantheon, and it struck me that what he was selling, really, was peace of mind. Aside from the historically horrendous conditions under slavery and colonialism for black people, there are modern-day links between first-generation immigrants and health issues connected to increased levels of stress, alienation, depression and chronic homesickness, not to mention non-psychosomatic issues resulting from socioeconomic factors like

---

* The drink I tasted, for instance, was kwasi bita, named after Graman Quassi, an enslaved healer and botanist taken from the Akan kingdom of present-day Ghana who passed on his secret recipe for treating ailments such as malaria.

poor nutrition and inadequate living conditions – very real leftovers from colonial subjugation. Gino's concoctions brought people together through a long tradition of resistance that had survived slavery and, however active the ingredients may or may not have been, no amount of Western science could discredit their role as something familiar, comforting and consoling there in the drab, grey, rainy hinterlands of Amsterdam.*

On my way out of the Bijlmer a few days later I saw a statue of the Winti Earth spirit Mama Aisa (Mother Earth), one of the most important Winti spirits, who symbolizes harmony among ethnic groups within Surinamese culture. Erected in 1986, she stood there resiliently in the pouring rain among the expanse of concrete high-rises, with pigeon droppings all over her face and in a sad state of disrepair. She'd witnessed poverty and plane crashes but, like the Surinamese community in the Netherlands, was still standing, defiantly.

* Western science is increasingly confirming the benefits of herbal remedies.

At the Black Archives I told Jessica about my trip to Bijlmer, and she juxtaposed that experience with the Surinamese community in Rotterdam, which she said wasn't as racially segregated but came with its own problems.

'Here in Amsterdam you have black people in the south-east and white people in the rich south, west is muslim and east is white working class. In Rotterdam everything is spread all over, because they didn't want what happened with Bijlmer to happen there. They didn't want to have black ghettos, so they spread everyone out. All of the Netherlands had this policy where only one Surinamese family could live in each building, but in Amsterdam it failed because of the situation with the Bijlmer, so the authorities in Rotterdam attempted to provide adequate housing across the city.'

Jessica told me that this had had a very distinct effect on the black community in Rotterdam, especially in terms of political consciousness: Amsterdam has had a pronounced history of resistance, whereas Surinamese communities in Rotterdam had been somewhat depoliticized but had a thriving black arts and cultural scene.

'People in Rotterdam tend not to want to speak about segregation as much, simply because they don't experience it as much. But in Amsterdam you are forced to question why being poor is so associated with skin colour. That was a question for me at a really young age, in a way that it might not have been growing up in Rotterdam, where everyone is dispersed. But as my mom says, the world is like a stage and everybody has their place. This is how I see the movement: you cannot take everything on by yourself, you cannot do the subtle and the dialogue then also the confrontation. Important work can be done by those resisting and those assimilating. I personally don't do the "dialogue" thing, but every year I've helped to organize the Kick Out Black Pete demonstrations, and it's actually a beautiful coalition of three organizations who do not always agree in terms of our methodology and how we should solve things, but we manage to build and collaborate with each other for a common cause.'

The Harlem Renaissance was also well known for its

high-profile disagreements between public intellectuals – I revisited a famous one later on in my trip in Marseille – but as long as these disagreements can coexist in a productive way, they can fuel debate and increase standards, giving a political hue to the sometimes naive pursuit of beauty or serving as a creative tonic for political bitterness, producing balance and excellence, as Joyce Moore Turner recounts in her book about the Huiswouds:

> Serious as they were, they had the ability to kid each other and laugh at themselves. There were marked differences noted as well: Huiswoud the quiet thinker who shunned the lime-light, Hermie the efficient collaborator and facilitator who got things done, Moore the bibliophile and extemporaneous 'orator of electrifying passion and clarity', Domingo the astute businessman and caustic and effective writer and speaker, Briggs the clever writer who used the absurd to shock and call attention to the ridiculous position of the opponent. Their names were frequently linked – a testament to the fact that they could work together and maintain their comradeship despite the contentious atmosphere within many organisations.[6]

Knowing *what* to do is one thing, knowing *how* to do it is another, and Jessica was proactive in drawing strength from black knowledge from all disciplines as well as fuelling the ventures of others. I personally sit more firmly on the side of dialogue, but I was inspired by Jessica's clear-sighted punctiliousness and found the reason she had adopted her specific position enlightening, especially with regard to how it was a response to a specifically Dutch brand of prejudice and racism.

'I always invest in black businesses. The largest section of our funding goes to rent, so why not support a black-owned building? It's the same with the graphic designers and curators, but that's my personal choice because I want to invest in marginalized socio-economic communities and communities of colour because we need money. We only have a small amount of funds to work with, because there is no funding to do something related to anti-racism in the Netherlands, they don't even call it racism, they call it "social exclusion". What we started to think about as we built our own archive – and this is only our own thesis – was that the Netherlands, like a lot of Europe, is a welfare state, and every time there is some kind of conflict within society a bit of money is invested and they say, "Okay, so there is a problem, we're gonna give you money subsidies and give you and your organizations a platform to speak about it, as long as you're polite." We found out that there has been a lot of money invested in various black organizations over the years, even here in this organization, Ons Suriname. What happens is that people get comfortable and think, *Maybe we are getting somewhere*, but then each new generation realizes that things really aren't changing so much in the grand scheme of things. In our opinion, whatever our generation does now, we don't want to be dependent on subsidies because it will frame the political goals that we want to reach. You need money, but the problem is that if you take that money there are certain things that you cannot do. Subsidies can be a way of keeping people quiet.'

What Jessica was speaking about is a common trend when it comes to black organizations dealing with funding in Europe, whose money often comes with a caveat that black events never stretch too far beyond what black scholars have begun to jokingly refer to as the three S's: saris, samosas and steel drums. I'd seen the ramifications of this sort of activity at SADACCA, an organization that was set up in the 50s in Sheffield. It is very similar to Ons Suriname in a way but was nearly run into the ground after half a century by an older generation who, unlike the people at Ons Suriname, had grown completely out of touch with the younger generation. It had become a place where nothing other than old gossip and the odd community dance happened.

Ons Suriname, however, is about to celebrate its centenary and, witnessing the work being done there, I could see it had a real reason to celebrate, and a future to look forward to, while many other similar organizations in the Netherlands haven't survived, their demise serving as a cautionary tale. In the 90s the Surinamese People's Information Office was subjected to huge cutbacks under a newly elected Dutch government, and a feminist organization called Flamboyant, which trained women to write letters and read, was closed down when the government stopped the money because it felt the organization was getting too radical. Dutch Surinamese scholar Gloria Wekker mentions the demise of another organization that was greatly reduced not by its own radicalism, but by the growth of the far right in the Netherlands:

> The National Institute of Dutch Slavery and Heritage past and present [was] founded in 2002. This institute, subsidized by the government and the city of Amsterdam, sadly did not live to celebrate its tenth birthday, because it was, like other memorials to the past such as the library of the Royal Tropical Institute and other institutions in the cultural field, abolished by the government Rutte-I, 2010 to 2012, in which the conservative democrats, VVD, in coalition with the Christian Democrats, were supported by Geert Wilders's xenophobic and populist Party for Freedom, PVV.[7]

Wilders is the Netherlands' answer to other xenophobic maniacs across the globe with bad hair and ideas, such as Donald Trump in the US and Boris Johnson in the UK, and his party has enjoyed exponential growth in the Netherlands, coming in second in the last general election, populists drawing on a misreading of national history to address the uncertainty of the future. What Wekker reminds us is that organizations too reliant upon the state are overly subjected to its whims, and she also eloquently explains how people like Wilders have gained a footing in the Netherlands through liberal arrogance. When a society has so convinced itself that it isn't racist, it feels vindicated and victimized when immigrants who are responding to very real racism raise their voices. For instance, despite wanting to ban Muslims entering the

Netherlands and forging close ties with Marine Le Pen's Front National, Wilders refuses to accept that he is racist in a way that is common across Europe and apparently acute in the Netherlands, suffering from what Gloria Wekker describes as 'White Innocence', 'the dominant and cherished Dutch self-image . . . characterized by a series of paradoxes that can be summed up by a general sense of being a small but ethically just nation that has something special to offer the world'.[8] This is a self-image woven around the Netherlands' status as a victim of German occupation during the Second World War, which embraces innocence and defends its innocence so vehemently that when struggling black communities, who, in the case of the Surinamese community, are physical evidence and an uncomfortable reminder of the history of Dutch slavery, are seen and heard, they must be silenced.

Gloria Wekker goes on to quote Afro-German scholar Fatima El-Tayeb: 'To reference race as native to contemporary European thought . . . violates the powerful narrative of Europe as a colour-blind continent, largely untouched by the devastating ideology it exported all over the world.'[9]

Here a distinction should be made. It is encouraged to celebrate signs of being from elsewhere, as long as they are contained and infantilized, segregated from any meaningful role in society – saris, samosas and steel drums to be stared at. It's why the word 'Afropean' irks some people; it inserts a provocative complication into ideas of ethnic absolutism and suggests an assimilation whereby the so-called 'other' doesn't segregate into ghettos or vanish into parody or invisibility but is firmly lodged within the notion of the European.

In the twenty-first century cracks in the façade of Dutch innocence are beginning to show, not only in the form of Geert Wilders's hateful rhetoric but perhaps even more potently with the controversy over an old Dutch fascination with a character called Zwarte Piet – or Black Pete – an underling of Santa Claus dreamed up by a Dutch teacher and poet in a book called *Sint Nikolaas en zijn Knecht* (*Saint Nicholas and His Servant*), which was published in the late nineteenth century. The character is supposedly a representation of a Spanish Moor, though no North African man I've ever met resembles the diminutive creature white men and women, with that odd and embarrassingly resilient old Western obsession, black-face themselves up for every year at the beginning of the festive season.

Even more bizarre than the obsession with Zwarte Piet is the level of anger and vitriol of large portions of Dutch society directed at black communities arguing how blatantly offensive the character is. Jessica and her colleagues, who have staged many non-violent protests at festive parades that include Zwarte Piet, have been on the receiving end of an incredible backlash that has included brutal arrests, widespread condemnation and, perhaps most creepily, 'innocent' parents who feel that these black people are spoiling the harmless fun during Christmas for their poor little white children. Most academic research supports the notion that Zwarte Piet is based on a North African Moor and has sinister slavery and colonial undertones – the character was, after all, brought into existence fifteen years before Dutch slavery was abolished – but Dutch society has woven these details out of the mythology of the character, so for many people it is considered well intentioned and positive, a jolly character kids adore as a fantasy creature made black with chimney soot. For anybody who is black, Zwarte Piet, with his frizzy pate of hair, his big red lips and goggly white eyes, is blatantly racist. I asked Jessica why she thought the suggestion that the character needed to be relieved of his festive duties had generated such a backlash from Dutch society. What was the big deal in getting rid of an out-of-date and divisive sidekick character?

'In the Netherlands, we're in this strange situation where, if you call somebody racist, it's like calling out their mother. It has to do with their self-image; the Dutch are known globally as tolerant because there is a soft drugs policy, the Netherlands was one of the first countries where same-gender marriages were legalized, and prostitution is legalized and controlled. Therefore, the white Dutch identity perceives itself to be liberal, tolerant and open, so how can it be racist? They think that 400 years of colonial empire didn't leave traces, but of course it did, especially structurally.'

Jessica and her colleagues have been working and collaborating on various projects to challenge Dutch structural racism – that is, racism that is inherent in a society, even if not consciously in individuals, because of the way it is organized to place white people in positions as bearers and inheritors of privilege accrued through exploitation. One such project is Decolonize the Museum, which aims to reframe and reinterpret museums with colonial histories and view their collections through a more critical, decolonial lens – a study and critique of those who studied and stereotyped others. The Black Archives project attempts to fill in the missing history of black people in the Netherlands but, as Jessica told me, it wasn't until the 'No Zwarte Piet' movement that the New Urban Collective began to face the very physical consequences of trying to challenge a system that promotes itself as just, egalitarian and progressive.

'As I mentioned, New Urban Collective started as an organization for students and young professionals. We started with a very positive attitude – we would study and work hard together and support each other and be young black success stories – but a twist came the year we formed because that's when Quinsy Gario, an artist who designed a T-shirt with a "Zwarte Piet is Racist" logo was violently arrested, just for having these T-shirts! That arrest gained a lot of attention because it was filmed and went viral on social media. It really spread among the black community because it gave form to our feelings – you always knew that you were being treated differently in this supposedly liberal society, but you couldn't pinpoint it because "racism" and "race" as words don't exist in our daily vocabulary. With the police, this invisible institutional and structural racism came out to play. Who is gonna protect you against the police? Who controls the way our arrests are officially reported and interpreted? Some of the young men on one of our demonstrations were depicted by an artist for one newspaper as tough middle-aged men, but they were really just teenage boys.'

Jessica, who had been so cool and composed, struggled to hold back her tears when she mentioned this story.

'It was emotionally hard because a lot of my friends, they were really brutally arrested. Their hair was pulled out, my friend Jerry was beaten up and others were dragged along the streets because they resisted. There was no reason for them to be arrested; just because you're standing up against racism, that's no reason to be arrested, so that's why they resisted. I still don't know how to think about that period, but at the same time I know I'm happy to be among these people because activism is a really lonely place. Not many people want to do it, it's not glamorous. Everybody is watched by the authorities, my phone is tapped . . .'

Jessica has sometimes questioned why she was drawn to activism but finds herself in a position where a certain Dutch veil has been lifted, and there is no going back. She reminded me why it was so important for black communities to stretch into the continent beyond their own nations, to offer emotional, economic and political support and let each other know that we aren't going mad when the nation state tries to frame us as such. Much of the Stop Zwarte Piet Movement produced literature and online blogs in English in order to reach an international audience, so that it could draw strength from other vilified black communities facing similar situations and share methodologies, tactics and historical considerations. The survivors of the Bijlmer tragedy, for instance, might connect and establish ties and networks of experiential support with the survivors of the Grenfell Tower fire in London.

Jessica showed me an entire cabinet full of documents she's been collecting over the years, piecing together a body of evidence and building a case against Zwarte Piet by collecting pan-European instances of the silly, jovial depiction of black people under various but closely linked versions of basically the same golliwog character – from Belgian comics like Tintin to Scottish children's books, to English jam labels, Danish cafés and Italian coffee, not to mention the ubiquitous dolls. Almost every European country has an iteration of it, and nearly every country has or has had a bizarre resistance to getting rid of it – as if not playing with black dolls with distasteful, exaggerated features would deeply affect their quality of life.*

The Stop Zwarte Piet demonstrations are growing year upon year in the Netherlands, and in a round-about way this silly black character has become something of an avatar for much bigger issues in Dutch society which until recently have remained latent under a liberal gloss. After my chat with Jessica, and having over-heard our conversation, Delano, who was a close friend of Hermina Huiswoud, took me to one side for about an hour and generously explained the history of the Huiswouds and the building to me, gave me his email address and told me that I was welcome to come back any time. He spoke slowly and carefully, with a deep Dutch-Surinamese timbre, and had weary eyes that wavered between stubbornness and demoralization. I found his work heroic and moving; to keep surviving as an independent entity marooned – pun acknowledged – in the Netherlands had clearly not been an easy task, but his legacy, and that of the Huiswouds, was in good hands with the Black Archives, and together they are repairing a powerful but broken black lineage. It was a lineage that was about way more than just the books – perhaps you can get them all on Amazon or eBay – it was the journey and curation of the books, the hands they'd passed through, the knowledge of how the information the books contained had a history of being put into practice and action and used as a source of empowerment. They contained stories, but they also embodied stories, and to pass through the space was invigorating. As I was about to see in Berlin, not all strands of activism in Europe felt like home.

---

* Yet, when I browsed various UK toyshops searching, unsuccessfully, for a beautiful brown-skinned doll in the form of a mermaid or a fairy for my niece, shop assistants looked at me as if I was mad. Someone even said to me, 'Oh, I suppose you want one with a Northern accent, too, do you?'

BERLIN

Whitegeißt

Where I'm from, I was raised socialist almost by default, but my experiences in Berlin unearthed a leftie atmosphere I felt nearly as out of tune with as anything I might find at a Conservative English country club or Republican American golf course.

I arrived in minus-degree weather at the enormous, functional, modern, very German central station that was once the last stop in the old West of the city, and marched east for over an hour through windy, concrete corridors of wide, gridded boulevards until the city's tidiness disintegrated and I found myself dishevelled in Friedrichshain. I may not have survived this journey before the fall of the Berlin Wall. The wall, an embodiment in concrete of the Iron Curtain and a relic of how Soviet Russia and the West divided the spoils of victory over Germany under the Potsdam Agreement following the Second World War, had created two Berlins. One side, ruled by the GDR under the Socialist Eastern Bloc, surrounded an enclave that was open to the West, funded and developed by the Allied powers-turned-postwar Russian rivals: the UK, the US and France. Berlin, then, became a key strategic battleground in a famously covert Cold War and was used to suggest whose vision of the future – the Communist East's or the capitalist West's – was the version the rest of the world might adopt.

During the second half of the twentieth century West Germany became known as something of a European success story thanks to its 'economic miracle', fuelled by commercial and industrial investment and prosperity partially funded by the US Marshall Plan (financial aid Russia refused to accept in order to limit American influence in East Germany). Though some former citizens of the German Democratic Republic lament the loss of what they considered a more egalitarian state, there's no doubt that, shielded from the capitalist democracies of their geographic neighbours for the best part of four decades and disconnected from the free-market economy of Western Europe, East Germany languished in comparison. That's why, despite the fall of the Berlin Wall in 1989, it's said that some citizens who lived through those forty years when Germany was divided (thirty of them by the wall for Berliners) constructed a mental wall in their minds that hasn't entirely fallen, culturally separating an East that is still poorer than its affluent cousin in the West. The reunification of Germany was, after all, younger than I was; I could have spent my early childhood in a nation, system and culture that no longer officially exists.

I have to admit that as I entered Friedrichshain I was guilty of constructing my own type of mental block, and it took a while to subside. Some of the people on the streets seemed to match their severe surroundings, with skin implants, facial tattoos, pointy

Hells Angel beards or extreme no-turning-back piercings, and there were brutal-looking white skinheads with demonic figures tattooed on their necks, wearing leather jackets or gilets with suspect symbols on them. Eagles, clenched white fists, demons and death-metal-band logos sometimes spell trouble for people who look like me. When I checked into the Odyssey hostel, the receptionist told me that Berlin was not a book to be judged by its cover; 'It is an ugly city full of beautiful, open people!' 'Open' was the buzz word in Berliners' mouths and was usually prefixed with 'super'; '*Ja*, Berliners are super-open people' or '*Ja*, we have a super-open society,' everyone would tell me. 'Open' really meant *closed* to anything that was conservative and didn't lean to the left, and very often the beautiful freaks I found down the alleyways of East Berlin were some type of creative, activist or anarchist – often all three.

I first realized that many of the harsher-looking East Berliners were 'open' at a large demonstration a couple of days after I arrived. When I saw the crowd I was on edge because, were I to imagine the scene of a Neo-Nazi march (Neo-Nazism had seen a troubling rise in Berlin in recent years), I'd have pictured precisely what I saw before me on the streets: hundreds of skinheads dressed uniformly in black army fatigues, steel-capped boots, complemented by the National Socialist-evoking colours of red and white on the flags they carried. Some wore hockey masks, balaclavas or scarves that covered their faces and held banners depicting pumped fists. As I tentatively approached the crowd I asked a striking woman who resembled an alien out of *Star Trek: The Next Generation* what was going on. Her hair was shaved and acid blonde, she had no eyebrows and large black contact lenses that made her pupils oversized and surreal. A metal spike protruded out of her chin and she wore a long black cloak with a huge angular collar. Her name was Agatha and she told me that most of the people on the march were members of Antifaschistische Aktion – or Antifa – an anti-fascism organization with roots in Nazi resistance

169

movements dating back to the 30s but which really took hold in the politically tumultuous 80s of Berlin as a response to a spike in far-right activity.

Agatha smiled at me and said, 'We are going to drink, party and fuck up some Nazis, it will be super-fun.' I confessed to her that at first I suspected *they* were all Nazis and she gave me a lesson in contemporary German Neo-Nazi fashion. 'They are not skinheads any more, that is the 80s depiction. Now in Berlin they are more subtle, of course, because they are cowards – they are in hiding, but if you know what to look for you can still tell who they are because they sometimes wear certain brands. There is actually a shop in Mitte called Tønsberg and they sell this one brand that is popular with Nazis called Thor Steiner. It's not just what it represents that is shitty, it's also just totally bad fashion.' I found out that the brand had been banned in Germany for using logos similar to those of the SS (all suggestive use of Nazi symbols is forbidden in Germany), but the company later rebranded and now sells the kind of stuff an armchair MMA fan or Games Workshop enthusiast would wear; lightning flashes and skulls with wings and B-movie slasher fonts. It's easy to forget that a lot of extreme Neo-Nazism is powered by teenagers, but then so is the Antifa movement.

As I made my way through the crowd and got a close-up view I saw that, while some of the demonstrators looked genuinely tough, with boxer's noses or facial scars, many of them could have passed for attendees at a sci-fi cosplay convention. They wore studded jackets with Japanese manga-style depictions of Antifa ninjas high-kicking a Nazi in the head, or swastikas smashed into pieces by comic-book-warrior-type characters. They carried bags with collections of left-wing pin badges and loved a good sticker – every square inch of Berlin was covered in Antifa adhesives. Nearly all the crowd appeared to be under thirty, many barely twenty, and now that I knew they weren't Nazis I started to find it all a little amusing. I also felt completely out of place in that way black people can in such situations, feeling *very* black suddenly, sandwiched awkwardly between the white-on-white violence, and the blackness I wore assumed a strangely conservative and uptight mood. I was embarrassed and unsure about anti-fascist etiquette in such circles; there seemed to be a specific way of dressing, talking and acting. I began to feel cynical about the methods and sceptical about the effects. It wasn't that only black people were allowed to be angry about racism, but this wasn't the rage that fuelled the Rodney King riots in 1992 or the emotionally charged riots in England that followed the death of Mark Duggan in 2011. Neither did it carry the energy of Black Lives Matter, responding to the unforgiveable frequency of unwarranted deaths and beatings of young black men and women at the hands of police, or the events in Ferguson, Missouri, in 2014, following the murder of an unarmed black man called Michael Brown. I think what unsettled me a little is that people seemed to be out there having fun, and I worried that this kind of protest legitimized the thing it was protesting against: policed societies and right-wing resentment.

Berlin's black community were conspicuous by their absence and, while their cause was implied, the mood of the march struck me as divorcing them from any agency within it. I can't speak for every black person, but the more I internalized my mocking of and uneasiness among the young white Antifa crowd, the more I had to admit it was coming from a certain kind of jealousy. Looking at these Antifa, I felt the same way I did when I'd see John Lydon in an interview or Liam Gallagher on a stage, disrupting, being 'real', creating a scene – being anti-establishment because the real establishment, the society at large beyond government, saw them as one of their own, would make them icons one day.* America had its mainstream black rebel icons, of course, some of them embraced by white Europe, but they usually had to become

---

* It turned out that many of those 80s rebels, John Lydon and Morrissey being the biggest examples, weren't left wing but merely contrarians, and have since made allegiances to right-wing politics.

martyrs to gain adoration, safe to embrace because they were no longer alive.

The notion of left wing and right wing emerged from the eighteenth-century seating arrangements in the National Assembly during the French Revolution; those on the left supported secularism and revolution, those on the right the established institutions of power such as the monarchy and the Church, but they were all white Europeans of a certain class. Karl Marx, for instance, who was introduced to the ideas of Hegel at the University of Berlin, was able to conduct his raffish rebellion because he was part of the institution, drunkenly debating in private members' clubs and student fraternities and getting away with shit that would have got others beheaded. When he rebelled it was fair game, a debate then a piss-up, at worst a slap on the hand and a loss of employment.

When I rebelled, even here in the 'enlightened' twenty-first century, I was lumbered with the feeling that I was rebelling on the behalf of an entire people, and when I refrained from rebelling it was to challenge the opinion that I was proof of a black problem; acts of resistance considered fair game when enacted by white people assume a dangerous, radical hue in the eyes of Western society when carried out by blacks. In essence, I wasn't comfortable enough in my own skin for this Antifa stuff, partly because I felt the colour of that skin carried its own surplus of surreality in the surroundings I grew up in; I could be wearing an Oxford shirt and chinos and driving a Toyota Prius, and still be enough of an outsider.

There were hundreds of heavily armed Polizei overseeing the procession, and they looked nervous and pathetic as they watched the Antifa kids drinking bottles of beer and dancing to a selection of out-of-date music booming from huge speakers on the back of a truck, all with a vague reggae rhythm, such as The Streets' 'Let's Push Things Forward' and Lily Allen's 'Shame for You'. The youthfulness of the Antifa movement, tied to alternative music and squatting, made me think of that horrible Tory saying that goes, 'If you're not socialist at eighteen you have no heart, if you're not conservative by forty you have no brain.' Along with the missing black demographic, I wondered where all the management-age Antifa were, and the absence of one spoke of the absence of the other. For most black people in Europe, the battle against prejudice is for life, which is why you have to pace yourself to run a marathon instead of exerting all your energy in a sprint if you want to survive – you can't be throwing beer bottles at police and telling them to go fuck themselves simply for the fun of it. There would be no one to rescue you as a black man or woman with a criminal record in Europe, no system or institution culturally geared in favour of your demographic if you decided you wanted to go on the straight and narrow later. And so the mean-spirited carnival I was witnessing looked to be less about fighting racism and more a chance to release some teen spirit without any repercussions: get hammered, dance to some music and brand it all as being for a good cause. This was a 'safe space' to be dangerous (there was an Antifa helpline for anyone arrested to call the next day), and early on I'd see people in handcuffs laughing and goading the police on as they were led to an armoured vehicle, enjoying the jeery cheers from the crowd.

When I found out who (not just what) the march was being held in the name of, the scene before me made more sense. Though the chants spoke of anti-racism, this demonstration, held annually, was in memory of a young white man called Silvio Meier who was born in Friedrichshain in 1965 and was active in the alternative squatter scene in the 80s, coming up in the radical left of East Germany before the fall of the wall. He'd been involved in a number of altercations with Neo-Nazis, but one fight with a gang of Nazi teenagers in a Berlin subway in 1992 proved to be his last – he was stabbed to death. Along with Davide 'Dax' Cesare, a white anti-fascist martyred in Italy, whose best friend was a guest of honour at the Silvio Meier vigil the next day, Silvio has since become a symbol for what the Antifa movement in Berlin stands for, a specific culture that sprouted out of the fight for a new German identity. Shortly after his death a vigil was held, and every year since then a huge demonstration – the largest in the Antifa calendar – has taken place in Berlin, with a commemorative plaque in the subway station where he was murdered, a Silvio Meier Prize for work in the community and a street named after him.

Though German reunification officially took place in 1989, the full dismantling of the Berlin Wall was only finished in 1992, and in those chaotic few years that have now been neatly packaged into a positive story of peace and solidarity and immortalized with footage of emotional reunions, for many black Germans there was little cause to celebrate. As one wall fell down, another was built; a wall of racism, with reunification becoming an opportunity for the far right to define a new brand of nationalism. This took shape in a surge of right-wing extremism in which members of the far right in West Germany linked with groups of a similar political persuasion in the East. Having suffered economically, the East German Nazis were often responding to the GDR's left-wing 'international' development abroad, which brought guest workers and students over from socialist-leaning African countries.

The Berlin Wall was originally erected in a single evening under the guise of an anti-fascism barrier against the West, and in fact its official title was Antifaschister Schutzwall: the Anti-fascist Protection Rampart. In reality it was built to prevent people defecting and, rather than shielding citizens from fascism, parts of East Germany became a breeding ground for it – there was resentment of the presence of Mozambican and Angolan guest workers during Communism and in 1987 Carlos Conceicao, an eighteen-year-old apprentice from Mozambique – and you won't find a huge annual demonstration in his name – was murdered in a racially motivated attack by German teenagers in the small East German town of Staβfurt.

For young people with reduced opportunities under the failing

German Democratic Republic, there were obvious ways to revolt; through an anti-state far-left movement such as Antifa or through Neo-Nazism, which, living under a left-wing state, was perhaps the ultimate form of rebellion. Sometimes the members of each group were interchangeable – reformed Nazis turned to the left; former leftists switched to the far right – but either way the fall of the wall became an outlet for the disaffection and anger of a generation, with black communities sandwiched uncomfortably in between in the scramble for this new Germany.

As well as the devastating far-right riots that torched Rostock-Lichtenhagen in 1992 and Magdeburg in 1993, and the numerous violent attacks on hostels housing immigrant workers, such as the Angolan hostel in Eberswalde, in the two decades after the fall of the wall over 130 people were killed in racially motivated attacks, including a Neo-Nazi arson attack on a Turkish family home in Mölln in 1992 which left two girls and a middle-aged woman dead, and another the year after in Solingen which ended in the death of another five Turkish women. The few black communities, from countries such as Cuba, Mozambique and Angola, who lived in East Germany before reunification were targeted, with Mozambican Alberto Adriano beaten to death as late as 2000 and, perhaps most famously, Antonio Amadeu, an Angolan worker from the GDR, butchered to death in 1990 in the first officially classified racially motivated murder on record in postwar Germany. Perhaps the most troubling thing about the murders was the light sentences handed down by the courts for the perpetrators and the refusal of the German government to appreciate how serious the situation was: one judge called the motive of a severe attack 'silly racism'. The ongoing trial in the so-called 'kebab murders', in which at least ten people of Turkish descent were murdered throughout the 00s, and which shows clear evidence of the collaboration of an underground far-right network, is being painted by some German press outlets as merely the work of three 'nut-job' serial killers – it's not terrorism when white people plot organized murders in the name of an extreme ideology. The establishment and quick rise of Alternative für Deutschland in recent years – the first far-right party in the country to have electoral success since the Second World War – suggests a troubling trend that goes beyond one-off instances and emerges as an issue at the heart of German society.

I learned about Silvio Meier from one of the demonstrators, Mikkel, as I walked slowly with the crowd after he warned me, 'You should be careful – sometimes Nazis organize a counter-protest and of course they will target you because of your colour.' I asked if that was why so few black people had attended, and he looked at me awkwardly, but I was beginning to realize this wasn't just some over-hyped party and why I'd seen so many worried-looking police-men and women at the start of the protest – unlike me, they knew what it was about to turn into.* As swathes of Antifa made their way down Warschauer Straße the crowd quickly began to swell, and what had been a couple of hundred people at the beginning was now easily a thousand. By the end there were over 4,000 demonstrators.

Mikkel could see I was feeling a bit out of my depth and said, almost boastfully, 'Don't worry – if there are any Nazis we will kick their ass, as we always do – as you can see this manifestation is *not* held from a defensive position.' I looked around. It was getting dark now and the music grew louder, and Bob Marley's 'Burnin' and Lootin'' boomed out of a van accompanying the procession with its own sound system and whipped everyone into a frenzy. The streets were charged and lit up by blue, red and green fireworks coming from all sides – smoke billowed from within the crowd and dispersed into the icy winter evening and rockets were let off from the rooftops of various buildings along the route of the march, where men in balaclavas had climbed and were waving Antifa banners to huge cheers from the crowd. Berlin was being set alight *Blade Runner*-style – all 80s-looking sci-fi punks dressed in black frolicking in neon fog over rain-drizzled streets.

---

* A wealth of new evidence backs up Antifa claims that there may be instances of collaboration between members of the German *Polizeï* and far-right networks.

As I ducked and wove my way through the shrapnel and red smoke I kept hearing Wilhelm-esque screams, usually signifying that a protester had gone too far and had been hit by one of the police with a baton and thrown into the back of an armoured vehicle – those being arrested weren't laughing now. Every time this scream happened, a little group of photojournalists I inserted myself into followed the noise in a compact unit, one of them bleeding from his forehead after being hit by a stray beer bottle. As the flashguns popped like bursts of lightning, documenting the arrests, the chants grew louder – 'Anti-fascista, anti-fascista!' – more reggae-tinged music blared, fireworks screeched and snapped and, in the buildings that lined the route, approving residents watched on in excitement, shouting obscenities at the police, waving flags in support, drinking cheap beer and enjoying the free entertainment. Unlike the American police in Ferguson, the police here were being patient with the white anarchists, I felt, and I saw an arrest happen only when one of the police had been physically attacked or someone had done serious damage to some street furniture. Judging from the anxious faces of the police at the beginning, and then the detached calm they exhibited in the heart of the storm, I imagined it must be the same every year – a silent agreement between people and state for an atmosphere-cleansing ruckus, in which the frustrations were being turned into a kind of frenzied reverie. By the time the march had reached the road leading up to Frankfurter Allee U-bahn station, things were completely out of control, even though the crowd was much thinner on the ground (most of the more reasonable Antifa had gone home by now) and all that was left were the press and the hardcore fanatics, some pissed out of their head, smashing street signs and fighting with the police in clusters.

The police were losing their patience and the arrests were becoming more frequent and more violent, and every time another anarchist was thrown into the back of the van the crowd chanted, 'This is what democracy looks like!' After a few more minutes a formal but polite recording of a female voice echoed eerily through the smoke and debris, repeating itself over and over again, saying something in German. It sounded like the type of inhumanly calm voice amid chaos you might hear before supreme devastation: 'This street will self-destruct in T minus ten minutes.' This assessment must have been fairly accurate, because I saw that it was coming out of one of the armoured police vehicles, and at it even the most hardcore members of Antifa started to panic and disperse. I asked someone what was going on, and he said, 'It will be dangerous now.' What did he mean? 'The police are now going to use serious force on us,' he added, and as he ran into the stairwell of a random building and I followed, I thought, *Well, at least they're polite enough to give you a chance to opt out*. The name of the activist was Markus, and when the voice stopped and an air-raid siren took its place, he led me out of a back door down an alley along a smoke-covered main street strewn with the remnants of the demonstration: torn banners, left-wing leaflets and various pieces of political propaganda. As a small crowd of us ran through all this, with the siren blaring in the background, I had a surreal moment when I felt like I was re-enacting the Battle of Berlin. Everybody was running in the same direction, on to the same U-bahn, getting off at the same stop, and I just followed the scattering bodies until I was firmly reminded that I wasn't in the Battle of Berlin as we arrived at a night club called K9, the official club of the demonstration. Yes, there was an Antifa afterparty.

I ended up partying with Markus and his Antifa mates at a legendary techno club called the Berghain, where there were rooms of white Rastas who danced like they were doing capoeira on crack, then another room full of men in leather chaps having sex (the Berghain started out as a gay fetish club), and a psychedelic moment watching the sunrise being turned into a dance floor strobe by the quick opening and closing of venetian shutters. Afterwards, as I stumbled back in the winter dawn to my hostel down a potholed side street, drunk, tired and exhilarated, I think I finally understood the virtue of Antifa. They made anti-racism, anti-fascism and anti-sexism cool for young white kids who, in the age of an alt-right trying to make racism hip, might well have been susceptible to other modes of antisocial behaviour. For all the reservations I had about Antifa, in the end I would rather they were there than not; as we have seen recently, their American wing has been battling the rise of fascism on the front line in America. We had gangs of skinheads chasing black people in the 70s; now we had gangs of skinheads chasing each other.

In the 70s, when Eric Clapton came out in support of Enoch Powell and shouted a slew of racist obscenities to his audience, including the reiteration of the National Front slogan 'Keep Britain White', and David Bowie was pictured making Nazi salutes and claimed Hitler was 'the first rock star', among a series of other dubious remarks in his Thin White Duke guise, they created a space for racism in popular culture.* It was left-wing organizations just like

* Interestingly, it was only when Bowie moved to Berlin that he ditched the Thin White Duke and apologized for the comments he made.

Antifa in Britain, charged with the music of The Clash and Steel Pulse, that created the influential Rock Against Racism events to demonstrate that racism wasn't cool to impressionable young white kids, especially those with reduced opportunities in a time of economic squeeze. If Antifa had confused hedonism with anti-racism, at least dancing, chanting and getting pissed against racism was better than doing those same things in the name of it. It takes a lot for someone who doesn't have to be personally invested in issues that don't directly affect them to stand up for something and, even if it was just a phase, maybe it's the best way to spend your youth while having the energy and inclination, before becoming more invested in existing power structures. Even if their methods didn't resonate with me, if nothing else, in the end Antifa was better company than the Neo-Nazis would have been. And I thought of what Mikkel had said: there was virtue in a group of people fighting racism who weren't operating from a defensive position.

Germaica

One typically arctic evening in Berlin I discovered a little piece of Afropea glowing in the darkness of Friedrichshain. Nil was a salubrious Sudanese oasis nestled in a land of endless currywurst cabins and doner-kebab takeaways and, though it was a tiny place with only a couple of small tables, during my time in Berlin it became my social hub, opening me up to a more multicultural side of the city. I'd chew the fat there with Israeli architects, Swiss-Ivorian accountants, Ghanaian-German musicians and the rotating Sudanese chefs on shift.

I found Nil by following my nose; the aroma drifting out of it as I passed by was unusual and pleasant, and I was ushered in by Hishem, one of the two men cooking and serving behind the counter. He handed me a small piece of grilled chicken covered in a delicious golden-brown Sudanese sauce called aswad, made with peanuts and fresh home-made yoghurt. I immediately asked for a plate of it and, after preparing the dish, Hishem served it up with hot potatoes and a crispy salad on a warm open wrap, with a glass of fresh hibiscus tea, and said, 'A Sudanese speciality – no chemicals or added sugar, good for you, brother.' It all came to less than five euros.

I sat by a window glazed with condensation, muting the myriad big-city lights outside into vague bokeh piercing the night, and felt comforted and relaxed by the sizzles and scents of Sudan. Berlin had been interesting but intense, welcoming in a strange, harsh, hard-to-read German sort of way, where the grim stares of strangers sometimes preceded an invitation to an epic party, and teasing/borderline insults often turned out to be a show of affection. I picked up one of the many Sudan-related books from a bookshelf that stood next to a large map of the country with local art hanging around it which had obviously been inspired by both sub-Saharan African and Arabic culture. The book was a big coffee-table publication from the 90s called *Der Nil* and, when Hishem saw me leafing through it, with no one to serve for a moment he sat by me and spoke about Sudan.

We looked at a map of the Nile, the longest river on the planet, running from Egypt down through Sudan and connecting North, East and Central Africa – Ethiopia, Eritrea, the Democratic Republic of the Congo, Kenya, Uganda, Tanzania, Burundi and Rwanda – and Hishem pointed to the east of South Sudan. 'That's where my father is from, my mother is from the north. It's really terrible what is happening there at the moment.' Sudan has recently been divided into two countries, roughly along religious lines – the Muslim north and the Christian south – after two civil wars that claimed the lives of one and a half million Sudanese people, but Hishem was keen to tell me about a country beyond the images of war and famine we've become accustomed to when we think of Sudan. Egypt has taken ownership of the Nile and the symbols of power all along it, but some of the Egyptian gods and shrines that the world has downloaded in its collective memory have histories that reach deeply into Nubia and the African interior. Sudanese civilization pre-dates Egyptian civilization, with some scholars believing that Sudan gave birth to pharaonic culture. Though the two countries have a long history (both have conquered each other in the past), when you look at the border of Sudan and Egypt on a map, like a lot of Africa, you see it is divided by an unnatural, perfectly straight colonial line; 'We'll take that part,' said some British lord, annexing off a section of Africa on the map in front of him with a ruler and a pencil back in London, splintering the organic topography of villages and communities he'd likely never visited or would visit. Hishem told me that social ties in Sudan ran deeper than political boundaries and then spoke proudly of how the country had its own pyramids and a glorious history that rose up from the Nile from East and Central Africa through Nubia and the once-powerful kingdom of Kush, which enriched the culture the world calls ancient Egypt.

Hishem didn't dislike Berlin, he said, but he missed home terribly: 'You know, I moved to Germany eight years ago because of the instability in Sudan. Things are very corrupt and dangerous at the moment. People leave because they either want to make a better life for themselves and their children or dream of making enough money to move back, but it doesn't happen that way. It's hard to save money here and, even if you do make money, the government back home is so corrupt you don't know what the future can be there.' Hishem became tearful and I changed the conversation to Berlin; he seemed to be doing well, with work in a job he clearly enjoyed, but he frowned.

'I love working here, and I dream of opening up my own place one day. But Berlin is not good for a person like me. I don't think it is a racist place, I don't get too many problems like that here, but I think that it is a bad life for everyone, not just immigrants. Germany is not a happy place. People work all day, travel to and from work and then sleep. Everybody is worried about having lots of things, but it turns them into slaves because they never have enough, they never stop. All I want is enough food, a nice lady to dance with and a home somewhere.'

A man with neatly woven dreads had walked in a few minutes earlier and had been eavesdropping on our conversation. I could tell he couldn't wait to get involved, and what Hishem said was his prompt. His name was Mohammed and, if Hishem was reasonable but fairly apolitical, Mohammed was passionate and reactionary, out of work and angry, and had turned his fear and precarious position as a black man in Europe into a sort of pseudo-empowerment. He said, 'Blessings, brothers,' and then, 'Europe is no good for the black man. Let me tell you something: we Africans, we are from a land of abundance. What they call laziness is our nature because

God provided everything for us in the motherland. When we were hungry we could just get up and pick fruit from the tree, we had gold and diamonds under our feet, sun in the sky – plentiful natural resources. The white man has learned different ways because of the bitterness of European weather and the unkindness of its land. He had to learn to be organized and work hard in the summer and think ahead for the winter – make plans so that his family could survive through the cold months. That is the big difference between the white man and the black man – we didn't need anything, we got everything handed to us easily by our land. But the white man needs more and more for his life because he is scared, so he comes to Africa to stock up and doesn't know when to stop. That is the system in Europe my friend is talking about, the system that is always hungry to be fed, and the more it feeds, the more it wants because it is always in fear of the future. The white man takes everything and then tries to make us live like him but under him.' Hishem added, 'But it is also a problem with black leaders, not just white leaders. In Sudan it's true that it isn't in our culture to want to spend our lives working. Many people aren't interested in university, they just want to live a simple life, be relaxed and be happy. But that is why it's such a mess – nobody takes an interest in the government, we just want to live for each day, so it's easy for the people in charge to take advantage of us.'

This stubborn generalization of black people as naturally lazy went against everything that I knew personally and everything that I'd seen on my trip, with black men working nightshifts to guard buildings, black women cleaning up after us idle travellers in the hostels, juggling work with parenthood and often education, enrolling as mature students to acquire diplomas for skills they'd already worked hard to be accredited for back home but which weren't recognized by European institutions. The Sudanese owner of Nil, Walid Elsayed, got a degree in horticulture while simultaneously learning German, his third language, cooking in the evenings and cycling his bike pulling a trailer around Berlin to sell food to

pay for his studies. While doing this he designed a menu specifically for his customers, selling Sudanese food to a German palate
by fusing traditional Sudanese dishes with pan-African and European ingredients. He then put together a highly strategic marketing
plan to target the young student clientele of Friedrichshain, before
setting up the shop and running it by himself for the first few years
from 11 a.m. until midnight.

Guyanese historian Walter Rodney once wrote, 'When an African
abuses an Indian he repeats all that the white men said about Indian
indentured "coolies": and in turn the Indian has borrowed from the
whites the stereotype of the "lazy nigger" to apply to the African
beside him. It is as though no black man can see another black man
except by looking through a white person. It is time we started seeing
through our own eyes.'[1] Rodney wasn't just talking about white
brainwashing but also about white structural racism; those unemployed black men I saw loitering all over Europe weren't inherently
lazy, but lost and low on confidence and opportunities, and their
crime was that they were visible, unlike the black staff who cleaned
the station and whose hard work had rendered them invisible.

While Hishem went back to preparing food Mohammed took
his seat and, seeing me flicking through the book about the Nile,
said, 'You won't find the truth about Africa in such books, my
brother. You won't hear about the powerful history of the Sudanese people, you will just see images of death and poverty that they
created and now are documenting as if they're saving it. But poverty is a circumstance, it is not an identity. You find the real Sudan
here in real life – you see, the food, the vibe, the power, they don't
want you to think of all this.' 'Who doesn't?' I asked. 'The Illuminati,' he said, and I suddenly wondered if I was in the midst of what
some in the black community describe as Hotep, from a wider
group mockingly named the 'Ankh-Right' – black extremists who,
like white extremists, are disproportionately men and come
attached with sexism, bigotry, prejudice, paranoia and misinformation while claiming to be the most enlightened people of all.

Hotep is from the ancient Egyptian saying meaning 'At peace', but so-called Hoteps are constantly at war, closing down dialogue with others. 'Hotep' was apt because it came with the Afrocentric desperation to claim Egyptian culture as its own, when the truth is that ancient Egyptian culture was likely a mix of many cultures: Persian, Arabic, African, Greek, and more. The Italian anthropologist Giuseppe Sergi called them 'Eurafrican'. But anyway, Hoteps didn't care about that; they stood as kings on a shaky foundation of dubious facts, and their independent position was curiously over-dependent on whiteness as a counterpoint: they gave white people too much credit, in other words.

In theory, the idea of using ancient Nubian culture as a source of pride and empowerment in the black diaspora made a certain amount of sense to me. Africa is a continent, not a country, but as Sudan was once the largest country in Africa, it was a sort of microcosm of the entire continent for a while, with many African cultures and religions represented and nearly all the major African languages spoken there. Mohammed had tapped into that history in a way that raised some interesting questions and produced searingly polemical speeches but would then be steered by a debilitating and paradoxical mix of self-aggrandisement and paranoia.

When we'd finished our food Mohammed invited me to go with him to see what he called the 'real black Berlin' and, thanking Hishem for the nourishment and hospitality, I followed Mohammed down to the East Side Gallery, one of the few remaining sections of the Berlin Wall left standing, which had now been covered in commissioned graffiti on one side and had an official sign threatening anyone who defaced or damaged the wall with prosecution, which I found somewhat ironic. We walked along the unpainted side of the wall, which was more evocative because in its blankness you felt its brutal and unsettling mood and size on a more visceral level – at around four metres tall it was too small to seem completely impassable but just tall enough to be oppressive and inhuman. Of course, the real problem trying to scale it would have been the border guards armed with AK47s, but its specific height made me feel claustrophobic and, as we neared the end of the 1.3 kilometre stretch of concrete, I heard the welcome off-beat thud of reggae music at almost the same time I was hit with the intoxicating funk of high-grade ganja, and it offered a huge relief. Mohammed led me into a place covered in red, green and gold called Young African Artist Market (YAAM), which I initially felt should have been named Jamaican Art Market, because as well as having a slightly cooler acronym, it would have been more accurate for the culture that had been adopted there in the bitterly cold German evening. There were palm trees and dreadlocked Rastas huddled round an open fire made in an old gasoline canister smoking sinsemilla, smoke and condensation rising out of their mouths as they exhaled in the freezing weather, bobbing their heads to Richie Spice's 'Earth a Run Red' which was booming out of a speaker. A hotly contested game of basketball was in full swing on an outdoor miniature court, with dreads flowing from black and white men swaying as they took each other on, and stalls selling Rizlas and merchandise covered in the faces of Haile Selassie and Bob Marley. Inside a covered section of YAAM were men and women skanking out, and I saw some of the tatted Antifa-crew types who were at the demo in a much more chilled-out state, one with a massive smile on his face, smoking a huge blunt rolled into a tulip.

As a grassroots non-profit organization offering a space for graff artists, photographers and other forms of independent creativity and commerce as well as live gigs and club nights, YAAM was in many ways the multicultural heart of Berlin. Originally established on the site of a former bus shelter by local youth workers in the early 90s, shortly after the fall of the wall, the aim was to create, as its website said, 'A place of multicultural encounters and integration through the provision of cultural, social, sports and leisure activities [and to promote] ... coexistence ... through its ... open, low-threshold approach, [helping] to provide cultural access and improve social integration and ultimately the quality of life in the urban area.' The location has changed through the years, but the ethos has always been the same. It had hosted gigs by everyone from Lee Scratch Perry to Tanya Stephens, ran Berlin's biggest multicultural festival, provided family support through youth work and crèche facilities, hosted the biggest graffiti festival in Germany and housed recording studios offering cut-price services to local musicians. As a place of networking, YAAM had an impressive legacy, and in fact gave Walid Elsayed, the owner of Nil, one of his first opportunities to sell food out of a trailer before he could even afford a car, YAAM being one of the few key hotspots where he was able to build an audience for his food on a low budget. The space also provided a local platform for Berlin reggae and hip-hop collectives like Seeed (who first met and formed at YAAM), who have three gold and two platinum albums to their name and have since found international acclaim, and Culcha Candela, who've had similar success on a domestic level. This is part of a wider, thriving national German reggae scene that also includes artists like Gentleman, Nosliw, Jan Delay, D-Flame, Jahcoustix and Patrice.

Reggae has long served as a counterpoint for hardline punks and anarchists to embrace as a chilled – but still subversive – alternative to the harsher sounds of rock. This may explain why it has taken root in Germany, particularly in the period after the fall of the Berlin Wall, to the extent that, when I spoke to German-born Nigerian-Romany singer-songwriter Ayo in my days as a journalist for *Blues and Soul* magazine a few years ago, she told me she had to leave the country because she felt stifled by a German record label trying to pigeonhole her into a lucrative and contemporary local reggae scene. But YAAM was the real deal, and for people like Mohammed a space that helped him survive the cold German winters.

I think it was his name and the fact he was from Ghana that made me miss it, but as soon as we stepped inside I realized that Mohammed was a Rasta, and it wouldn't have surprised me if he had found his faith there at YAAM. We joined the group of men huddled around the fire. One of them was preaching in German and Mohammed said, 'We got an English bredda wid us,' and another said, 'Brix Tan toon,' affectedly. I asked the man if he'd ever been. 'No, but wan day Gad willin, this is no place for a Black man.' He was Ghanaian, too, and in fact almost all the Rastas I spoke to at YAAM were West Africans who'd assumed Jamaican accents and a reverence of East Africa through their Rastafarian faith. Looking around at black men grinding with black women, white women grinding with black men, white men grinding with black women, the Antifa crew skanking out next to African Rastas, I had to ask what was so bad about Berlin. 'I been here ten years,' said the preacher man, 'and all the time I'm getting harassed by the police. I am like many other Ghanaians who have come to Europe hoping to make a bit of money – in Ghana you can build a nice big house for only 20,000 euros.' His face grew full of anguish and his voice turned bitter. 'What happens is we don't ever make enough money to go back. So we end up drifting in Europe, getting stuck in the European way. Europe has a way of getting into you, even though you feel worse than you did back home, because it's too shameful to go back empty-handed, and anyway you've come too far, you're bitter like a European.' Mohammed pointed to one of the T-shirts and said, 'Don't worry, brother . . . the King of Kings. One day the black king shall return and, without violence, take you, me and all these black men you see here and around Europe back home to Africa to build a great nation. That is what our prophets told us.' I thought about this and wondered what the black king would do with those of us who are mixed race and/or feel mixed-cultured. Would we be selected for his African ark? And what if we did get a golden ticket? Would we choose to board? After all, members of the motherland may well have been complicit in the sale of my ancestors to the Europeans. What about building a great non-separatist community and supporting Africa from right where we stood? But I could see the lure of this story of a black king as a fascinating and empowering mix of mysticism and irrefutable fact that all black people living in Europe could make use of, linking the recent histories of Europe with ancient African folklore, decolonial struggle, the history of Christendom and perhaps the most mainstream black diaspora culture across Europe, Rastafarianism – a faith that was a fuel, keeping people like Mohammed going.

Ras Tafari Makonnen was raised as an African royal and educated by a French Capuchin monk as a child (French was the only European language he could speak fluently), and it's said that his roots can be traced back through an unbroken 3,000-year link to King Menelik I, who, legend has it, was the son of the biblical King Solomon and Makeda, the Queen of Sheba. Records of this lineage date back millennia and their union is even mentioned in the *Kebra Nagast*, a text written in Coptic in the fourteenth century which suggests that Ethiopia was the location of the Ark of the Covenant. Ras Tafari was certainly part of a powerful history of African excellence (if we're judging excellence by European standards) and his royal Ethiopian heritage could boast its own script, Ge'ez, and seventeenth-century castles commissioned by its own emperors in the northern medieval city Gondar, which earned the nickname 'the Camelot of Africa'. It had Christian churches older than any in Europe and a stunning architectural heritage, with the sites at Lalibela and Axum among the most impressive in the world, given UNESCO world-heritage status in the last century. More impressive than any of this, though, was the fact that Ethiopia had long been powerfully independent: the only African country that had never truly been colonized. Ras Tafari's father had led Ethiopia to the famous victory over Italy at the Battle of Adwa in the late nineteenth century, which was the first time an African country had beaten a European nation in a major recorded battle since the legendary Hannibal fought the Romans 2,000 years earlier.

When Ras Tafari was immodestly crowned 'By the Conquering Lion of the Tribe of Judah, His Imperial Majesty Haile Selassie I,

King of Kings of Ethiopia, Elect of God' he was at the seat of not only the Ethiopian empire but an entire global black diaspora movement asserting itself after centuries of slavery and colonialism at the hands of Western powers. One of the most powerful voices of black empowerment at the time was the Jamaican writer, philosopher, activist and Pan-Africanist Marcus Garvey, who, in the 20s resurrected a Back to Africa movement that had been attempted in less convincing terms since official abolitions of slavery across the world in the nineteenth century. The goal for Garvey was to unite all black peoples of the African diaspora who were displaced by the West and repatriate its members back to Africa, to create an Israel-style African Zion and completely split ties with the culture of their former captors. Preachers across the diaspora, notably Leonard Howell in Jamaica, believed that in the crowning of Ras Tafari as emperor of Ethiopia, an ancient biblical prophecy of a black king emerging to return a 'chosen people' – the black race – to Africa was coming to pass, a belief that chimed powerfully with the decolonial mood at the time.

Rastafarianism, which suggests that Ras Tafari, also known as Haile Selassie, was the Messiah returned to Earth, was considered improbable by many, including the Jamaican authorities (even after colonialism) and Ethiopian citizens, and was quietly refuted by Haile Selassie himself, who said on his trip to Jamaica in 1966, 'We are not God, we are not the prophet, we are a slave of God.' This did little to waylay the Rastafari movement, and it's easy to see why; here was an African king tied to a religion that had been bleached and used to indoctrinate black diaspora cultures in the belief that their own subjugation was part of God's plan. With Rastafarianism, a belief in a higher power that *did* help black communities get through tough times was now transfigured into one that was also in their own image and changed the trajectory of 'God's plan', which now said God didn't want you to serve anyone but Him, that He is great and good and He looks just like you. For those attached to a people who had been forced to worship a white

Jesus and serve white plantation owners, Rastafarianism merged Christianity, African history and folklore, black power politics and Pan-Africanism into something deeply empowering, with symbology and legends every bit as convincing as anything that came out of the Vatican, and with much catchier hymns in the form of roots reggae.

As someone who came of age in the early twenty-first century and considers themselves agnostic, I was interested less in Haile Selassie as an embodiment of God and more in his actual reign as a political leader throughout the tumultuous twentieth century and the potential he embodied but perhaps ultimately failed to live up to. His father, Ras Makonnen, built Harare's first hospital and state school and instilled in his son a strong belief in education, which made him a great reformer. Haile Selassie went on to establish Ethiopia's state-education system, Ethiopian Airways (said to have inspired Nelson Mandela, who saw his first black pilot while on board an Ethiopian Airlines plane), build a United Nations African HQ, establish an official church and organize Ethiopia's first parliament and the country's first constitutional government. He created a cosmopolitan, multicultural, educated African capital city built on collaboration; where there was a reported 73 students in the country in 1950, by 1973, near the end of his reign, there were over 10,000, with a boom in local educational establishments at home as well as funding for Ethiopian students to study abroad. All of this made Ethiopia's capital, Addis Ababa, a modern, forward-thinking African city which refused to reject the input of other cultures across the globe while, relatively speaking, keeping it largely out of the hands of the global superpowers.

Selassie managed to do this by cleverly playing the circling vultures from the West against each other. He was the first Ethiopian royal to travel outside of Africa, entering France through Marseille then travelling to Belgium to recruit financiers, to Italy, the Vatican City, and Sweden, where he gained the allegiance of Swedish doctors, and ended his tour in England, where he received an honorary degree from Cambridge University. He used Britain and, covertly, even the Nazis (who supplied ammunition and tanks) to fend off Mussolini in the 30s, before Italy eventually allied with Germany in the Second World War. When Britain began to slowly sink its teeth into Ethiopia by introducing the British colonial currency of the African shilling as thanks for the extra muscle against Italy, Selassie persuaded America to hold Britain at bay by introducing a more favourable Ethiopian dollar, then fended off American influence by working with the USSR, albeit at a cool distance, in each case negotiating favourable trade deals, often revolving around Ethiopia's world-class coffee crops. He signed Ethiopia up as one of the founding members of the Non-aligned Movement, that transcontinental coalition of countries attempting to maintain sovereignty in the midst of the Cold War in a way that refused to pledge allegiance to Eastern or Western superpowers.

Selassie even managed to make Italy give reparations and return the statue of the Lion of Judah in the 60s, which Mussolini had shipped to Italy during a five-year occupation the Italians managed to secure using illegal chemical warfare, forcing him briefly into exile in Bath, England.*

At the outbreak of the Second World War, with Italy siding with the Germans, Selassie, who'd been lobbying for military assistance from European powers throughout his exile, finally got the support he needed to take back Ethiopia, and did so in a triumphant procession in 1941, five years to the day after Italy captured Addis Ababa during the Second Italo–Ethiopian War. He wanted Ethiopia to move forward in harmony, even with the remaining 15,000 Italian citizens who still lived in the country. Selassie's savvy, outward-looking manoeuvres to establish Ethiopia as a

---

* Rita Marley, Bob Marley's first wife, recalls being convinced of Haile Selassie's role as the earthly Messiah when he waved to her and she saw stigmata on his hands. In fact, these marks were damage caused by poisonous mustard gas during Italy's attacks. Fairfield House, bought by Selassie, now serves as a day centre for elderly ethnic-minority citizens and is a site of pilgrimage for Rastas across the world.

modern African country eventually undid him; while he sat on his throne with his honorary degrees and international prestige, by the 70s, his country was floundering through famines, and after suffering the loss of his wife and daughter he grew further and further out of touch with the needs of the Ethiopian poor, deploying high taxes on farmers with agriculture on increasingly privatized land. His biggest sin, like so many African leaders in the twentieth century, lay in not knowing when to retire and pass on a leadership base that was larger than a single leader, one that stretched beyond a cult of personality. In a round-about way, though, Haile Selassie did produce leaders, with many of the major proponents of the Derg – the military party involved in the *coup d'état* that ousted him in 1974 – the recipients of the educational reforms and military academies he'd established in the 30s. When you look at Addis Ababa today, beneath the dust and the poverty there is an idea of a modern city that never really moved beyond Selassie's vision; 60s modernist and brutalist government buildings attest to this, built in the international style and commissioned not by colonial powers but by Haile Selassie himself. In this way Addis Ababa was the centre of a fleeting manifestation of an African Zion, when the hopes and dreams of an entire diaspora concentrated on one man and one country . . . and still do for some, as evidenced by the iconography and German-African Rastafarians praising him in the chill of Berlin. For people like Mohammed – black and living in Europe but feeling stranded and estranged, the question of adopting any kind of Europeanization was unthinkable, bordering on reprehensible, and Rastafarianism was an energy that could carry him through 'Babylon', the term Rastas use to describe colonial and post-colonial societies. I spent all evening chatting, dancing and smoking and emerged out of YAAM at three in the morning, stoned and sleepy, leaving a party that didn't look like it was about to finish any time soon. When the big metal gates of YAAM opened up and released me back into the city I felt disorientated – in a flash I was back in the Babylon of Berlin.

When the socialist Derg government took control of Ethiopia after Selassie, the East German Democratic Republic was one of its biggest allies, training its secret service, reaching favourable trade deals with it, swapping weapons for coffee. Hundreds of Ethiopians enrolled in East German universities and the GDR sent over academics to teach in Ethiopian universities. Today in Addis Ababa a GDR-funded and -designed Karl Marx memorial stands rusting in the city's subtropical climate, long after the political energy that once surrounded it had dissipated, when the Derg, like many other socialist states at the time, including the one in East Germany, began to dissolve in the 80s.

This connection between the GDR and Ethiopia speaks of an alternative history not just of East Germany but of Germany in general, because the socialist, international attempt at German influence in Africa was by no means the country's first foray overseas. Rather than the French and English imperial pomp that still lingers (both countries secretly, sometimes explicitly, proud of their colonial endeavours), in Germany there appears to be something of a cultural aphasia about its history beyond its own national borders; it prefers to pretend it had no colonial history at all. When in 2010 German Chancellor Angela Merkel talked about how 'multiculturalism had failed' and that immigrants weren't doing enough to fit into German society, she was talking about German society as if it had always been a solid, monocultured thing.

While East Germany cordoned itself off from the West and attempted to forge international socialist ties, capitalist West Germany faced a labour crisis because of the restricted flow of cheap labour from the East of the country, so the government began a huge recruitment drive encouraging *Gastarbeiter* (guest workers) from Turkey in the early 60s. These workers were so integral to West Germany's labour force that employers pressured the state to abolish a two-year limitation clause so that Turkish workers could stay for longer. The 'economic miracle' of West Germany, then, wasn't such a miracle after all. Despite playing their part in the creation and economic success of contemporary Germany – not to mention the fact that Germany and Turkey have links dating back to the 1500s, when the Ottoman Empire invaded Europe – in the official German narrative Turks are still considered foreigners who don't fit in.

The narrative of blackness in Germany has been equally glossed over, and it's almost as if, having had to deal with their defeat in the Second World War, the legacy of Nazi cruelty and the Holocaust, there isn't room to talk about the black Germans who were neutered under the Nazi regime so that they couldn't procreate, or the atrocities against the 17,000 French *Tirailleurs* largely made up of African soldiers, who, fighting on the French frontline, were killed – even after surrendering – in unofficial executions, their bodies dumped into mass graves like animals. Not a single German officer connected to these events, named the Thiaroye massacre, was ever convicted of war crimes.

Not only did Germany have its own large colonial empire,

which included the acquisition of Chad, Nigeria, Cameroon, Ghana, Togo, Namibia, Burundi, Rwanda, Mozambique, Tanzania and more, the city of Berlin was in fact the birthplace of colonialism as we know it. The Berlin Conference of 1884, orchestrated by German Chanceller Otto von Bismarck, resulted in the famous 'Scramble for Africa'. The Germans, by and large, weren't successful colonialists, and the beginning of the end of German colonialism came with the Herero genocide just twenty years later, when, after anti-colonist rebellions, German troops massacred 70 per cent of the Herero tribe of modern-day Namibia (at least 25,000 people) and performed horrific scientific experiments on Herero men and women left starving and riddled with scurvy in concentration camps, injecting them with arsenic and opium, and using their body parts for the type of eugenics and craniometry that would foreshadow Nazi Germany's crimes against humanity. When word about the genocide got out, national support for colonialism dwindled in Germany, and the First World War put a nail in the coffin.

Today, Germany has no Commonwealth like the UK or International Organization of the Francophonie like France, but in many of Germany's old African territories you can find hints of this hidden history of German colonialism through the large presence of German NGOs, and I was about to meet a family who could shed more light on it.

I arranged to meet Ulli and Ayellet Helmstetter and their daughter Shira at a small café in Mitte after noticing them at a service by the Afro-gospel choir Ndembe Spirituals at Berlin's French Cathedral. The choir was Pan-African and the singing that filled the ornate interior was ethereal, but as soon as I walked in I saw that the black worshippers and white worshippers had divided themselves, each sitting on either side of the church aisle. My choice of which side to sit was made easy for me – the only seating available was on the black side. The white Germans in attendance looked like Ladysmith Black Mambazo liberals, dressed almost uniformly in mildly earthy white cotton tops, linen scarves with a splash of African print here, a necklace of beads there, and smelled of incense. Sitting with me in the black half of the church were five huge Ghanaian women who made strange noises to signify their approval at what the pastor was saying in between the singing. They were with many children, who played noisily, and their husbands were standing at the sides, disengaged or immersed in their smartphones. The white Germans, who easily outnumbered the black contingent, were getting miffed at the women's noises and the children playing, shooting passive-aggressive looks at them, or smiling through pursed lips in a way that said, *Halt die Klappe!* They'd come to experience that abstract notion of 'Africa', not Africans, and their imaginings of what that meant were affirmed by the soaring harmonies of the choir, not the people they were distancing themselves from who'd shout at their children in a mix of German and pidgin English. The Helmstetters were sitting a couple of rows in front of me, and I saw them operating in the middle space like I was and we exchanged details at the end of the service.

Ulli was a sturdy, balding forty-something white man from Münster who had the physique of a rugby player and the aura of a *National Geographic* photographer – one of the few men in the world who looks great in cargo trousers. Ayellet was from Israel, had silvery cropped hair and embodied a similarly worldly air, though in a less physical, more scholarly way. The Helmstetter who really caught my attention was their young daughter Shira, who was from Kenya, with skin that was almost literally black and big, beautiful brown eyes. It was Shira who most personified this powerfully global vibe the Helmstetters were giving off, and could there be any better family to talk to about the state of multiculturalism in Germany than one comprised of a white German man, a Jewish Israeli woman and a black Kenyan daughter?

'We met in 1998 while travelling in India. I was learning yoga and Ulli was . . .' Ayellet looked at him playfully. 'Actually, what *were* you doing?' Ulli smiled. 'I was just travelling, trying to find myself . . . but I found you.' It was, to me, the perfect way to meet someone, and I think I secretly hoped I might have such fortune on my journey through Europe, that out there somewhere on my travels was a home and another lost soul looking for true love, but while Ulli and Ayellet may have strolled off into the Indian sunset together, later came the reality of everyday life.

'We knew we wanted to make it work, but we just didn't know where. When Ayellet finished her yoga training she agreed to give Germany a go, which changed everything.' Ayellet said that their relationship was never an issue; in fact, it was the rock that got her through some tough years in her new adoptive home. Recently, Münster won an award for most liveable mid-sized city in the world for its placid lake, low-rise architecture, cobbled squares, low crime rate, bike-friendly streets, baroque palace, German markets and progressive university. But the liveability, the Helmstetters told me, didn't seem to extend to those who weren't white Germans or students. Ayellet's face was fraught with the memories. 'That place nearly broke me. I lasted four years and, honestly, I'm not sure how I did it. I completely lost my capacity to smile. I felt so alone, was constantly singled out because of my skin colour and made to feel like such a fool the whole time. Everybody looked down at me, which was so different to how my life in Israel and as a traveller had been. In Münster everybody keeps themselves to themselves and conforms. If you're a foreigner or an outsider, it's just a grey, rainy, lifeless existence.' As Ayellet spoke, Ulli bounced Shira on his knee with a look of guilt. 'What she's saying is true, and what really troubled me was that Münster had provided such a nice life for me as a white German before. Here was the very same place, the same buildings and squares, that suddenly took on a new form. I saw a completely different face of Germany, not only through Ayellet but later also through Shira. I had absolutely no idea how prejudiced the system was against non-whites and non-Germans, and I think this is a problem; it took having a wife from Israel and a daughter from Kenya to make me see this reality, but so many Germans don't get the opportunity to see the subtle ways Germany has of keeping outsiders at bay, so they wonder what others are complaining about. I was always such a proud German before, but I started to feel ashamed.'

The Helmstetters packed their things and Ulli took up an opportunity to teach in Nairobi, Kenya, part of a large, extended German NGO presence in the country. Ayellet felt that they'd finally found a home: 'Those first days in Nairobi were wonderful. Compared to Münster, it felt like this really fertile place – everything was alive and shining, friendly and soft. The house they put us up in was incredible, 200 square metres of space. There was a real feeling of contentment for a while. We were settled and happy, good money was coming in and I found my smile again.'

Ulli taught physics at the German school in Nairobi to what he described as disinterested, arrogant and lazy German expat teenagers, but initially he, too, was happy with their new set-up in Kenya. Slowly, though, they began to realize that the shoe was now on the other foot – the Helmstetters were welcomed, but as part of an inner circle that put up walls against others.

Ayellet said, 'We had maids, which made me feel a little uncomfortable in the first place, but even more so when they'd ask for things and start to snoop; they thought we were super-rich. One year we went through fifteen different maids. We were living in this huge house surrounded by a fence and barbed wire and it wasn't long before we had to open our eyes to the huge gap between our expat experience and the experience of the people living in poverty in Nairobi.' Ulli agreed and said that they started to feel like they were living in a bubble, in the same way those people back in Münster had been living in one. Their bubble was smaller and they were in the minority – Ulli was often dismissively called *mzungu* (a Bantu word which translates as 'aimless wanderer' and sometimes used in an insulting way by locals to label white people), but name-calling and prejudice mean little when you're the *powerful* minority and still living in the best houses, getting all the best job opportunities, have all the social capital and are likely to be treated with more respect by the state.*

'Like the other Germans in Nairobi, we were pretending that just beyond the fences of our big houses wasn't Kibera – the biggest slum in Africa. It was difficult because after having such a horrible time in Germany we had found personal happiness. It is easy to shut off from the misery of other people when you have everything you need around you and never have to come in contact with it. There was no public transport, all our social scene and even the kids I taught were white, there in the heart of Kenya, but we just couldn't pretend for ever.'

As the writer and developer David Gaider once said, 'Privilege is when you think something is not a problem because it's not a problem to you personally,' but wisdom is acting upon knowledge, not turning a blind eye to it – which is how I came to see the Antifa I'd initially been dubious about. It's also easy to be cynical about transracial adoption, and perhaps some sort of guilt did play a part in Ulli and Ayellet's decision to adopt in Kenya, but there's no doubt that love was the driving force – it had to have been, because adopting Shira wasn't like choosing a new puppy in a pet shop. It took three lawyers, three judges and three years of Kenyan and (mainly) German bureaucracy.

'You know, Ayellet had mentioned children back in Germany and, with our age, adoption was always an option. But I said no because I'd never wanted to be a father, I enjoyed my freedom too much. My experience of parenthood had been a German one – I saw the way German mothers were with their children – stressy and strict – but after my few encounters with Kenyan parents I started to change my views: things seemed more relaxed, there

---

* I once had a lively discussion with Alanna Lockward, a Berlin-based scholar and film director of Dominican descent who has done much work under the Afropean banner at university level. She believed that reverse racism (black to white) can't really exist in any meaningful way because it doesn't come with social and economic power on a grand scale, and that reverse racism is only name-calling if it doesn't play a role in the systematic oppression of the person it is aimed at.

seemed to be more harmony, less pressure on the children, unlike back home. Being a parent actually started to look appealing. Then we thought about it and came back to that feeling of happiness we had – we wanted to find a way to share it and thought it would be a good foundation for a child.'

Shira was an orphan; the Helmstetters became her guardians when she was just seven weeks old and by then both her parents had passed away. As I watched Shira, who was now six, mischievously wriggling all over her father, Ayellet said, 'She remembers being alone. If you have watched her this entire time, she has never left this area. Even now, at six years old, she hates to be more than a few yards away from us.' As Shira grew, the Helmstetters began to think of her future, and where they might be able to sustain their multicultural family unit. Ulli told me that increased intertribal warfare in Kenya, mixed with local resistance to their adoption, meant that attempts to take part in Nairobi in a more meaningful way were hampered, and they felt it was time to leave Kenya and give Shira, who by that point was speaking German at home, the opportunity to get a German passport.

'At first everything went well. I told them I wanted to bring my partner and my daughter over and that they needed green cards. The German embassy were so helpful and made life very easy for me. Until, of course, they realized that my partner was Jewish and my daughter was Kenyan. Then it became hell!' Ulli, who'd handled himself with a restrained dignity throughout the retelling of their stories, struggled to hold back his anger, the battle with the embassy still raw.

'One of my colleagues at work applied at the same time as me – his family was white. It took them two days to get a passport, and we battled for two months just to get a three-month visa – even when it should actually have been a two-year visa. The German ambassador . . . oh man, she was cold as ice! She took one look at Shira and decided she was going to make it as hard as she could for us, so we just said fuck them and I travelled to Germany to sort things out myself in person.' Ayellet carried on: 'And during this time we moved to four different places in three months! It was a crazy time, but we refused to give up. We had a shipping container full of all our things ready to ship back to Germany.'

This time, the Helmstetters decided on Berlin, hoping that a larger, more diverse city might accommodate them for a while. They weren't sure they'd stay, they said, but they felt that Berlin was very different to the rest of Germany. That even though it was poor it had energy, was 'open', and Ulli had a theory as to why this was the case.

'The rest of Germany has been heavily rebuilt after the war, and in the rebuilding and reunification it's as if a solid identity had

been built into the buildings and social spaces. But Berlin still feels a little underdeveloped for a big city . . . and that allows capacity for change and the possibility for us to take part in shaping it. Wherever we end up living we will expose Shira to her environment and to as many cultures as possible, so that she knows she is our child but also a child of the world who can take part in shaping her environment.'

It seemed to me that the big challenge for Germany, being at the centre of the Eurozone, is to stop using the idea of multiculturalism as and when it sees fit, when it's convenient to use it for political or economic purposes, which both exploits and scapegoats multiculturalism for its own political agenda. The future of Europe depends on transparency – governments should clearly state how Europe benefits from diversity, open up and admit when the financial sector has failed society, teach colonial history with nuance and honesty and face up to the past so we can all understand the present and move towards a truly unified future, the potential of which I saw in the eyes and smile of little Shira Helmstetter. Her generation will have to tear down some of the new walls that are sprouting up, drawing, perhaps, some inspiration from the late Afro-German poet May Ayim, who, shortly after the fall of the Berlin Wall, defiantly asserted her intention to insert plurality into German national identity in her 1990 poem 'borderless and brazen: a poem against the German "u-not-y"', which begins:

> i will be African
> even if you want me to be german
> and i will be german
> even if my blackness does not suit you

STOCKHOLM

Let the Right Ones In

Travelling through the cities of Western Europe during the winter months, I got the feeling I was witnessing a slow decline, that the continent was looking backwards, dining out on a warped, sentimental view of itself. Buildings that were still being used to suggest European power struck me as absurd. The Eiffel Tower, designed as a monument to science, industry and the French Revolution, had been reduced to a tacky tourist trap; Buckingham Palace housed a redundant royal family; the Vatican City was more museum than moral guide. Europe was creaking under the burden of its own history and, when I thought about it, its central powers were suffering a crisis of identity much worse than those of us living at the periphery of those old ideas and used to navigating the fluidity of change, the uncertainty of the future, the discontinuity of tradition, the fallibility of the nation-state.

Standing on the platform in Cologne waiting for a sleeper train called *Borealis*, I felt (naively, as it happens) that I was about to leave the haunted grey mass of this old colonial Europe behind for something more neutral and egalitarian, bound, as I was, for the northern and snowy pastel-coloured cities of Scandinavia. Aside from Oslo, where a psychopath – no, a terrorist – called Anders Breivik, in an attempt to 'annihilate multiculturalism', had massacred seventy-seven people in 2011, to me, Scandinavia's cities had always suggested a certain respite from racial tension, their soft-sounding syllables sung in pronunciation filling me with an inner calm: Copenhagen, Gothenburg, Malmö, Bergen, Tromsø and my destination, the so-called capital of Scandinavia, Stockholm, a place that had long been one of my favourite cities.

I loved Stockholm for its clear blue skies, low levels of pollution, world-class national healthcare, free education, healthy vitamin-B-rich diet and the rivers and ravines that pass through its low-rise urban archipelago of islands so clean they are safe to swim in. Whether a Stockholmer's ethnic heritage was Nordic, African or Arabic, the people I'd met there over the years had a certain Swedish glow that came with a healthier lifestyle. I'd see successful black and Arabic Swedes on billboards, all over national TV on chat shows, as newscasters and chefs, in music videos, and they always looked self-assured, respected, together; weren't confined to tower-block imagery or hyper-capitalist vulgarity. I'd often see young black professionals in slim-fitting suits and woollen pea coats, fine-spun scarves draped elegantly around their necks as they headed for work as lawyers, graphic designers, videographers and accountants.

I know all this shouldn't sound revolutionary, but it did feel that way to me as a working-class black Brit – in the social scene I'd tapped into in Stockholm, Afropean creatives were the predominant black identity on display. Over the years all this positive, successful imagery was such a relief, Stockholm such a figurative and literal breath of fresh air, that I'd never bothered to look much beyond these romantic notions. The city had always treated me well, giving me lifelong friends, inviting me to its best parties, playing me excellent Afropean music and soothing me with its warm cinnamon buns and great chai lattes as I'd meet for fikas with friends or people-watched through the steamy windows of its cosy cafés.

The proliferation of elegant, middle-class, brown-skinned celebrities was contemporary, beginning in earnest in the 90s and 00s when a generation came of age who were often in Sweden not directly because of the history of colonialism but rather as the offspring of esteemed travelling black jazz musicians and artsy Swedes who'd got together and had beautiful babies in the liberal 60s and 70s. They laid the foundations for a creative Afropean community that had massive influence not just in Sweden, but internationally. This scene included Quincy Jones III, son of legendary American producer Quincy Jones and Swedish model Ulla Andersson. Jones Junior grew up in Stockholm and, as a producer, along with Danish duo Soulshock and Karlin, contributed much to 2Pac's uniquely melodic brand of hip-hop. Then there was Neneh Cherry and her Swedish pop-star half-sister Titiyo, both daughters of Ahmadu Jah, a legendary Sierra Leonean drummer. Neneh's platinum-selling singer-songwriter half-brother Eagle Eye shares the same mother as Neneh, the Swedish artist Moki Karlsson, who later married famed African-American trumpeter Don Cherry; together the family lived in an idyllic-sounding multicultural artists' commune in an abandoned school in the Swedish countryside.

On a more domestic level, Timbuktu, whose dad is an African-American journalist and scholar, is still one of Sweden's biggest hip-hop artists, Trinidadian-Swedish singer Jennifer Brown won Swedish Grammies in the 90s and Awa Manneh, of Gambian and Swedish heritage, also a singer, was given the dubious honour of 'Sweden's Sexiest Woman'. This centre of Afropean excellence was small, home-grown and collaborative, with artists often working on their friends' projects behind the scenes, controlling production and aesthetics. Tarik Saleh, a Swedish-Egyptian former graffiti artist turned director, is responsible for a wave of inventive music videos such as Lykke Li's 'I Follow Rivers', acclaimed Swedish-Ethiopian documentary maker Teddy Goitom produces highly stylized documentaries about Pan-African artists, and the late Algerian-Swedish director Malik Bendjelloul won an Oscar for his hugely successful *Searching for Sugar Man*. I was introduced to the city by a friend, the singer-songwriter Stephen Simmonds, son of a Swedish mother and a Jamaican father, and through him, what I have experienced in Stockholm year after year is unlike anything else in Europe. Stockholm was my little secret, my city break of choice when I had some spare money, and I'd always return feeling

refreshed and inspired, things I was in need of at this halfway point in my journey.

Stephen was educated at the prestigious music school Södra Latin, grew up in the bohemian (though now utterly gentrified) south island Södermalm and told me that he never really felt pigeonholed as a 'black' artist, and this seemed to extend to his position as a Swedish citizen. Whenever we'd go out, whether eating at his Algerian friend's restaurant or partying at a chic soul club with his best friend, who is Korean, there was rarely a need for what I call the 'black nod of solidarity': an unspoken rule enacted when you see a fellow brown-skinned citizen on the street in a majority-white environment and acknowledge the minority struggle. Stephen's music, which he calls 'alternative soul', reflects the balance in his own life, unburdened by a market lust for reductive black street-posturing, and over the years his albums have included sitars, rainsticks, Swedish orchestras and the type of ambient Moog patches you'll usually hear in down-tempo

European chill-out music. He was obviously heavily influenced by the Motown, Blue Note and Island Records LPs his dad exposed him to at a young age, but also takes pride in Swedish pop music (even Abba), the legendary Swedish pianist Jan Johansson is an influence, as well as the strong tradition of melodic nursery rhymes and festive folk songs Swedish children are raised with, born from that historically important ingredient in a soul singer's soup: the church. Markedly different to the black Baptist and Pentecostal churches that produced a wealth of African-American musical talent, Stephen's sound is likely infused with the Lutheran branch of Protestant Christianity that took hold in Sweden. Though church attendance continues to dwindle in the country, the values of Lutheranism, along with some other key philosophies, underpin the mood of city life at large in Stockholm, which, at first glance, appears to revolve around tolerance, modesty and moderation. Some see the guilt and work ethic of Protestantism as the driving force behind capitalism, but Sweden's free-market economy is disciplined (within Sweden, at least) by a tradition of balance through democratic socialism and its *folkhemmet* – a sort of social contract between people and state that promotes the idea of country as family – as well as other very Swedish concepts that suggest balance and restraint, such as *lagom*, which can't be directly translated but means something like 'enough is sufficient', and *jantelagen*, a kind of restrictive etiquette that says the individual should never stand out from the crowd.

Another uniquely Swedish term is *mys*, a pop philosophy which has become wildly popular in lifestyle consumerism, like the East Asian concepts of feng shui and wabi-sabi, through its Danish incarnation *hygge* (the cultivation of cosiness), which at first suggested warmth and conviviality when I'd read about it in books on interior design. Certainly, I felt there was a degree of snugness in Stockholm, but on this trip I began to see these uniquely Scandinavian ideas as private pleasures that had a way of alienating anyone outside an inner circle of friends. What did it take, exactly, to become part of that *folkhemmet* family of citizens? As I looked to link my experience in Stockholm with a wider black experience in Europe, Stockholm's tapestry of tolerance began quietly fraying.

Stephen Simmonds was holidaying in Jamaica, so on this trip, instead of hanging out with a pop star, it looked as if I'd be spending Christmas with two middle-aged strangers. Hostelling in Europe suggests youthful escape, but I was travelling off season and my experience was overwhelmed by stinking men-feet in disintegrating socks, overweight fifty-year-olds snoring, bad tattoos, loners, drunks, belligerent football hooligans and unwashed blond dreads drooping from hippies who'd been on the road far too long. Most of the hot young people were backpacking around Southeast Asia about now, or waiting for Europe's summertime festivals. The few I saw on this trip, especially Americans, were locked in their own cyber-bubbles, talking in the reception areas to concerned boyfriends, girlfriends or family members over Skype and Face-Time. From a distance, Americans say, 'Have you seen what's happening over in Europe? It's terrible!' While their college campuses are being shot up because of insane gun laws, their police frequently and indiscriminately kill black people, their Midwest and Deep South are rotting in poverty, their politicians and leaders are interchangeable with Hollywood actors and reality-TV stars, their privatized healthcare creates opiod addicts and their country is increasingly subject to frequent natural disasters as powerful lobbyists deny the effects of climate change – they worry about the safety of loved ones who are backpacking through Provence, Bavaria and Scandinavia.

In Stockholm's Mosebacke hostel I'd finally found cleanliness and privacy, but there was still no suggestion that the hostel came with a 'youth' suffix, and among the list of house rules I almost expected it to say, 'No admittance to anyone attractive and under forty.' No sleeping bags were allowed (fined if caught), any persons not staying at the hostel were prohibited at all times (fined if caught), and there was to be no noise after ten, when the lights in the common area were switched off and the door to the kitchen was locked. Forget hostel-organized piss-ups and pub crawls, there was barely any staff presence at all, other than a timid and tired-looking Kurdish woman who'd sometimes come in to clean at night.

I was sharing the entire place with Gus, a Greek man looking for work, and Saleh, a nightclub bouncer from Tunisia. During two echoey weeks at the hostel I never saw them at the same time, their itineraries so out of sync that both men would talk to me as if the other was a myth: 'It's quiet, huh? I hear there is also a Greek staying here' and 'I have seen a big Arab guy, but I don't know if he is a guest or security.' I, too, initially mistook Saleh for security. He was built like an ageing boxer refusing to retire; powerful-looking but a bit flabby, with a big, tough, broken body; his knees looked sore when he walked, but he could still kick the shit out of you. He'd come to Stockholm from Tunisia at the age of twenty and had been living in the city for twenty-three years but looked at least ten years older than the maths suggest. 'I came as an import, met a Swedish woman, she buy me from Tunisia. It's where Europe get all its best fruit,' he said to me, smiling. Saleh was the one who initiated the conversation and, though a big bouncer cornering you in a darkened room (the reception) at 11 p.m. might sound terrifying, he had the presence of an even-handed alpha male. Tough, yes, but relaxed in himself, as if he'd proven his masculinity on enough occasions throughout his life to now have no time for posturing. How did he find Sweden?

'Swedish people racist, of course, you know these fascists get in government now, but it's much worse in Denmark, Holland and Finland. People say Scandinavians are peaceful. Ha! That's bullshit! You know here they have what you call double moral. This Nobel guy who make peace prize invent explosives! And still they make many weapons here used by America.'

I knew that Alfred Nobel, who the famous peace prize is named after, also invented dynamite and had made a fortune from its sale. By chance, he'd got hold of an obituary written about him that had accidentally been published before his death, criticizing how he'd made his money, the headline rejoicing, 'The merchant of death is dead!' Feeling disturbed and guilt-ridden, he bequeathed his mass wealth to a foundation which, after his actual death, distributed most of his money through the Nobel prizes in peace, physics, chemistry, physiology, medicine, literature and, more recently, economics. Until meeting Saleh, though, I had no idea that, despite its neutral, peaceful reputation on the world stage, Sweden was still one of the world's biggest exporters of weapons. There are two huge multinational chemical companies still in existence that can trace their lineage back to Nobel himself, and one of them, Dynamit Nobel, powered the Nazis during the Second World War, though it's not just Nobel's legacy. Per capita, Sweden is currently the third largest arms exporter in the world (behind Israel and Russia), and most of those weapons are made by a company we've all heard of, because until recently it also made cars: Saab. The Swedish political system has little anti-corruption legislation in place for what may be the world's most corrupt industry, which has meant Swedish weapons have in the past armed everything from illegal wars to bloody dictatorships. The reason the government turns a blind eye is no doubt partly because the defence industry currently employs 30,000 highly skilled Swedish workers; the industry is worth trillions of euros. That's what Saleh meant when he talked of 'double morals'; what kind of money, exactly, was funding those clean and safe streets and the peaceful reputation I'd fallen in love with? And Saleh wasn't finished.

'Swedish people will always live good, they are only 9 million people, but they have slaves, they need people like me to make sure only the right people get into their clubs. And you see Kurdish woman who cleans here? You can't find her in the daytime, enjoying the shops or cafés, she is used only for this purpose. All these people in Europe, they think they give immigrants a favour. But they don't realize that we are only here because they destroy our countries. America is like big dog, and in Europe it has its little dogs, Sweden supplying weapons, UK following to Iraq, creating war to steal oil. Then when Iraq is turned to shit and an Iraqi has to leave for America or Europe, they don't let him in or think they doing him a favour if they do!'

The West's aggression overseas, its plundering of natural resources and unnatural division of foreign lands, advanced its economic prosperity; the wealth of its knowledge is also global. When we write numbers, we are writing in Arabic characters; many of the defining art movements of the twentieth century have an African lineage, born from geometric, figurative and graphic art from Europe's newly acquired colonies. Most modern pop is the musical descendant of the twelve-bar blues created by African slaves in the American Midwest, and 'algebra', or 'al-gebra', isn't a Latin word. The entire Industrial Revolution wouldn't have been achieved anywhere near so quickly or on such a large scale without the toil of the colonies. I mention all this not to discredit some of the undeniably valuable cultural and scientific advancements of the West, but just as a reminder that the West, too, has historically and consistently drawn from the world pot, has always advanced itself by moving beyond its own home territories and borders. International development has been anything but a one-way stream between the West and the 'Third World'. When you think of where so many natural resources have been sourced, it leads you to the question: who has really been developing who these past two or three centuries?

One of the few things that disappointed me about some of the communities I visited on my trip was that they hadn't managed to connect with each other to solidify some kind of meaningful trans-national grassroots movement against the structural oppression of their new home. I was frustrated at how comically disorganized and corrupt African consulates in Europe were, and constantly shocked by how divided the Arab world was, how the Turks looked down on the Kurds, how Ethiopians and Eritreans sometimes despised each other, how Moroccans often loathed Algerians. Back in Sheffield I have heard Yemenis say that Kosovanis are lazy and dirty. I've heard Jamaicans use the word 'Paki', seen privately educated Africans look down their noses at people of Caribbean heritage, not to mention the shadism that exists within black communities. Of course, in some cases, the tension was a hangover from colonialism, or connected to old wars and aggressions that had reverberated over from the motherlands – just because people have brown skin or share a certain faith doesn't mean they are naturally compatible – but the division was also sometimes a reminder that it isn't only white westerners who suffer from this 'historical amnesia'. There are many black people serving up, to other black people, the type of discrimination their own families and communities suffered (and still do suffer) at the hands of white people when they first arrived in the country. The prejudice was always rooted in fear, exacerbated by money troubles and directed at the easiest targets: those people near us who are new and different to us. After twenty years living in Sweden and, now, telling me all about its racism and oppression, Saleh, for instance, hadn't found any camaraderie with the Swedish Somali community. He lived in the suburbs, he said, and was staying in the hostel to make some extra money by renting out his place over Christmas. I asked him about Rinkeby, a Stockholm suburb with the highest population of immigrants in all of Sweden.

'You know, Rinkeby used to be nice place but now too many Somalians! If you are going to do crime, do it properly – but these guys are stabbing kids for mobile phones.' He said this in a way that led me to believe he knew all about 'doing crime properly', and increasingly reminded me of Marlon Brando's Godfather, with a husky Swedish-Arabic accent that wasn't a million miles away from Don Corleone's American Italian in both tone and intonation. I was curious about his prejudice.

'I work sometimes on door of nightclub and, you know, the

only people I have fight with is Somalians! They always get too drunk, and when I tell them they can't come in they say I'm racist and want fight with me. And sometimes I say, "Yes . . . I am racist!" He laughed, then pulled a face full of indignation. 'But they are the ones that are racist! They are Arab people, like me – I'm an Arab! But you call them Arab and they say, "No! I am Somalian!" Now me, really, I am Berber, but still I say I am Arab. They have problems with Arabs.' I asked Saleh for an example.

'Okay, I make many friends with young people who came to the club where I work – they see me like uncle – I split fights and protect them from trouble. One girl who is half Somali, half Arab, I not see her for a while and she remembered me from the club so we talk on the street. Then this Somali guy I know . . . he was friend, you know, he call me "brother" when I see him. He walks past and say something to this girl . . . and I can't speak the language but he says something about "Arab". I ask girl if she knows him and she say no, and she say he asked her, "Why she is talking to an 'Arab'!?" He call me Arab, but what is he? He is Arab! You know, it is peaceful here, nobody make problem apart from Somalians!' Saleh carried on. 'But the Swedish are very clever . . . they make place like Rinkeby and keep all the immigrants together so they don't have to see them! When Libya have problem with Gaddafi, Sweden and other places in Europe only get few immigrants . . . Tunisia get 1 million! You know, we are not rich country and we have only just finished rebellion, but Tunisia take them in . . . UN tell different story, but I know, I was there, Tunisians give things from their home to help these people, feed these people. A van used to come around to help, with food and clothes, and people would give anything to help, but Arabs never thank Arabs. If Swedish man comes to help, they all love him, but they don't have respect for each other.' Saleh had finished his speech and, before I could reply, he looked at his watch and said, 'OK, it is late now, I must go to bed. It's quiet, huh? I hear there is also a Greek staying here.'

Just as Saleh the owl, with his wizened Godfather voice and sobering tales, suited the darkness of the night-time, so did bright, chirpy lark Gus suit the daytime as he bounded around with limitless energy, speaking in torrents. It was as if their characters had been crafted from their timetables. Saleh was what you needed at night – big, tough and streetwise; whereas Gus was designed for the daytime – small, and skinny and approachable, a bit foolhardy, perhaps, a networker. His days were born to be seized. What both did have in common was their age, and Saleh and Gus reminded me of the saying, 'When you're eighteen, you worry about what everyone thinks of you; when you're forty, you don't care what anyone thinks of you; when you're sixty, you realize nobody ever was thinking of you!' They were both in their mid-forties and, like most men of their age, both were opinionated and spoke authoritatively in their own way. I often felt that I had valuable things to add to our conversations, but they never listened, always cutting me off, which sort of suited me.

I first met Gus at what was breakfast for me and lunch for him. He wore spectacles and a bumbag and was fidgeting over the cooker, preparing a meal that looked disastrous (plain pasta with plain meatballs in tomato ketchup and a side of dry lettuce with no dressing). He didn't look geeky, exactly, but close. The bumbag is always a sign that the person wearing it is more concerned with convenience than aesthetics, and Gus's style was that of a man too preoccupied with higher thoughts to care too much about his appearance. Before he even spoke I immediately guessed he was an academic, and when he did speak it was elaborate and usually included some kind of mild trivia. When I later relived and wrote up what he said in my notepad, I noticed that the cadence of his sentences demanded constant exclamation marks. 'Hello, I'm Gustus! Or *Gustav*, as we're in Scandinavia – same root, and the root is Swedish, actually. Of course, you can just call me Gus, that is fine too!' His words over-analysed themselves, his whole demeanour Woody Allen-like, and he kept talking over me, not out of rudeness but because he'd just remembered a point he had tried to make earlier that had trailed off into a point about something else. He would be staying for another week. When he started talking about his children I wondered why he was in Sweden, especially over Christmas, but never needed to prompt a story out of him. 'I'm thinking of moving here, actually! I am from Greece so I guess I don't need to tell you why I'm trying to get out, and why I'm choosing a country that doesn't have the euro!' He smiled resignedly and continued: 'There is no point leaving a place and going to another place where the same could happen. We were targeted because we were low on the index and had nothing to export, but they are now talking of Italy and even Spain!' He pointed to his lettuce. 'I mean, this is probably from Spain, they have agriculture, but they could still be in trouble!' I asked Gus what line of work he was in. 'Well, there is the work that I did, and then the work I am looking for, of course! I taught physics in Greece, but all the work stopped. Seriously, it's like the Middle Ages there; this last couple of years people's lives have been destroyed. All my friends in their forties now have no jobs, and you know that is a bad age to be unemployed with no welfare and no opportunities . . . there are families that need to be supported, pensions that need to be saved for. People don't realize just how bad it is. It's crazy, the taxes just keep getting higher and higher, but last year I had a wage cut of 40 per cent! And, you know, I go to Lidl here to buy my food, and it is good for me to judge because we have Lidl in Greece also. In Sweden they earn three times as much but the prices for the food are the same! In Greece taxes are going up, wages are going down and everything else is staying the same, it doesn't make sense, is impossible situation!'

I mentioned that Sweden is notorious for high tax rates (up to 60 per cent), and Gus cut me off again: 'Yes, but people here don't mind because they can see where their money is spent; in the street lights that always work and the roads that have no potholes, so they can say, "If I don't pay, then the lights go off!" But in Greece it is not the same, our money seems to fund nothing but banks and politicians!'

He hadn't mentioned what his wife (who I gathered he was still with) thought of the idea, but I suspected it was partly why he was alone at Christmas, that she thought he was insane and the whole idea hare-brained, especially when he described his home as 'the type of place small and tranquil enough to be named only by its proximity to another well-known place! So I'll just say, "It's between Thessaloniki and Athens and then three hundred kilometres to the West!"' Gus told me that his youngest daughter, who was ten, had absolutely hated the idea, and was in floods of tears when he told her his plan, worried that she'd lose touch with all her friends. When I suggested that sunny Greece to freezing Sweden was a bit of a lifestyle shift I heard the first and only bit of defensiveness in his voice; his sharp response was as though he'd had to defend the idea to many people many times before. 'Greece is not all just resorts, you know! This place where I live is very cold too, there was fifteen centimetres of snowfall before I left! It's eight hundred metres above sea level, in the mountains ... with a stream ...' And then his tone saddened and his voice tapered off at the thought of the beauty and idiosyncrasies of his home. 'I am from Athens originally and used to move so quick, and in the village I live in now I am known for being a really quick walker. I have seen everything in the village, so why do I need to waste time by slowing down? I just like to get to where I'm going! But here in Stockholm even the slow people seem too busy!'

That's when I found out things were so bad that this charming, intelligent teacher of university-level physics was considering uprooting his family to become a coach driver. 'You know, it's a job that there is a demand for and I already have my class-D licence and am studying for my Class C,' he said proudly, the eagerness in his voice poignant. When Gus spoke of his situation, and that of Greece, it wasn't with anger, exactly, but amazement, and his optimism was iron-clad. I imagined the faces of his wife and kids when he had told them his plan, and his demeanour was that of a man who was going to work as hard as possible and show them his masterplan beautifully realized. His ultimate goal, he said, was to integrate into Swedish society, but he was currently finding it a little elusive so kept visiting a place on the outskirts in Sölna, where there was a community centre founded by Greeks who'd started a new life in Sweden in the 70s. It was somewhere to watch Greek TV, make friends and network, a potential entry point into Sweden.

'The main issue is getting started, it will be okay after that, but it's so hard to get in here. You first need a national-security number and to get that you need a job, but to get a job you need national security! I came so close to getting one, but it fell through and I kind of gave up for a little bit. I have no relatives in Sweden but made connections by spending some time in the Greek community centre. Its members welcomed me in until I asked if I could use their address as somewhere to get my documents sent to, and then these people vanished – it was like an impressive magic trick! But I don't blame them, it's a lot to ask. It's fantastically impossible to get a place in Stockholm, and they paid their dues. It's not even the price, it's that there is nowhere to live! No space – there is like a three-month waiting list and people are actually renting out their rental properties. I think I will go to see Uppsala.'

I told him about Saleh, the 'Tunisian Import', who was renting out his place over Christmas, and Gus told me that most of the immigrants he knew had made it in Sweden by marrying locally.

'Yes, a Persian gentleman I met said, "The best way is the bed way!" But for me it is obviously out of the question, because I am already married. It's a shame because it would help me practise the language too – it's like English without consonants. But I am taking a course and feel I have an ear for languages.'

Later on I told Saleh about Gus and his plans, and he was dismissive of them. 'I tell you, people come to Sweden and they think they are gonna live like Swedish people, but it's impossible, even if you finish university they save all the jobs for Swedish people and keep all the jobs they don't want to do for immigrants. It used to be better here but, just like all of Europe, things are getting worse, more racism, more discrimination.'

People like Gus, who are not self-pitying at all but enterprising and industrious and trying to do the best for their families, are my heroes. He wasn't a dreg. Like most immigrants, he was a human being willing to leave his beautiful home, uproot his family and swap his skilled career for something menial so that his family could survive. He wasn't a coward who was incapable of fixing his country and had decided to run away, he was a trailblazer ready to sacrifice so much so that his children might have a chance at a better life, having had his own life ruined by a greedy international banking system and warped politics beyond his control.

To make Gus feel better, I'd told him, 'Give your daughter a few months and she'll have new friends and will have forgotten all about home,' but, really, I felt worried for Gus and his family. There were perhaps times when I was guilty of self-aggrandizing my journey, but at the end of the day I was travelling out of my own free will and without any dependents. Here was a man on a mission with *real* problems, whose travelling hinged on providing food for his family to eat. In the introduction I mentioned Hishem, the Sudanese man I met in The Jungle, who, as someone with brown skin, I felt pressured to write about, even though I didn't feel I could do justice to his story. But this Greek man, living in and highly educated by Europe and yet in such a desperate situation, was a reminder that, in an era of climate change, xenophobia and economic uncertainty, any one of us may be closer to the landless Sudanese man in The Jungle than we realize.

Rinkeby Swedish

Wandering through Södermalm on Christmas Eve, there it was again: the peaceful ambience, the successful-looking people of all shades chit-chatting in their mellifluous dialect, everything before me pleasant on the eyes and ears. It wasn't even one in the afternoon and it was already early twilight, and the crisp winter twilights in Stockholm are lovely and long-lasting. The sky was pearlescent, pinks, purples, silvers and creams mingling dramatically as overhanging streetlights began to glow, along with the omnipresent lantern-like Swedish star of Bethlehem in the windows of busy cafés and heaving bars that lit up and spilled out on to the sidewalks, turning the snowy semi-pedestrianized thoroughfare of Götgaten into a glowing river of gold.

Over some *chokladbolls* (delicious spheres of chocolate covered in shredded coconut with a subtle hint of coffee, a Swedish specialty that I later learned used to be known as 'Negro balls') and a cappuccino at one of my favourite cafés in the open-plan Bruno galleria, I made conversation with Lucille, one of those well-heeled mixed-race people who seemed to proliferate on Söder. Lucille was born and raised in Ostermalm, which is a little bit like saying you grew up in Mayfair in London, or the 8th arrondissement in Paris. She lived with her white Swedish father who'd divorced her Afro-Cuban mother when she was little, and told me that, first and foremost, she considered herself Swedish. She wore her hair naturally, in a large Afro, had my complexion, which is to say she was the same colour as my cappuccino after I'd sucked off the froth, had the same type of retro-soul-influenced knitwear as me (earthy and bohemian but young and urbanite). She was what I'd describe as being 'of my tribe', but right from the start of our spirited conversation we politely disagreed on nearly everything, especially when the conversation turned to class.

'People in Rinkeby, even of the second generation, absolutely refuse to lose their immigrant accent,' said Lucille snootily, one eyebrow raised in disapproving condescension. All her opinions were delivered axiomatically, like one of those pipe-smoking anthropologists or scientists you see being interviewed as unquestionable experts on serious matters in footage of TV shows back in the 50s. 'Of course, these people think it's "cool" to talk with this broken "Rinkeby Swedish". I don't understand why they don't take the time to learn Swedish language and culture properly and take part in society,' she said, again with that arrogantly raised eyebrow which by now seemed to signify she was mildly concerned by such matters. Rinkeby Swedish is something like Ebonics, and had entered into the popular lexicon nationwide as meaning 'Swedish ghetto-slang', even if the person speaking it wasn't from anywhere near Rinkeby. Lucille said that she didn't believe Sweden was an inherently racist society, and that immigrant communities were mostly to blame for any kind of divide. If an educated, mixed-race European felt this way, was there any hope at all? Had she not faced *any* racism or discrimination that had made her empathize with the immigrant struggle?

'Well, not really, but it's because I don't look for it. I'm twenty-eight and have had perhaps two occasions in my life where I could say I've had racism directed towards me, and that's in *Ostermalm*, where there were only two other mixed-race kids in the entire area. But I notice with black people a kind of obsession with race. Even my own mother looks for racism everywhere, and so what happens? She finds it! I think people need to work harder to take part. Despite having lived here for forty years now, my mother still hasn't lost her accent – she absolutely refuses to, and I just don't get it. To hold on to the old culture holds you back in the new culture you live in. Why hold on to the past?'

'Perhaps it's something to do with class,' I suggested. Maybe holding on to an accent *is* sometimes an act of defiance against a society that refuses to let you truly blend in because of your skin colour but, more than that, keeping an accent is about remembering where you came from and keeping a part of you alive that may help you navigate through places that are rejecting you. It was quite easy for Lucille, who embodied subtle middle-class Swedish etiquettes and was backed by economic power and an elite education, but just the previous day I'd spoken to a young man called Ishmael who'd grown up in Rinkeby, and when I asked him whether Sweden was racist he'd had a different experience that chimed more with what Saleh had been telling me. 'It's a difficult question, with perhaps more than one answer,' he said charitably. 'I personally have had many obstacles trying to get ahead in Sweden, but it's because I wasn't born here, and have an Arabic name. But the story is different for my best friend, who I grew up with since I was three years old. He is half Eritrean and half Swedish, but we look so alike that people often mistake us for brothers, or at least cousins. We were neighbours so my mother practically raised him, and his mother me, and we have very similar values when it comes to work ethic and morals. We went to the same school and studied at the same university . . . in almost every way we are "cut from the same cloth", you could say. After uni, though, things changed. We both applied for lots of jobs, and he kept getting interviews and eventually got a job in a junior position at a really great firm, but I hardly ever even got to the interview stage. Now he is doing really well. He has worked very hard for what he has, so I just thought that maybe he had some special way about him. But when I said this to him recently, he took me to the side and said, "Ishmael, we both know that, if anything, *you* are the smart one. Do you know what the only difference is between you and me? You have an Arabic second name while I inherited a Swedish one from my mother.'

Was the onus to change really on the person speaking with a

slight lilt, or on the society that judges someone based on something as trifling as an accent or a second name? There is also no reason for immigrants to think what they are bringing with their own culture can't enrich Europe, as it frequently has done throughout history, and anyway, hadn't European colonial powers tried to impose their own languages and dictions on the world? Even though Swedish colonial history is relatively small, it opened many missions in Africa that tried to educate the local tribespeople in the ways and words of Christianity. It seems they hadn't factored in any resistance, or that by their conquests and 'civilizing missions' they themselves might need to change or be accommodating, allow leeway and be open to influence by other cultures. Lucille still wasn't convinced.

'Okay, so it's about social systems and class, but what does that have to do with race? Certain families do well and then help their friends, and so on. It's natural. What does race have to do with it?'

I said that I felt nearly all those families in Europe were white, working within a white infrastructure that had benefitted from the undermining of other peoples and, because of that, race is often a badge people judge class on. I brought up the small group of Stockholm yuppies known as 'Brats' who you can find in certain upmarket clubs. Much like the very poor, the very rich were often hidden in corners of Swedish society, but a culture among certain young women, and particularly men, had emerged in the economic boom of the late 90s where overtly expressing one's wealth and privilege became fashionable even in Sweden – they were a precursor to the neoliberal Instagram #lovinglife #blessed #veganbrunch crowd. These 'Brats' can still be found in VIP sections in Stureplan's upmarket nightclubs such as Berns, Café Opera and, by now, probably places I've never heard of. They were nearly always white, blond and tanned with slick-backed hair and Ralph Lauren shirts, and initially comprised only Stockholm's upper classes, with connections to Swedish royalty and aristocracy. Now they're mostly just minted twenty-somethings who either made a fortune as bankers or are living off their parents' hedge funds. Why, if it was only about class, did you never see a black Brat? I asked Lucille.

'Well, you know, I grew up in Stureplan and you actually do get black Brats! Both boys and girls who straighten their Afros and wear it in exactly the same way as white people, slicked back with gel. And at the moment, within the Brat circles it's very popular to have an exotic-looking boyfriend or girlfriend.'

That Brats like to fuck blacks doesn't mean they have accepted them as equals any more than a man wanting to have sex with a woman proves he isn't a misogynist. But I wondered if that had been why, as a young man with brown skin and an Afro, I had felt so comfortable in Stockholm. I did feel that it was fashionable to be mixed-race there, but had never realized I might only have been a fashion *accessory*. I would later be told by one Brat that the East Asia look was now more *à la mode* anyway.

It all sounded a bit like Paris in the 20s and I wasn't sure how deep and meaningful the cultural exchange between the French bourgeois and the appreciation of African culture was back then either. The ironic proliferation of imagery of the black woman as sexy and savage didn't always speak of racial enlightenment but was often a perverse objectification that can still be seen today, and was certainly very evident in the influential 80s work of Jean-Paul Goude and his book *Jungle Fever*, in which he turned Grace Jones into a caged and prowling panther woman. 'I'm not saying a superficial or physical appreciation of something is all bad,' I said to Lucille, 'but I don't think it necessarily signifies respect or equality.'

'Yeah, but you mentioned Paris, and I have to say I don't like that city. I have tried to live there twice now and there is such a pressure that keeps you down, and it is very unsafe. I stayed with some cousins in the suburbs and they told me that I might get shot if I were to go out alone after eight at night. My mother went to Paris to be a model but she couldn't settle either and that's why she came to Stockholm. I'm so glad she did.'

Lucille was fascinated by how a place can influence a people and took my observation that Stockholm's infrastructure and cleanliness had made its citizens healthy and beautiful a stage further. She was studying something called epigenetics, a new science that had initially been discredited but was now making a comeback, thanks partly to the work coming out of a small Swedish university in Umeå. I'd never heard of it before meeting Lucille and, though I found it fascinating, it immediately struck me as something that could be problematic and susceptible to pseudo-scientific interpretation.

'Epigenetics is less about our genes and more about the *expression* of those genes . . . for instance, you might carry a gene for an illness from your father but, because of your environment, it isn't expressed. And if you don't express that gene, then it might miss a generation. But it's also about the information transfer across generations. We inherit chromosomes from our parents, but only half of those chromosomes are DNA, the other half are proteins that carry epigenetic information. I think of my mother and her heritage, which is linked to slavery and which, you know, is not so long ago, and I sometimes think those memories and experiences are entrenched not just within the black psyche but in black people's very biology. So many black people, including my mother, have this kind of latent slave mentality, even though there is no slavery now, but I got brought up here in Stockholm by my white father, so I guess it's different for me.'

Lucille seemed to be suggesting that her upbringing in an affluent part of Stockholm had saved her from a life-long chip on her shoulder, not just psychologically but at the very core of her DNA. But all I could think of were the noble faces of African America, of Maya Angelou, Miles Davis, Michael Jordan, Henry Louis Gates Junior, Oprah Winfrey, Neil deGrasse Tyson, Stokely Carmichael, Audre Lorde, Muhammad Ali, James Baldwin, W. E. B. Du Bois. Of the gene pool of slavery being, if anything, a nucleus of black excellence. Award-winning writer Malcolm Gladwell, who also carries 'slave DNA', had suggested a correlation between mathematical excellence in Chinese students and the long history of rice cultivation in difficult environments by their forefathers – the level of concentration and attention to detail it took to cultivate rice in China, Gladwell says, is the same kind of mindset needed to be an excellent mathematician. If Lucille was on to something, I am glad I carry the lived experiences of survivors, despite the worst odds. And for the record, I'm also glad I've still got my northern English accent, which I get remunerated for as a continuity announcer for a major television network.

I wished Lucile well and, before stepping out into the cold, looked back at her briefly as she gazed thoughtfully out of the window. Seeing her sitting there alone with her brown skin in the middle of snowy Stockholm, I realized that in the past I, too, had bought into the Stockholm she'd been mentally occupying, and in our oblivious privilege we had been just as lost as those members of the black community in Europe who, like Mohammed back in Berlin, defined themselves only in terms of their own blackness.

With this acknowledgement I began to assume a more equitable middle ground and came to see Stockholm with new eyes. For instance, on the many trips I'd made over the years I'd noticed that Stockholm was a city of dog walkers and interpreted this as a sign of prosperity, an outdoorsy lifestyle, excellent public parks, and so on. But out of his desperation to assimilate, Gus back at the hostel had studied the Swedes more meticulously than I had and had noticed that the dog walkers were often solitary and, rather than being a symbol of success, to him, the dogs signified something else, namely *loneliness*. Then I remembered that my friend Stephen's most successful album was entitled *Alone*, the stark title track full of haunted vocals and melancholic lyrics suggesting displacement, longings to feel at home, yearnings for warmth, friendship and love that is absent.

As tradition has it, when shops close in the early afternoon on Christmas Eve, Stockholm settles into an outward silence and turns inwardly festive, everybody retreating into their homes for family time and *mys*. Candles are lit, folksongs are played, food is cooked, friends are invited over and hot wine is served. All my friends were out of town, staying at their folks' second home in the countryside or enjoying a novelty non-white Christmas on a beach somewhere, and until Christmas Eve I'd felt okay about being alone in Stockholm, which was more like peaceful solitude than depressing isolation. But with no busy cafés to sit and write or eavesdrop in, or street scenes to photograph, wandering solitarily through the falling snow and getting glimpses through apartment windows of festive, private conviviality, I felt almost deliriously dejected. The idea of spending Christmas anywhere alone is a bit depressing, but there is perhaps nowhere on earth more Christmassy than the winter wonderland of Stockholm – you're practically in Santa's stomping ground, with Lapland just over a thousand kilometres to the north – yet I felt I was witnessing all the merriness behind a sheet of frosted glass, and no matter how much I scratched I couldn't get in and take part in all the fun. There are so many people living in Europe who must feel like that every day, close to a beautiful dream but quietly – and increasingly not so quietly – denied by it, and I had to acknowledge that I was often on the comfortable side of this equation. I had an early night in the

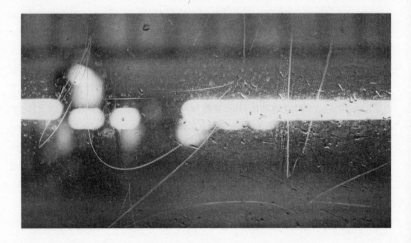

hostel with the two other lonely men who were, in their own way, also being excluded by Swedish Christmas.

On Boxing Day I found myself trudging through an area of town where nobody was or had been celebrating Christmas at all and life was going on as usual. In the turquoise twilight were signs that appeared like mirages, lit by the low sun, in various scripts, and with words like 'Ethiostar', 'Naima' and 'Barwaaqo' on shopfronts. There were symbols and semiotics from all over the Muslim diaspora: crescent moons and stars, the predominant colours white, red, black and green in various configurations; flags of Iran, Iraq, Ethiopia, Turkey and Kurdistan displayed in apartment windows without a Christmas candle in sight. Low-key mosques in makeshift buildings looked more like council-estate youth clubs and were open, and the Byzantine twang of Arabic music was spilling out of poor-quality but sufficiently loud speakers. There were women dressed head to toe in niqabs and chadors of brilliant colours, drifting through thick white snow and a maze of 60s Scandinavian modernism.

En route to Rinkeby I'd had an odd encounter. A woman called Caroline, who I suspect was a little drunk from the night before and who had a massive bull mastiff with her, started chatting me up. In eight years of travelling to Stockholm it was my first meeting with any white Swede who I knew could be described as 'working class' – in certain parts of the city it can feel as though the only demographic is the middle class. She was particularly enamoured with my black Britishness and her sentences were littered with profanities, which is often a sign that someone has learned British English as a second language through local immersion. Her accent had a more Swedish bounce than most other Swedes I met, who, growing up watching Hollywood movies, had acquired a more American accent when they spoke English, but Caroline's also had a very slight hint of Jamaican.

'I focking love you guys,' she said, 'I lived in Totten-ham for a year and hung out with all the Yardies. Went to some crazy parties to skank out. You know this one guy Dennis Bovell? I focking love roots reggae music.' Though Dennis Bovell is an icon among afi-cionados, Caroline's somewhat niche reference threw me a bit. I'd never heard anyone in England profess their love for him in casual conversation.

Caroline had long, almost pitch-black hair and big, pretty brown eyes, but her features wore the type of toughness Walker Evans would have made a portrait of, the bottom half of her face sunken slightly, as if she'd done a lot of smoking or Class-A drugs and – I placed her in her early thirties – it was now starting to show. When she asked me where I was going and I said Rinkeby, she said, scathingly and without hesitation (I could have had relatives there, for all she knew), 'It is focking disgusting there, I would hate to live in these focking places, it is so depressing. And you can't see one Swedish girl there, it is all foreynjers coming here to take our jobs.' Caroline told me she'd grown up in Varby, a lower-middle-class suburb of Stockholm, and started complaining about a place called Fittja, near to where her childhood home was, which had seen an insurgence of immigration in recent years. But like a lot of immigrant-bashers, she was contradictory and hadn't thought deeply about what her argument really was, other than it having something to do with a hatred of 'foreynjers'. 'I pay my taxes for these focking foreynjers to live in a nice place – they live just as good as me but I work to pay for them!' she said, to which I replied, confoundedly, 'So are they stealing jobs and living like shit, or milking the social-security system and living like royalty? You ignorant fool!' but only in my head. I wanted her to tell me how she really felt, so I egged her on, wanted more racism, more prejudice, more xenophobia, more things to write about. Good, Caroline, good! 'Swedish people pay a *lot* of taxes, too, don't they!' I said.

'That is my point exactly! This is bullshit! I pay my 40 per cent but it doesn't go to the Swedish, it goes to these focking foreynjers. Not everyone should live the same! I work harder, so I should get more, but then these focking Turkish come and they live in a new apartment and they get all these new fittings. That is why Sweden is so focked – they let too many foreynjers in.'

Our chat was cut short when she got off the train a few stops before me and said, 'So you want to chill one time? We could take a smoke and listen to reggae,' then, because my phone had run out of battery, she gave me a piece of paper with her number on it, and I smiled, flirtily, and said, 'Sounds fun,' knowing there would be a trash can for me to put it in when I arrived at Rinkeby.

On the twenty-minute trip from Central Station, I noticed that there were other working-class white people as well as first-generation immigrants who didn't necessarily have that Stockholm sheen I'd seen in the centre of town. These passengers were the type of people I'd seen all over Europe, and definitely growing up in Sheffield, but hadn't noticed at all in Stockholm on previous trips, and their clothes were less fashionable, their hair less manicured, their postures slightly more hunched, their faces more weathered, their expressions more strained and stressed. I looked outside; gone was the low-rise dreamscape and in came the familiar austerity of European peripheries: bland and monotonous tower blocks in greys and browns, slightly different to the ones you see at the edges of London or Paris because they were clean and still in good condition, and in a way their clinical appearance had the effect of making them look even more featureless and inhuman. People interacted with slightly less discipline, too; the type of daytime chat I had had with Caroline would have seemed a bit out of place in central Stockholm but was in keeping with the mood on the train. A young, hard-looking white woman with a pitbull got into an argument with a grumpy old white man who'd had to step over her dog, who was lying across the carriage, to get to a seat, and a group of Somali teens were loudly bantering with each other over trap music being played through a smartphone speaker. By the time the train pulled into Rinkeby there was barely a white face, a precursor to what was above ground, where 90 per cent of the local population identified as immigrants.

My initial impression of Rinkeby was that it was quite pleasant, and I sort of expected it to be. On its Wikipedia page, one of the first things mentioned is that it was the site of a murder in 2002. Where I was from in Sheffield, murders happened every year, and some years every month, and even that was better than lots of other places across the UK.

An aromatic smell from a Turkish restaurant next to the 'Muslim Centre' spiced the cold breeze that hit me as soon as I exited the station. I went inside a shop called Rinkeby Bazaar that sold very different, but equally gross-looking ingredients to the ones you'd find on an average Swedish smorgasbord. In place of pickled herring, the shelves were full of things like smoked lizard fish, dried giant catfish, bitter leaves and whole ogbono (West African seeds used to thicken and enrich soups and stews). There were dented and dusty cans of coconut water, papaya juice and mango nectar, looking like they'd just about survived the treacherous journey as cargo coming in from more tropical climes on the other side of the world. There were broken biscuits with strange names in trampled packages and meats hanging off the same dusty shelves that housed tinned produce and looked capable of giving you weeks' worth of food poisoning, if put in the wrong hands. I knew that in wise hands these ingredients would be used creatively, cooked to perfection and served as part of a mouthwatering dish. I knew this because I was home – if Afropea could be found anywhere, it was in a store like this one, where my Arabic neighbours in Sheffield bought the ingredients that made some of the best meals I've ever tasted, where Jamaican grandmas found the magical, authentic spices that make their food so different to that disappointing jerk chicken recipe in Jamie Oliver's *30-minute Meals*. This store, nestled in the snow fifteen kilometres from Stockholm, was exactly the same as those that can be found all over Europe, that help power up the appetites of weary brown-skinned outsiders who can't afford wholefoods and don't have any desire to eat the soggy cheese-and-tomato sandwiches from Tesco or Carrefour. The store was a connection to back home in more ways than one and, as well as all the ingredients and huge sacks of rice people were buying, almost everyone in a fairly long queue bought phone cards. All these people had smartphones with apps that could call internationally for free, but of course very often the people on the other end of the line, in Somalia or Ethiopia, didn't have those apps, so the phone cards were still essential. That's why in London, other than as advertising space for pimps, our rapidly decaying public telephone booths are now used almost exclusively by people to call family members in the Global South.

I wandered around Rinkeby Torg, the main square, taking pictures, and people mostly left me to my own devices, giving me nothing more than a disapproving frown if they caught me taking a photo of them. As dusk settled, Rinkeby livened up a little, as bored and aimless young men hung out in the freezing cold by the Metro station entrance and older men filled up the cafés with lively discussion and arguments that, to someone like me, who couldn't speak much Arabic, initially looked like they were about to erupt into fist fights, but instead erupted into laughter. Arabic language and expression can be like that. The grocery-shop owner was playing a radio show with a monologue of a depressed-sounding monotone voice that could have been one of those war reports on 40s radio, except that it was interspersed with canned laughter. When I asked him what it was, he said, 'Arabic Mr Bean.'

Piercing this mildly affable atmosphere, there was some shouting. It didn't sound aggressive, and I listened again to hear that it was singing – really bad singing. The song being sung was 'Free Nelson Mandela' by The Specials and, as I turned the corner around the side of the main square, I saw that it was coming from an old black man hobbling through the snow with a walking stick, though the loud singing and his chunky frame had the effect of making him appear strong and sturdy. Between the 'Free Nelson Mandela' choruses he was shouting, 'Nelson Mandela! I am Nelson Mandela's brother!' at anyone he passed. I followed him at a slight distance as he walked up to the young men at the entrance of the Metro, who I now saw weren't all young but a mixture of ages and mainly Somali. As he shouted, 'I am Nelson Mandela's brother!' over and over, they humoured him, at the beginning, but quickly grew tired of his ranting. He was desperate for an audience, and when one of the Somalis tried to walk away he grabbed the young man by his arm and was then essentially told to 'piss off' as the group moved away from their Metro entrance hangout to avoid any further confrontations with the old man, who was now shouting, again in English, 'You are cowards!'

Impressed with the blasé indifference of the young Somalis, who I'd heard so many bad things about, I stood strategically in the man's line of fire. I am sure his performance was old hat in Rinkeby by now, but a loud, elderly African wandering alone in the Swedish snow desperate to speak to a stranger was exactly the kind of person I wanted to hear speak. He had a wide face and high cheekbones, and I knew that Nelson Mandela was one of many siblings (his father had thirteen 'official' children). Just imagine if . . .

When he noticed me he gave me a curious, wry smile, as if to say, *You've just seen me in action, why aren't you running away too?* 'Brudda, you hif to understand,' he said to me, quieter now. 'Ah am di bruddah of *Nelson Mandela*!' His voice was rich and gravelly, and rather than being 'crazy', it appeared his loneliness had driven him to distraction, and he realized it didn't matter what he did, how outrageously he acted, he was locked in an eternal wheel of rejection and isolation. But he had got more than he'd bargained for with me. Like lots of lonely old men, he was desperate to recount his life story to someone, and I was that rare someone who wanted to hear it, though he was so used to being ignored that getting beyond first base was strange and uncharted territory, and it took him a while to know what to say: '. . . At sixty, you realize nobody ever *was* thinking about you.'

'Really? Do you mean his real brother or his brother in spirit? In arms?' I asked. He looked at me, perplexed, and then slipped back into the comfort of his old refrain, 'Nelson Mandela, ah am Nelson Mandela's brudda!', but after looking me in the eye and waiting for a 'piss off' that would never come, he switched to a more thoughtful, coherent and conversational tone. 'He is my *real* brudda. We are from kings. The original kings.' He was being ambiguous but getting frustrated with me for not understanding. I guessed he wasn't a long-lost sibling and was instead saying that all people of the Xhosa tribe were in effect 'brothers', and I asked him if he was indeed Xhosa, and he looked at me in a sort of comically offended way. 'What? What do you say? Say that again,' he said, so I did: 'Are you Xhosa? Mandela's tribe?' 'I am Thembu,' he answered, then he grabbed the side of my arm softly to comfort me, smiled, looked directly into my eyes and added, in the most visceral way, 'And you mean *Xhosa*.' With the correct pronunciation, which includes the loud click of the tongue right where the X and H meet – 'N TOCK ZA' (I had been pronouncing it

Zoh-sah) – it rung out into Rinkeby, and in a silly way really spooked me. It was something to do with it being said so fiercely amid the white snow, and the darkness, and the slight echo, all of which evoked the reality of this old man's migratory path across cultures, generations and geography. Before, he was a bit of a clown; now I took him seriously as an elder with a real story to share, even if it was unlikely I was speaking to the long-lost brother of the world's most famous South African.

'Oh, the laif ave had,' he said with a big sigh, and told me that in 1980 he'd been jailed in Botswana after becoming embroiled in the anti-apartheid struggle. 'They catch me because ah fight for Mandela – fight against apartheid – ah am ANC freedom fighter . . . Free Nelson Mandela. Free Nelson Mandela!' He started singing The Specials song and a brief smile flickered across his face before he became serious again. 'But they try to kill me, so ah flee to Botswana, but when ah arrive they put me in jail for three years! Oh, the laif ave had!'

Botswana, having newly won its independence from Britain in the 60s, but poor and landlocked between the warring territories of South Africa and Namibia, became a place of exile for many ANC freedom fighters in the 70s and 80s, thanks largely to the sympathetic new president Seretse Khama and a Botswana national called Fish Keitseng who'd seen first hand how bad things were in South Africa when he'd done some work there. Keitseng helped facilitate a safe passage for ANC members into the country and set up refugee camps providing meagre – but considering the circumstances heroic – food and shelter. Politically and economically, Botswana was in an impossible situation, trying to position itself as vocally anti-apartheid and Pan-African while also attempting to protect its important relationship with South Africa, which offered friendlier customs tariffs and work for Botswanan citizens and businesses. During this time there were cross-border raids, the kidnapping of ANC members and illegal military operations by the apartheid government. In an attempt to appease South Africa, while still accepting ANC exiles the Botswanan government banned the training of liberation movements or the planning of strategic attacks on the apartheid government's South African Defence Force on Botswanan soil, which is what my new friend in Rinkeby had been found guilty of.

He told me that he was glad all his fighting eventually amounted to something – the freedom of Nelson Mandela and the end of apartheid – but expressed a deep regret at how difficult his own life had turned out because of it. He grabbed me by the arm and said, 'Young man, don't live laif like me! Meet woman, have pretty babies, be quiet and get a job.' He'd originally studied economics at Cape Town University, had steady work at a mining firm called Tarry and Company and dreamed of working as a lawyer. But then he got caught up with politics when Mandela was jailed, and especially so after he himself was exiled and imprisoned. After serving his time, he continued the struggle against apartheid by training as a guerrilla, joining what he called the 'People's Liberation Movement of South West Africa', which is modern-day Namibia. They teamed up with the Fidel Castro-backed People's Armed Forces of the Liberation of Angola, and he fought once again against the apartheid government's South African Defence Force, this time for Angolan autonomy.

'We fight with the AK47 in '88! We beat them! We get New York 1988! AK47!' he said, and made a machinegun noise. He was talking about the Battle of Cuito Cuanavale, the biggest war on African soil since the Second World War, later called 'an important step to free [South Africa] of apartheid' by Nelson Mandela. 'New York 1988' was in reference to the New York Accord signed at the end of that year which granted Namibian independence from South Africa, something Fidel Castro claimed the apartheid regime was forced to do after being driven out of Angola. With African liberation movements armed with decent Soviet weapons and empowered by Fidel Castro's knowledge of guerrilla warfare, South Africa faced increasing pressure to loosen its white-minority rule over African countries demanding the right to be governed by their own native population. And though the South African Defence Force and its allies had been covertly supplied with arms by Ronald Reagan's America in Cold War manoeuvres against the Communist-backed resistance movements, and Margaret Thatcher went on record to call Nelson Mandela a terrorist, there was general worldwide pressure on South Africa's apartheid regime and few countries as vehemently opposed to it as Sweden.

From the bold move of advocating the award of the 1960 Nobel Peace Prize to Albert Lutuli, the ANC president, making him the first person outside Europe and the Americas to receive the honour, to the establishment of the Swedish South Africa Committee set up by writer Per Wästberg, who'd made connections with Nelson Mandela through the writer Nadine Gordimer to influence action by Swedish politicians, there was a long history of resistance to apartheid emanating out of Sweden. Through the 60s, 70s, and 80s Swedish student movements and other groups boycotted South African produce and ultimately convinced Olof Palme, the Swedish prime minister, to ban any Swedish business investment that could benefit the apartheid system, and to provide valuable non-military aid to the ANC. A week after giving a keynote address in Stockholm to the Swedish People's Parliament against Apartheid, where he loudly denounced the South African government and reiterated his support for the ANC, Palme was assassinated on the streets of Stockholm in 1986, and the perpetrator is yet to be found.

Sweden's struggle against apartheid underpinned what Sweden was at its best, in my eyes: non-violent, fair, liberal, organized. But it was sad for me to speak to this old man, who was given political asylum in Sweden, like a number of South African freedom fighters, and then think of Sweden now. It was engaged in what broadcaster and former chairman of the Equality and Human Rights Commission Trevor Phillips once called 'passive apartheid' when speaking of the racial divide in Britain to describe how 99 per cent of

Britain's black community lived in big cities, while the countryside was almost exclusively white – a form of congenital cultural and racial separation.* Sweden's passive apartheid was more about immigrant communities being out of sight and mind. More than a few people, some of whom I haven't included, corroborated Lucille's opinion that the people of Rinkeby kept to themselves and liked it that way, but I wondered if something slightly different was going on. In Clichy-sous-Bois, people had been completely neglected and shunted out to the middle of nowhere, which bred an angry community. But Rinkeby wasn't the worst place I'd ever visited, was only twenty minutes from Central Station on the train and seemed to me to have *just enough* – almost like the people in the working-class north of Britain – to neuter the desire to leave.

The area was one of many born out of a hugely ambitious housing scheme overseen by Olof Palme's Social Democrat Party and known as Miljonprogrammet (The Million Programme), which in England might be described as something similar to the New Towns housing scheme. The goal was to build a million homes over a period of ten years from the mid-60s to the mid-70s to combat the country's chronic housing problems, as jobs shifted from agriculture to industrial work. Not only did the Social Democrats achieve this goal, they surpassed it by 6,000 homes and completed the project a year ahead of schedule, and the work was of the highest standard: coveted architects and planners of 60s Sweden attempted to create not just Corbusier's 'machines for living' but machines for Swedish social democracy. Each area had its own public spaces, nurseries, libraries and schools, encouraging an educated, localized, harmonious society and promoting a better work–life balance. The programme was generally seen as a success, and the apartments I saw in Rinkeby (similar to the ones I saw at a distance on the train) were pleasant up close. The shopping

* On this trip I only visited big cities, which were the places I could find black communities, and I frequently thought that it would also be fascinating to travel through Europe's right-wing rurality.

area was low-rise and open plan, the housing that surrounded it a mixture of large housing blocks and smaller maisonettes. It didn't feel at all like a rabbit warren, a trait some British and French architects were guilty of imbuing into their vast social housing schemes in the postwar era. But Rinkeby's self-containment seems to be working against it, due in part to 'white flight', after successive conservative governments of the 90s and 00s privatized public housing, which created economic division in the city's geography, or what I'm now calling 'passive apartheid'; those – nearly always white – who could, bought up specific areas and apartments in some of Stockholm's more desirable neighbourhoods, for private ownership or to let, which meant huge and uncontrolled increases in rent, making it increasingly difficult for poorer people to occupy the centre of town. Owen Hatherley, writing for the *Guardian*, suggested that in Stockholm 'social democracy was abandoned only for the poor, its innovations were retained for the bourgeoisie'.[1] And that was it, exactly. If you have enough money, the right breeding and etiquette, then Stockholm treats you fairly and you can live a balanced 'social democratic' experience full of *lagom*, *mys* and *folkhemmet*. I still sensed the mood of social democracy in central Stockholm, but gone are the days when Sweden would try to produce these qualities that might be used to encourage integration within the minds of its citizens through innovation in design and even-handed fairness in policy. The people of Rinkeby, who naturally want to create some of the things they knew back home, have been left to their own devices in a space and time warp.

'Nelson Mandela's brother' refused to let me take his photograph or even give his name. When I asked if he'd been back to South Africa since Mandela was released and the ANC got in power, I realized he was still scared for his life, claiming that if he ever went back he'd be assassinated. I asked if he'd managed to contact any family since leaving, and this old man, buoyant with wild proclamations and militant chants, went quiet and closed his eyes for about twenty seconds, and it brought him back down to an all too sombre and clear-sighted sanity. 'My mother and father, ohh!' He held his hands over his heart, keeping his eyes closed. 'I miss them.' When he opened his eyes they were glossy with unshed tears and he took a deep breath. 'I can't . . . it hurt. Ohh, it *hurt*!' He hadn't seen them since 1976, and they were in their sixties then. He couldn't think about them because he recognized the inevitable, and never had chance to say goodbye, or give them grandkids, or take care of them as they entered old age. And I couldn't help thinking about his parents. What was the last they heard of their son? Would they have ever guessed he'd end up alone here on the outskirts of Stockholm? After telling me one last time, 'Don't live laif like me,' and wishing me a merry Christmas, Nelson Mandela's brother wandered off alone into the snowy shadows. After hearing his stories I thought that if anyone ever had a right to claim Nelson Mandela as their brother, it was that man. His adventures, which involved escaping apartheid in South Africa, jail time in Botswana and guerrilla warfare in Namibia, before descending into incoherence and invisibility in this enclave of ice-cold Europe, wasn't so unusual here in Rinkeby. When I thought of the demographics of the area – Eritreans, Somalians, Ethiopians – it hit me that these people hadn't arrived suited and booted in their Sunday best on a boat from the colonies at a colonial motherland but had all fled from war, famine and devastating corruption. The things they must have seen or heard. Call it epigenetics or post-traumatic stress disorder, there were psychological wounds at the core of some of these communities and, all things considered, I thought they were keeping it together, and that it was Swedish society, not these immigrants, who might be doing more to help them integrate.

It's all relative, isn't it? I may have come to understand my Afropean Stockholm utopian fantasy as just that, but it wasn't until I left to cross the Baltic and continue my trip in Russia that I realized Sweden could also be doing a lot worse.

MOSCOW

I Worry as I Wander

On the evening before I was set to leave Sweden I received a call from a private number: 'Hello, this is Mr Pitts?' said a voice on a crackling line so dourly Russian I initially suspected it was a friend from back home winding me up. 'I call to inform you of change of plan,' it carried on. *Leon is that you, you nobhead?* 'Boat has been cancelled, there will be email with explanation.' I'd booked to travel from Stockholm to St Petersburg on the *Princess Anastasia* ferry, a two-day voyage across the Baltic costing thirty-five euros, but in the promised email was told that it had been cancelled because of bad weather. This 'act of God' meant that the ferry company wasn't liable, so I wouldn't be receiving a refund or offered an alternative mode of transportation, but as a consolation could travel for free on the next service, which set sail in February. It was 28 December.

If I'm being honest, when I realized I'd been given a reasonable excuse for leaving Russia off my itinerary, I was a little relieved. Search 'black culture Moscow' or 'African in Russia' online and it isn't long before you're led down a path of racial hatred via Neo-Nazi snuff films, white-power discussion forums and racist blogs, some of which are connected to mainstream, government-owned Russian radio and TV stations. With only a few clicks of the mouse I found myself surfing the Dark Web, watching a grainy home-made video with harsh, dramatic orchestral music and scenes of an anonymous forest somewhere in the Russian wilderness which cut to two young brown-skinned Tajikistani men on their knees, bound, gagged and trembling, a swastika flag tied between two trees in the background. A Russian Nazi dressed in a balaclava and army fatigues walked into the scene behind the two men and began to slowly saw one of the men's heads off with a blunt knife. I couldn't watch much, but the description read that after cutting the young man's head off the Nazi tried unsuccessfully to balance it back on the decapitated body, before shooting the other man (who in the last few minutes of his life had had to listen to the awful wailing of his tortured friend) in the head with a shotgun. The rise of racist aggression among Russia's native Slavic communities extended mainly to members of former USSR colonies – Armenians, Kazakhstanis, Tajikistanis and Uzbekistanis – as well as African students making the most of the comparatively cheap high-level education that is still available in the country, though to a lesser extent than it was under the Communist scholarship programme. Blog posts by some of these black students and academics painted a depressing portrait; fear of being seen in public with their white friends or partners, being forced into staying in at night, verbal and physical abuse and, in some cases, brutal murders, with a justice system offering little or no punishment to the offenders. The member of staff who'd taken in my visa application at the Russian consulate in London a couple of months earlier (where I'd had to answer the question 'Are you a member of Al Qaeda?') had expressed concern as soon as I walked up to the counter, and told me not to walk alone at night or go out on football-match days, and to avoid national holidays, though the only way to fit it in with my schedule was to arrive on the biggest Russian national holiday of all – New Year's Eve.*

It was mostly Russia's recent history that would fill any solo brown-skinned traveller with trepidation upon entering the country. Despite all the anti-Soviet propaganda that seeped into my

---

* When, full of bravado, I later tried to impress a love interest with my Russian story, she said, 'Wow, *so brave!* You went even though you were told not to go out at night, and to avoid going places alone, and felt you constantly had to be alert to unwanted attention!?' She didn't even need the sarcastic tone to tell me what the point was: much of the planet holds those concerns for the solo female traveller.

psyche as a child of the West born in the 80s, through films such as *Enigma*, *The Hunt for Red October*, *No Way Out*, *Avalanche Express*, *Red Dawn*, *White Nights* and, of course, *Rocky IV*, I knew that Russia hadn't always been such a foreboding place, at least for people who weren't invested in a Western status quo. There was Russia's alliance with numerous African independence movements who set out to overturn Western imperialism and also voluminous accounts of travels in the Soviet Union by black writers and thinkers who almost always had a positive experience there. Though he later became disillusioned with Communism, in a 1923 essay entitled 'Soviet Russia and the Negro' Claude McKay wrote, 'Those Russian days were the most memorable of my life . . . Russia is prepared and waiting to receive couriers and heralds of goodwill and interracial understanding from the Negro race. Her demonstration of friendliness and equity for Negroes may not conduce or produce healthy relations between Soviet Russia and democratic America.'[1] A few years later Paul Robeson proclaimed, during a visit to Moscow, 'Here I am not a Negro but a human being . . . for the first time in my life.'[2]

Perhaps one of the most memorable accounts by a black traveller to Russia was by Langston Hughes, who echoed the sentiments of both McKay and Robeson in his autobiographical travelogue *I Wonder as I Wander*. The book was published in the 50s and retells his journeys across the globe in the politically charged 30s, with Hughes recounting one particularly hilarious trip to the Soviet Union with twenty-one other African-Americans to film what was to be a doomed Communist propaganda movie. Alarm bells rang for Hughes as soon as he boarded the boat, when he realized that most of the movie's 'actors' were completely inexperienced and mostly comprised young African-American students in their early twenties snapping up an opportunity to get paid to summer in an exotic part of the world. They were to travel to Russia for a big-budget movie called *Black & White*, playing poor African-American workers in the segregated South who, by joining trade unions and connecting with their blue-collar white 'comrades' in the North, and thereby empowering the proletariat, manage to overcome the evil exploitative factory owners in the South. For Hughes, who only got the chance to read the script outline weeks into the trip, there were three main problems. One was that the young, upwardly mobile, educated blacks from New York and Chicago – the only people who could get together the boat fare (to be refunded at arrival) – didn't much relate to the story, weren't at all familiar with any of the old black spirituals that were performed throughout the movie and in fact had never even travelled south of the Mason–Dixon line. The second was that the Soviets supposed that all African-Americans were by their very nature gifted singers, but only two members of the group could hold a note so, even after the numbers had been learned, they sounded awful. Third, and importantly, the storyline wasn't rooted in any kind of reality connected with 30s America. Much as Ronald Reagan had never stepped foot in Russia before delivering his famous 'evil empire' speech condemning the country in 1983, the acclaimed Russian writer of this film had never visited the States and had based his story on American history books about the Civil War, shoehorning in Communist ideology as a one-size-fits-all answer to America's problems, which distorted Hughes's home country beyond his recognition. Though Hughes was connected to communist movements back home in Harlem, he took particular umbrage at the idea that white American workers from the North, an area of the world still grossly unequal and racist in the 30s, would ever jump to the rescue of black workers in the South. The notion of the American Dream, of individual responsibility for one's own destiny and the racial hierarchies that allowed working-class whites to chase that dream while refusing all but an elite group of blacks, was too embedded in the mood of the country to be upturned overnight in favour of interracial worker solidarity.

Despite the confusion and calamity of making the movie,

Hughes and his friends had a ball in Moscow. They were addressed as '[our] Negro-worker comrades', while also seemingly exalted by the supposedly egalitarian system, Soviet society proving a far cry from the Jim Crow laws back home. Two decades before Rosa Parks brought North America's segregated bus journeys to international attention, this was what Langston Hughes experienced in Russia:

> On a crowded bus, nine times out of ten, some Russian would say, 'Negrochanski tovarish – Negro comrade – take my seat!' On the streets queuing up for newspapers, or cigarettes, or soft drinks, often folks in the line would say, 'Let the Negro comrade go forward' . . . of all the big cities in the world I've ever been, the Muscovites seemed to me to be the politest of peoples to strangers. But perhaps that's because we were negroes and, at that time, with the Scottsboro' case on world-wide trial in the papers everywhere, folks went out of their way to show us courtesy.[3]

The case Hughes mentioned would have been of particular interest to the Soviet Union, being an early instance of the type of empowering collaboration between Communist ideology and black resistance movements that defined much of the civil-rights and decolonial processes of the twentieth century. The Scottsboro' Boys were nine African-American teenagers wrongly convicted of raping two white American women after a fight broke out between them and a group of racist white men trying to throw them off a train because of their skin colour. When, via the black teenagers' self-defence, the white men were left bruised and battered, they immediately went to the local sheriff and made up the rape story, and all but the youngest member of the group of black kids – a twelve-year-old – were convicted of rape and sentenced to death by an all-white jury. It wasn't until the Communist Party of the United States of America (of which Otto Huiswoud was a signed-up member) joined forces with the NAACP (National Association for the Advancement of Colored People) that the case was appealed and received international attention, exposing gross injustices in the American federal court system. After numerous scandals and retrials this ultimately meant that none of the Scottsboro' Boys would receive the death penalty, and most escaped serious jail time. They were all eventually pardoned.*

This Russian friendliness wasn't merely born out of a political agenda, though. Hughes became friends with a middle-aged African-American woman called Emma Harris, who was the life and soul of the town long before the Russian Revolution of 1917: 'Everybody in Moscow knew Emma, and Emma knew everybody. Stalin, I am sure, was aware of her presence in the capital,'[4] wrote Hughes.

Harris had journeyed to Russia at the turn of the twentieth century with a theatrical troupe, married a Russian grand duke and lived in a huge Moscow mansion before Lenin and the Bolsheviks overthrew the Tsar, and Emma's duke in the process. The mansion they had shared together was divided into a dozen apartments, but Emma was allowed to keep a large section of the house as her home and still managed to enjoy a lifestyle that was beyond most Muscovites, as Hughes recounts Harris half-heartedly bemoaning: 'Things ain't what they used to be here since these Sovietskis come in . . . why, I used to have me six servants and a boot boy. Now, best I can do is one old baba older'n me, part time.' In the middle of the capital of the Workers' Republics, Emma did not work. And although freedom of speech was felt to be lacking in the USSR, Emma said anything she wanted to say . . . She had not been home for so long herself that she had lost all personal consciousness of color . . . Russians of all color accepted her wholeheartedly.[5]

In a world where unemployment was illegal and shop shelves were sparsely stacked, Harris's Soviet Union was a leisurely land

* The last three posthumously, as late as 2013.

of plenty and, while others were rationed, her dinner table boasted roast chickens, hot apple pies, corn bread, collard greens and even on occasion barbecued spare ribs – unthinkable in 30s USSR. She had one foot in high society, as the toast of Soviet functions with her stirring speeches, delivered in perfect Russian, against the great injustices inflicted upon her fellow black countrymen in America, denouncing US segregation and lynch law while privately sharing dissenting jokes about Stalin and offering Hughes black-market hospitality with after-hours brandy in illegal blues joints, lock-ins and speakeasies.

Throughout the ups and downs of the Soviet Empire – the ruthless black-market economy, the great toll of the Second World War, where an estimated 24 *million* Russians lost their lives, Stalin's gulags, which continued right into the 50s, and the subsequent crumbling infrastructure and decimated economy – even by the 80s a certain Soviet spirit survived which encouraged and welcomed waves of African and Asian students to study in Russia and produced a number of important African leaders, engineers, pilots and scientists. My brother Richard, who is eleven years older than me, enjoyed a state school trip to Moscow in the 80s without noticing any hint of tension at all, and black British writer and editor-at-large for the *Guardian* Gary Younge spent time as a student in the USSR as late as 1991, when Communism was crumbling all around him. He spoke of the bureaucracy and propaganda of the period, but also of collective dog walks and weekly swims in a trade-union-cooperative-sanctioned pink hat with flowers on it. Clearly, as a black student in Russia, he wasn't afraid for his life.

It wasn't until the final collapse of the Soviet Union that so many African students, academics and home-grown black citizens began to experience frequent, overt racism. The biggest concern for most students coming in from the tropics had once been the minus-degree Russian winter, but now it was racist attacks and murders, the very presence of black students a charged reminder of a failed system.

In 1992 the largest university participating in the African scholarship programme, named after the Congo's first democratically elected prime minister Patrice Lumumba, changed its name – which it had had almost since its inception in 1960 – to the People's Friendship University of Moscow, and the dropping of Lumumba's name ties in not just with the end of the Cold War but with a change of Russian sentiment towards Africans and foreigners in general. Russia became insecure and inward-looking, and a secular society (religion was suppressed in the USSR) was now finding meaning in an almost militant Russian Orthodox branch of Christianity, encouraged more recently by Vladimir Putin and embodying that old idea that has become synonymous with historical amnesia, inequality, homophobia, racism, violence, bigotry and ignorance: 'Let's make our country great again.'

Even the proudest of black Russians, James Lloydovich Patterson, a poet and actor who was once the very symbol of Soviet racial harmony and had enjoyed life as a Russian intellectual and member of the Soviet Writers' Union, fled Russia shortly after the fall. Interestingly enough, Patterson is the offspring of one of Langston Hughes's travelling companions on that Moscow movie Soviet trip, Lloyd Patterson, who'd stayed on in Moscow, fallen in love with a Russian woman, got married, had two sons and built up a respectable career at a Russian radio service until dying of injuries sustained in the Nazi bombing of Moscow during the Second World War. His eldest son, James, rose to fame as a child in one of Soviet Russia's most famous movies, *The Circus* (1936), about a white circus performer forced to flee America after giving birth to a mixed-race child. The movie ends happily, with the young woman finding a home in the racially tolerant Soviet society where all races were supposedly considered equal. It was, in many ways, the perfect Communist propaganda movie which had originally been sought in the unfinished movie Hughes wrote about. James Lloydovich Patterson, still a loyal Russian at heart, decided it was best to leave his beloved home for his fatherland of America in the mid-90s. His motives may have been partly economic, but the idea of where one might be able to exist as a mixed-race family had shifted in opposite directions in a very real sense for people like Patterson and his now elderly real-life white mother.

During the 30s trip to Russia, Hughes noticed how the idea of being Soviet, part of something bigger than oneself, had in its early years created a tolerant, civil society: '"Ne sovietski" was a phrase one heard often. If somebody was pushed too brusquely into a bus or a streetcar, others would turn around and say, "Citizen, that's not sovietski."'[6] But as I would find out first hand, that couldn't be further from the truth in twenty-first-century capitalist Russia. I knew I wouldn't find the flashes of Afropea I'd seen in Stockholm, Paris, Brussels or London, but the question of how a society goes from being racially tolerant to being scarily bigoted and xenophobic was worth investigating, and in the end it was Saleh, the bouncer at my Stockholm hostel, who convinced me to book a last-minute flight to Moscow. He'd been before and had had no problems, he told me, so I booked the cheapest flight I could find with an airline I'd never heard of for the same day.

When I mentioned the airline, Rossiya, Saleh gave me a wry smile then reassured me, 'Don't worry, plane shit, pilots good, they are all old Soviet airforce employees,' and it wouldn't have surprised me if the tiny plane itself had also been reclaimed from the Soviet air force. There were still ashtrays in the backs of the seats, ancient TV sets hanging from the roof of the plane with slots for VHS tapes, none of the reading lamps worked, the carpet was badly frayed, the soap dispensers in the toilet cubicle, which also had ashtrays in it, were broken and the toilet lid was missing, all this while some in-flight classical muzak was quietly playing in the background on what sounded like a cassette tape, making everything seem absurd, like I was in some ironic 70s sitcom. If all this was going on in plain sight, what was happening under the bonnet?

The plane flew through the forecasted bad weather that had cancelled the ferry I was supposed to take, and as it rocked violently side to side my anxiety was compounded by the evacuation card I looked at, noticing the Cyrillic script of the Russian alphabet, its characters like futuristic hieroglyphs from an alien species more advanced than our own, an evocation destroyed by the crushing evidence of the creaky old plane I found myself trapped in. And I suddenly thought, I really know absolutely nothing about contemporary Russia, the language, the cuisine, the customs, the history beyond its relationship to black communities – it was all a huge ball of mystery that had been swallowed and spun by the West and regurgitated to me as propaganda.

The storm had been so bad that, when the plane landed, it was still surrounded by a thick black cloud, so everybody in the plane thought we were still in the sky when the wheels thudded against the runway, and I finally got a bit of emotion from the middle-aged man sitting next to me, who raised an eyebrow and had a mild smirk on his face.

On landing, nowhere came close to the initial culture shock of Russia, partly because I kept waiting for the dramatic clichéd images I had of it to burst, and they never really did: the staff at Arrivals looked like Russian models playing Bond villain parodies and were fascinatingly rude. The weather was awful and, while snow had beautified Stockholm, covering everything in a layer of fluffy whiteness, the ice on the streets of St Petersburg that day was slushy and brown with dirt and pollution. Low storm clouds turned imposing buildings into gloomy spectres, boxy, 70s-looking Lada cars (which I thought dated from the 70s but were still being manufactured, apparently) filled congested roads and, as I headed along the pavement of one boulevard, someone strolled past me walking a brown bear – yes, I swear: a *bear*, on a leash. St Petersburg was a metropolis on cheap under-the-counter steroids – the boulevards twice as wide, the brutalist buildings twice as brutal and dramatically oversized, built originally as a reminder that the city and state were all-powerful, that this was where everybody's money was going, and in that way a failed Communism still loomed large, haunting and hanging over the atmosphere. Had Communism been so easy to comprehend and relate to because of my democratic distance from it?

Before catching my overnight train to Moscow I found a small restaurant and eventually managed to bluff and mumble my way to a dinner of potatoes and sausages with a shot of vodka to wash it down (yes, of course, *that* was what Russian cuisine was). As I walked across a bridge afterwards a mustard-yellow Lada ambled up beside me and drove very slowly a couple of metres in front. I stopped and it stopped. I walked forward and it continued a little until stopping, again when I stopped, then the driver leaned across and opened the passenger door without saying a thing. If it was a taxi, it certainly wasn't a legal one, and I'd heard that one of the methods Neo-Nazis used to kidnap African students was masquerading as taxi-drivers.

It was probably a handful of seconds, but I stood paralysed for too long, completely bamboozled, on a quiet, snowy road with an old Soviet car a few metres in front of me with its passenger door wide open, beckoning me in, and though I didn't know what was happening, when I leaned down a bit to see the driver and saw the silhouette of a skinhead I turned around and walked briskly in the opposite direction, and the car just waited there with its engine idling, its brake lights on and the passenger door still open. Keeping an eye on the car until I was out of its sight, in the midst of my panic it struck me as a strangely beautiful scene, almost like an Edward Hopper painting, or a scene in a Wim Wenders film, and after being transfixed for a moment I realized I'd been walking without my hat on for the first time in Russia and my Afro was out. The hot meat and potatoes and vodka had warmed and relaxed me and I'd forgotten to take my woollen hat out of my jacket pocket. Concealing my hair was a way of concealing my race from a distance, as my skin in deep winter is almost as pale as Slavic skin (a comedian I once went to see live spotted me in the crowd and said, 'You're mixed race, aren't you? But having an Afro sort of makes you *more* black'). I immediately put my hat back on, giving it ten minutes before paranoiacally crossing an adjacent bridge towards the train station.

Some of the names of the overnight trains to Moscow sounded like crime novels or films about espionage – the *Red Arrow* (famous for shuttling the wounded between cities in the Second World War), the *Grand Express* (posh and privatized by Putin), the *Northern Palmira*, the *Megapolis*, the *Lev Tolstoy* and the *Nevsky Express* – and the prices ranged from nearly 1,000 euros for 'grand class' on a Firmeny (or brand-name) train to twenty euros for third class on the less cinematic-sounding 267A. I opted for one of the cheaper seats on one of the slightly more expensive trains, which promised a restaurant car, clean carpets, well-trained staff, better toilets and, boasted the train's official leaflet, 'on-board Russian militia'. This stunning blue-and-white *Northern Palmira* train (Palmira being an old name for St Petersburg, and no connection to the Palmyra in Syria under siege by the Russian army) was a huge, satisfying iron horse of a locomotive, idling on the platform, steam rising into the minus-degree deep-winter night. I made my way through drunks and loiterers under the dim tungsten-lit platform and, with my woollen hat low and a scarf covering my face, avoided the attention of a group of tattooed skinheads who, it turned out, would be my travel companions, and convinced myself that, as I hurtled through the Russian wilderness the guards carrying AK47s would ensure my safety.

I boarded and passed through the buffet car to look at what was on offer on an English/Gibberish language menu, and it contained the following: beef tongue, fish dainties with trimmings, vegetable all-sorts, Russian canned mushrooms, smoked meat scrab and cold-cut compound trimmings. In my couchette, which sort of resembled how you'd imagine a Soviet living room might look in the 70s – chintzy patterns, gaudy colours, huge curtains, wallpapered and carpeted – food packs were laid on a table with bread rolls and vacuum-packed salami and salmon, with metal cutlery and a large samovar used to boil hot spiced tea. It wasn't the most long-distance-train-friendly food but I was happy I wouldn't have to find out what 'scrab' or 'compound trimmings' entailed, and glad of the company of a travelling companion, Sayana, a young Buryat woman who'd grown up in Siberia, just across the border from Mongolia. She was studying and working in Moscow and spoke near-perfect English. As well as being a throwback to the golden age of train travel, the entire scene enlightened me a little about Russia – the spices, the samovar, which was bulbous and ornate in that Asian way, and Sayana's story and roots were all deeply connected to Russia's history but spoke of a huge Asian influence often missed off the Cold War propaganda we received in Britain. As we ate together, rattling through the frozen Russian night and drinking hot tea, Sayana and I spoke of shamanism and swastikas, a conversation which began when she saw me looking at a book next to her bunk with the symbol all over it, smiled coyly and said, 'Don't worry, I'm not a Nazi.'

Despite being an ancient spiritual symbol used by many peoples throughout millennia, Hitler chose the swastika as an emblem of the National Socialists because of its connection to Indo-Aryan culture, a culture prone to pseudo-scientific misinterpretations by some Western anthropologists and encouraged by a misreading of German philosopher Friedrich Nietzsche's *Übermensch* concept – that we are our own gods, or capable of being superhumans. In the late nineteenth century Aryan culture was promoted, for political and military purposes, as an all-powerful, superior white master race with origins in a geographic area in India. Both Hitler and the Third Reich's minister of propaganda Joseph Goebbels accused various rivals of *die große Lüge* – telling an audaciously big lie often enough until the masses believe it, despite contradictory evidence – but it was they who ultimately came to extol the concept in Nazi Germany, through the notion of the Aryan master race. The swastika is still used widely in Hinduism and Buddhism and across Asia, with mostly peaceful connotations, and for Sayana was connected to Mongolian shamanism. 'For us, the swastika symbolizes eternity and, as a culture, we have used it for centuries.'

Like so many Muscovites I would meet (Sayana had been living in Moscow for five years and was studying information technology while working part time in a hostel), Sayana was amiable on a one-to-one level but riddled with political worries, distrustful of Putin and an apologist for Slavic racism, especially when it came to the Caucasus. When I asked her about the Nazis she said, 'There is a saying, "Moscow is not made of rubber," meaning it can't expand and keep holding new people. We have a lot of illegal foreign workers who come to work in Russia and I think these Nazis target them because they take a lot of jobs from the Slavic people. It's the government's fault, they exploit the workers from Tajikistan or Uzbekistan because they're Muslim and don't drink and work very hard for so cheap, and the work they do is required. You can find one of these guys and he will do ten times more work than a Russian who you have to pay double or triple the amount of wages. They live maybe eight or ten in a room and live on 3,000 rubles per month [£40] and they send money back to support their families, so there are a lot of them in Moscow. But the thing is that they can sometimes become really arrogant, sometimes they fight with Slavic people and can be aggressive, sometimes they walk around with knives.'

I felt like saying, *If I had to sleep in a room with ten men for months on end and work for a pittance against a backdrop of violent racism so that my family could survive in a ravaged country in the middle of nowhere that had been abandoned by the Soviet Union, I think I'd be exactly the same.* But I didn't have the same cultural purchase as Sayana to voice my disagreement. Sayana was Russian, but only *just*, and despite having faced Russian racism herself and being raised in the Republic of Buryatia, near Lake Baikal, an area at a precarious distance from the Kremlin both culturally and geographically, she clung to her Russian nationality for all it was worth. If she didn't, she might be set adrift as a cultural nomad in a very different way to her ancestors.

'You know, we Buryats are from nomadic people, but if we find ourselves in the same group somewhere, say a classroom or something, it's not like "Ah, my brother." I think people get afraid because nobody has much, and they worry that a fellow Buryat might try to make a claim to your property, or want to eat your food. Not all Buryats are based in Russia, some are in Siberia or other towns that used to be part of USSR. It was like European Union back then, but it changed, and some of the Buryats now outside the Russian territory aren't doing so well.'

I couldn't work out how old Sayana was, and when she spoke of the Soviet Union I didn't know if she was speaking from her own memories or those of her grandmother, who was clearly a hero.

'Now, in Russia, everybody thinks only of themselves. My grandma feels sorry for me, she says we are living in a very terrible time in Russian history. It's scary because unless they have money, the youth can't look forward, and even if you work hard you might not be able to build a future because there are several people who have all the connections. That is why there is so much alcoholism here, because people don't feel that they have a future.'

Sayana told me of recent cases of Russians, both men and women, killing their families and then committing suicide because they either went insane through alcoholism, owed money to gangsters or simply felt that they literally couldn't afford to live, and Sayana thought that, though things had been tough under Communism, they had been better.

'Gorbachev ruined everything, and Putin made it worse. People used to feel that the state was working for them, you know? And I think now Russians forget this and only remember the tough times under the Soviet Union, how there was nothing in the shops and products were sold under the table, the long queues and the criminals who were everywhere. But Putin privatized all the national resources, stealing them from the people and giving them to his friends. Even though we have gas, we have the oil, our prices for both are getting higher all the time, and I don't think it has to be like this.'

Sayana wasn't the first person, and wouldn't be the last, to suggest that Putin's Russia was a kleptocracy, and it's true that his close circle of friends, many from his days as a member of the KGB, have been turned into billionaires by little other virtue than their proximity to the president. But with corruption, isolation, poverty, mafia gangs and so many other issues to navigate, what was the alternative? Sayana answered me bluntly:

'There is no alternative. The thing is they create a circle of power so they have no opposition. They put in people to pretend they are opposition, but anyone who is real gets killed or imprisoned.' Sayana reeled off name after name, some of them powerful oligarchs or politicians with a new vision for Russia – Mikhail Prokhorov, Mikhail Khodorkovsky, Sergei Udaltsov – and they had all been exiled or thrown into jail at key moments during their challenge to Putin. Scarier still, when Alexei Navalny, a lawyer and politician who perhaps represents the biggest challenge to Putin, asked people to donate money to his cause through a kind of Russian version of PayPal, Putin's government allegedly tried to get the names of the people who donated.* Putin isn't just hacking elections abroad, it seems, he's hacking his own people. Sayana believed that elections were rigged and approval ratings were fixed, and the government found a way to control people through chaos: better to have anti-West sentiment, religious zealotry, xenophobia, misinformation and racist attacks than a focused challenge to 'United' Russia.

If the state could no longer be relied upon, the people of Russia

---

* Navalny was recently the victim of an acid attack which caused him to lose much of the sight in his right eye, an attack he blames on the Kremlin.

and the former colonies had to rely upon themselves; there was a free-for-all at every level of society, billions made, poverty, imprisonment, police corruption, illegal immigration into Russia from some of the poorer former states set adrift after the fall, and a rise of nationalism, as there always is when there are huge insecurities around national identity, severe economic pressures and a realization that the people in power don't have your best interests at heart. In that way, Russia struck me as a kind of oracle, its existential crisis ahead of its time, and everything that has been happening there in the last couple of decades was now starting to happen to America and Europe. Before neoliberalism and globalization took hold and widened the gulf between the haves and the have-nots, and began to challenge local identities and encouraged reactionary politics from those feeling slighted by an international outlook and an overarching project (Europe, the UN), Russia knew all about such insecurities. Sayana mentioned how, in the wake of this new dog-eat-dog Russia, the Buryat community she belonged to lacked solidarity – it was every man or woman for themselves – and I saw it as a cautionary tale. If, as the trend suggests, white Europe does splinter apart into insular nationalisms, black Europe must be more unified than ever if it is to save its communities from implosion.

Strangers in Moscow

Before sleepily disembarking the *Northern Palmira* in morning darkness at Moscow's neo-Baroque Komsomolskaya station, Sayana gave me her contact details and the usual tips about staying safe in Russia, and then said, 'It's so stupid I have to do this, you actually look like one of Russia's biggest national heroes.' She didn't mean literally, but was hinting about the heritage of the godfather of modern Russian literature, Alexander Pushkin.

Later that day, under the falling snow, I saw the statue of Pushkin on Pushkinskaya Square, which was built with public funds and unveiled by Ivan Turgenev and Fyodor Dostoyevsky in 1880, and remembered part of the poem Claude McKay wrote about it:

> In Moscow, in the old Strasnaia Square,*
> I wondered at a frizzly mat of hair,
> Gazing upon the image of the man
> In whom a nation's flowering began.
> The very greatest Russian of his race,
> I saw the Negro plainly in his face.[1]

Pushkin was proud of his African heritage, and the noble lineage was indeed something to speak about, inspiring an unfinished semi-biographical novel called *Saint Peter the Great's Negro*, which, when it was published posthumously in 1837, the year of Pushkin's death, might well have been the most complex and nuanced portrait of a black man in literary fiction since Shakespeare's Othello. It is an elevated, slightly aggrandized version of

---

* Strasnaya Square was the previous name of Pushkinskaya Square.

the very real story of Pushkin's great-grandfather Abram Gannibal, who some say was born in the ancient Ethiopian empire, Abyssinia, but the respected work by Dieudonné Gnammankou (a Benin-born Patrice Lumumba University-educated historian) convincingly argues he was the son of a prince from the border town of Logone-Birni, between what is now Chad and Cameroon. What all sources agree is that Abram was kidnapped from his African home when he was around the age of seven and taken to the heart of the Otto-man Empire, Constantinople, modern-day Istanbul, to work as a servant for a sultan. Incredibly, Abram (or Ibrahim, as he'd just been renamed by the sultan) was later acquired by Count Peter Tolstoy, a Russian ambassador at the time and the great-grandfather of that other giant of Russian literature, Leo, and gifted to the Russian Tsar Peter the Great. Because of his high intelligence, Abram found favour with Peter, and what seems to have begun as royal folly on the Tsar's part became close mentorship bordering on sur-rogate fatherhood to the young Abram. Officially, the Tsar took the role of godfather and enrolled Abram in the finest schools in Russia, where the young student excelled in mathematics and geometry before being sent to the very decadent Paris of 1716, right in the early years of the Enlightenment, to study military science, and later enrolling in King Louis XV's prestigious artillery academy. He rose to the rank of captain, fighting for the French under a name he ascribed to himself, Hannibal, after the legendary North African general Hannibal Barca (in Russian this became Gannibal), one of many gestures suggesting that, while Abram pledged loyalty to Russia, he never forgot Africa.

When Peter the Great died of illness three years after Abram's return to Russia, Abram fell out of favour with the xenophobic new monarch Prince Menshikov, who distrusted the young black man's foreignerhood and was insecure about Abram's reputation for military excellence. Abram was exiled in Siberia for three years but was later pardoned and essentially spent the rest of his long life (he died at the then ripe old age of eighty-five) at the top of Russian society as a general, governor and landowner, known by his peers as 'the black Lord'. He was awarded the rank of Russian nobility and given his own coat of arms, which he designed himself, depicting an African elephant and the inscription FVMMO; there has been speculation that it means anything from 'homeland' in the Kotoko tongue of his African ancestors, to the Latin motto *Fortuna vitam meam mutavit oppido*: 'Fortune has changed my life greatly.' He left behind an Afropean dynasty of sorts, with his second wife, Christina Regina Siöberg, a young woman of the Scandinavian nobility who he married in 1736 and who bore him ten children, among them Ivan Gannibal, a famous figure in the Russian military, who rose to the rank of general-in-chief and founded the city of Kherson in what is now modern-day Ukraine. Another of Abram's sons, Osip, had a daughter who became known as *Prekrasnaia Mulatka* in Russia, or *la belle Créole* in France; her real name was Nadezhda Osipovna Pushkina, and she was Alexander Pushkin's mother. Through this lineage, members of aristocracy across contemporary Europe, including many British aristocrats, such as the Mountbattens (George Mountbatten being a cousin of Queen Elizabeth II), Natalia Grosvenor, the Duchess of Westminster, and Alexandra Hamilton, the Duchess of Abercorn, can all trace their heritage back to Abram Gannibal, a black man from Central Africa who became an important figure in Russian history.

Pushkin's own story, though one of tragedy, is consoling for a self-pitying writer like me. Despite being born into nobility (though without much money – his grandfather had squandered much of Abram's wealth), he produced his writing with a background buzz that makes my own financial worries, heartbreak and cultural disjuncture pale by comparison. He was debilitated by disease and produced a number of famous works, including *Eugene Onegin*, while convalescing after a bout of cholera. He started an important literary journal while pushy in-laws forced him to put up two of his wife's unmarried sisters shortly after his wedding and, after helping to pay off his own hopeless brother's debts, fell into serious financial struggles himself. During this time his flirtatious wife Natalia, known as 'the most beautiful woman in all of Russia' (beauty and fidelity once again seemingly the only measures of success for a woman during that time), was constantly the source of scandalous rumours of infidelity, and Pushkin found himself invited to VIP parties merely because everybody, including the Tsar himself, had his sights on the young bride. In the end a handsome suitor from France was so open about his infatuation with Natalia that Pushkin was forced to challenge him to a duel, and was mortally wounded, dying two days later at the age of only thirty-seven.

Because of the subversive politics in his poetry, during his lifetime Pushkin fell out of favour with a number of dignitaries, including the Tsar, and was exiled, just like his great-grandfather, for a period, in the Caucasus. In him I saw a sort of kindred spirit of the liminal terrain, rooted in Russia but at a poetic distance from it, too; an Afropean wanderer with a story other Afropeans could tap into. It is empowering to 'see' yourself written into European history in such a way, because being taught in a European school, few of the stories are about people you can identify with, even the few that are about black people. We have no Martin Luther Kings or Malcolm Xs. We have Frantz Fanons and Stuart Halls but, unlike the way the American Dream integrated the civil-rights movement into its own mythology, our heroes aren't overtly embedded in the narrative of European history and identity. Maybe that's a good thing, meaning the stories aren't commodified and stripped of their power, but it does mean they often reach us too late or not at all, absent from our formative years and our deeply entrenched ideas about 'authentic' national identity.

It's not just that Pushkin wasn't a slave or a colonial subject, it's also the fact that it was impossible to reduce him to a two-dimensional figure of fear or victimization, and the toil of his complicated mind had been embedded and preserved in mainstream Russian society, so much so that he transcended his own mixed heritage, though that in itself can also pose a problem. The racist football hooligan will throw a banana at a black football player on the opposing team, and if you bring up the fact that their own star striker is black, they'll say, if not in so many words, 'No he isn't, he's *Paul Pogba*.' It was the same when, during one of his documentaries, Louis Theroux pointed out to a deeply racist South African Boer woman that her favourite singer, Lionel Richie, was black and, with the realization, the woman nearly had a meltdown on camera. This reiterated to me again what the Afropean term might embody: a complicated, integrated form of blackness in Europe that refused to be bogged down by stereotypes while also refusing to deny its brownness and plurality; the Afropean as a teller of transgressive stories, hybrid histories and complicated cultural allegiances like those so embedded in the personal histories of Pushkin and Abram Gannibal.

Having said that, nowhere else on my trip challenged my ideas of a shared Afropean consciousness more than the outskirts of

Moscow, where I visited the university once named after Patrice
Lumumba and wondered what kind of comfort or inspiration the
many anxious-looking African students I saw there might draw
from either the term 'Afropean' or from Alexander Pushkin.

Shortly before the collapse of the Soviet Union in 1991 some
50,000 students from across Africa studied in USSR universities
as part of a thirty-year tradition, with much older seeds of cross-
continent international solidarity having been planted by Lenin,
as Russia and the US began their battle to steer the twentieth
century in their own image. By 1992, when it became clear who'd
won the fight, the amount of African students in Russia was barely
a fifth of that number, indicative both of economic realities in
post-Soviet Russia and a dramatic shift of national intention. The
scholarships offered to African students had always been largely
at the whim of foreign-policy agenda rather than Soviet altruism
or philanthropy and were set up initially to promote friendship in
the fertile soil of an Africa in the throes of upending its long-time
colonial rulers from the West. Friendship or, if you're a little more
cynical, *soft power*. The USSR was certainly intent on replacing
Western colonialism with, at the very least, 'Third World' governments with closer ties to communism than to capitalism. They set
about doing this by arming the African independence movements
fighting for liberation from Western oppression with Russian
weapons, but it was no good giving people weapons if they weren't
at least partially sympathetic to your cause, and where better to
ensure that than in a Russian university. It wasn't that students
were indoctrinated into a regime – the subjects were less social
sciences and more applied sciences: engineering, medicine, agriculture, and so on, skills desperately needed by newly independent
African societies with a huge unskilled workforce emerging out of
the shadows of colonial inequity. It was more that through being
well treated (students were given huge grants for clothes and trips
to France and East Germany and free education at an elite level,

while strict Soviet legislation ensured Russian nationals were, for the most part, on their best behaviour in the company of these foreigners), and becoming fluent in Russian (free intensive courses ensured most students reached degree-level fluency within a year), a global bond could be built in the scramble for a new world order.

In the midst of this scramble, some say that Russia forgot about its own citizens, who had held on to the idea of Communism as if there would one day be some payback for their patience and hospitality, and when it became increasingly unlikely – and impossible after the fall of Communism – that there would be any long-term reward, years of frustration seem to have been unleashed on those same black people who were once celebrated by Russia. In the same way Britain in the 70s dealt with the loss of empire, black people were now reviled as reminders of the failure of the grand cause; told to go home, sometimes spat at, at worst attacked, with goodwill towards 'negro comrades' having run dry.

Communism wasn't as bonkers as Westerners, particularly Americans, like to suggest, though, and it certainly wasn't helped by a number of devastating covert operations by the CIA and former colonial powers to undermine this 'friendship' and create a neo-colonial Africa, which history shows that they largely succeeded in achieving. The key was to supplant European colonial leaders with African leaders who would effectively continue the course of European colonialism in all but name, and at times that's essentially what happened: white leaders went home, African leaders came in and then employed all the same white Europeans behind the scenes; independence for show, of benefit for only a few self-interested black African leaders willing to play the game.

The obsession with the 'Illuminati' among some black (and white) people, such as Mohammed, who I met in Berlin, which suggests, at its most severe, that there exists an elite group of devil-worshipping white men who have secretly controlled Western civilization for millennia with the sole purpose of oppressing black people, is born of stuff like this. When the Illuminati theory gets really wacky, it says that members of the black community who provide contradictory evidence of the Illuminati's existence – Oprah Winfrey, Barack Obama, Jay Z – are merely those who, with ancient daggers and blood oaths, have signed a secret and elaborate pact selling their souls to the dark side in order to . . . well, I'm not exactly sure what, to be honest with you, but it involves making a diamond sign with your hands in music videos and making money. Most of the YouTube conspiracy theories seem to be based on Dan Brown novels and 2Pac lyrics, but in reality are, I think, used subconsciously as a glamorous alternative to a depressing reality: that there *are* self-interested black leaders and celebrities serving merely as token avatars for a system prejudiced against black communities;* that many black people *are* struggling economically, often because there *is* institutional racism and a legacy of systematic oppression by white men. Looking into the FBI's role in tearing down the Black Panthers through COIN-TELPRO, the CIA in Africa during the postwar African fight for independence and, more recently, contemporary Russia's own hand in hacking at the highest level, you can see why a black fear of some unseen and malevolent white force isn't necessarily as unreasonable as it might first appear. It is incredibly hard not to get caught up in a grand conspiracy theory aimed at the continued subjugation of the African continent when you unpick how it has been both overtly and covertly undermined and over-mined.

The thinkers, revolutionaries and leaders most probably assassinated by Western secret services during the second half of the twentieth century, particularly in the twenty or so years after the Second World War, when there was a golden opportunity to create a new Africa, show that the probable ramifications for black people were immense. To name a few: Martin Luther King, Malcolm X, Fred Hampton and John and Robert Kennedy in America, Maurice Audin of Algeria, Che Guevara of Cuba, Félix-Roland

---

* Black Lives Matter and Ferguson happened during Obama's time in office, and while the rich grew richer, average black wealth decreased.

Moumié of Cameroon, Mehdi Ben Barka of Morocco, Eduardo
Mondlane of Mozambique, Amílcar Cabral of Guinea Bissau,
Olof Palme of Sweden, Kwame Nkrumah of Ghana, Walter Rodney of Guyana . . . the list of unnatural deaths of people in whose
hands Africa's future may well have been better off is vast.

Perhaps one of the biggest losses was that of Patrice Lumumba,
a young, intelligent and dedicated Pan-Africanist whose father was
a farmer and who wrote poetry and studied philosophy in his spare
time. In a touching letter to his wife, Pauline, sent from Thysville
Prison, after being overthrown in a Western-backed military coup
only four months into his premiership, Lumumba wrote:

> Whether dead or alive, free or in prison by order of the colonial-
> ists, it is not my person that is important. What is important is
> the Congo, our poor people whose independence has been
> turned into a cage . . . History will one day have its say; it will
> not be the history taught in the United Nations, Washington,
> Paris, or Brussels, however, but the history taught in the coun-
> tries that have rid themselves of colonialism and its puppets.
> Africa will write its own history and both north and south of
> the Sahara it will be a history full of glory and dignity.[2]

As the first democratically elected prime minister of the Congo,
Lumumba proposed a series of progressive reforms and deposed
former Belgian colonials from positions of behind-the-scenes
power, while attempting, in vain, to create a politically neutral
African country in charge of its own resources and to hold the
mighty powers of both the West and the East at bay. When he
approached America and the UN for help to stabilize the country
during the inevitable uprisings in the wake of the election, he was
denied and had to gain assistance from the Soviet Union, which
ultimately made him a marked man because neither Belgium nor
America could let the mineral-rich land of the Congo fall under any
kind of Soviet influence. America was the first international power
to officially recognize King Leopold's brutal Congo Free State in

the 1880s, and later mined all the uranium from Congo soil to power the atomic bomb that annihilated Hiroshima and Nagasaki. In an attempt to appease a new non-colonial military, Lumumba appointed only black African military leaders, but one of his promotions included that of a former soldier named Joseph Mobutu to the rank of colonel and chief of staff of the army. Rumours were rife even then that Mobutu was working with US and Belgian intelligence services, and in the end it was Mobutu who, backed by the Belgians and sponsored by the CIA, led a military coup that ended in Lumumba's assassination. Mobutu's dictatorship would last over three devastating decades, during which he left what was then Zaire corrupt, kleptocratic, in dire poverty and in huge debt, while turning himself into one of the richest men on Earth. Later in my trip, en route to Marseille, I would visit one of many huge palaces, villas and mansions he bought himself across the world, in a billionaires' playground on the Riviera, while his country crumbled.

Lumumba's death and Mobutu's reign were templates of the African tragedy. When I went to get a visa from the Sierra Leone high commission in London recently, I perused sparsely stocked shelves which held some leaflets about various sectors of industry. The one on the fisheries sector said, 'There is a lack of infrastructure to support this growing sector, specifically access to cold storage facilities, landing sites, drying facilities and service centres for trawlers,' while another leaflet promoted the Sierra Leone mining sector and gave evidence of the country's rich land: gold, diamonds and titanium are in abundance, but the names of the companies it said were in charge of mining the land told a familiar and depressing story: London Mining controlled Iron Ore exports; Vimetco, a company largely run by Russian oligarchs, acquired the biggest bauxite mining contract (bauxite is the mineral most aluminium is extracted from); Cliff Gold, another London-based company, had one of the country's biggest gold mines; and Octet, yet another company with its headquarters in the UK, holds the exploration licence for the diamond-rich Tongo field. Soviet internationalism must have seemed a bold alternative to Western capitalism for many Africans during the fight for independence, and in the twenty-first century, all one can really ask when it comes to this friendship between Africa and the Soviet Union is *what if?*

Needless to say, things are a little different for black students in Russia today. Moscow had been freshly covered in a thick layer of snow overnight and yet still refused to look in any way quaint. Even the bulbous St Basil's Cathedral, one of the most impressive buildings I'd ever seen, had a sinister edge, as though it could have been the palace of an evil clown – it was, after all, commissioned in the sixteenth century by Ivan the Terrible to honour the conquering of the Caucasus peoples that were now so maligned in Russia. Wandering round central Moscow, on my way to catch the Metro to the People's Friendship University, the one formerly named after Lumumba, I saw a Nigerian man dressed as a Russian tsar who beckoned me into a souvenir shop and tried to sell me a matryoshka doll with a painting of Barack Obama on it. He was one of a few African men I'd seen dressed up in such a way in Moscow, and also across Europe; I saw an Algerian Spartan in Rome, a Senegalese picador in Barcelona, and a Kenyan barmaid in full Bavarian get-up in Berlin. They were first-generation immigrants surviving, essentially, by playing the role of court jester to European society, juxtaposing old European national identities with their non-European faces. This was a parody of the Afropean, a surface-level interplay more widely accepted and even enjoyed by Europe because it ironically contradicted the idea that an African could ever really be European. Some other cultures had it worse than Africans, and were so under attack that even an ironic gesture about national identity wouldn't go down well; I often saw Bulgarian, Romanian or Arabic men and women hide their heritage by painting their faces silver or gold and pretending to be statues on London's South Bank or along parts of the Seine in Paris, a way of making money by literally being silent and invisible.

The Nigerian tsar's name was James and he promised me a 'nice price' for the Obama doll. James was buoyant and full of banter, a charmer/bullshitter type who later told me that it was those very qualities that had helped him survive in Russia. When he asked me what I was doing in Moscow, I told him I was thinking of studying there, and asked what he thought of my plan: how was it for black students? He took me to the side and dropped his song-and-dance act, looking at me seriously and saying, 'Brother is fucked here. In last three weeks they kill two blacks from Ghana . . . this is no place for a black man,' then, seeing his boss, a young white woman with blonde hair standing behind a counter looking over at us absent-mindedly, his expression turned from one of desperate anxiety to desperate jolliness again. 'Come have a look, we make a good price for you,' he continued, but I wanted to know more about being a student in Moscow: if it was so bad, why not study somewhere else? James told me that he was studying to be a forester at the Moscow State Forest University and, though it seemed a random subject at the time, I later learned that logging is a huge boom industry, especially on Russia's black market, worth billions each year, especially with the Chinese as neighbours, who are both the world's biggest importers of logs and the world's largest exporters of wooden products. Sayana had mentioned this on the overnight train to Moscow; China was taking Russia's raw materials, empowering its own manufacturing industries then selling the finished product back to Russia and the rest of the world. James wasn't necessarily in it for these reasons; it was just that with Russia having more forest than anywhere else in the world it had an excellent university and, anyway, it was too expensive to study anywhere else. He hoped that after surviving a few years in Russia and coming out with some decent skills and qualifications he might be able to find employment in Britain, France or Scandinavia.

'This is not a good place for me,' he said, again conscious of his onlooking boss. 'Trust me, brother, they don't like foreigners, and if they hear a black man speaking English they won't like it. I am here, working like this, because I know the language, I know what to say to get away from trouble. Please be careful walking around at night.' Trying to prompt him, I said that I'd seen a lot of police patrolling Moscow, that surely it was safe? 'Ha! Fuck that shit! Never carry your passport with you, just a photocopy, because they will bribe you. And if they see a black man getting killed by a gang they are going to go like this . . .' James turned his back to me, mimicking what he believed to be the police's response, and then said that the Nazis were bad, but he thought the people in the Caucasus were also troublemakers making it more difficult for Africans. 'You know, apart from these Nazis, I think Russians are good people in their heart. It's the former USSR people that make problems for everyone.' I couldn't help feel that James was buying into Russian-media demonization, but it was also likely that as an African student he was simply keen to distance himself from a deeply unpopular demographic, because the Nazis had a way of shoehorning Mongolians who were Russian nationals, Africans and Indians attending university and exploited Tajikistanis working illegally into an amorphous group causing the same 'problems'. I asked James where I might find a place that was safe for black people in Moscow, and he told me that he sometimes went to the Moscow State Chaplaincy at St Andrew's Anglican Church to meet up with other African students. When I researched the place online it seemed shrouded in vague details. I eventually found a website, but the contact number didn't work and the email address bounced back, saying, 'Email unknown.' I did find a short documentary online filmed in the chaplaincy, with an interview with a Ghanaian man who, when asked why he didn't return to Africa despite having finished his studies, tearfully replied, 'I can't go back with an empty hand,' and that was perhaps the one thing all of the non-Slavic people in Russia did have in common: pressure from all angles to achieve, with an extended family or even an entire village ravaged and resting their hopes on the one person who'd managed to get a golden ticket to study or work abroad.

This devastating situation always reminded me of the 2003 Armenian film *Vodka Lemon*, one of the most poignant and illuminating fictional accounts depicting the impoverished economic reality for so many former USSR fringe towns after the fall of Communism, which is both humorous and tragic in its authenticity. In it, Hamo, an old widower with three sons, is waiting with bated breath for a letter with some news and money from the one son he's managed to send abroad to work in Germany. After months a letter finally does arrive, but contains no money; on the contrary, it is a letter of desperation asking for money to be sent.

As Polly Savage recounts in an excellent essay, 'African Students in the USSR', this pressure to succeed was amplified for African students in Russia during Communism, who found themselves at the centre of various political forces and grand plans much bigger than themselves, their families or even their towns. Diplomatic relationships between nations were at stake and an African future free from colonial rule was riding on their success, and these forces at times contradicted each other. Fidel Castro was in the end unimpressed with the schooling his Cuban Communists received in Moscow, and stopped sending them over, claiming they returned disillusioned. The Soviet Union's friendship with Africa was based upon Communism eventually taking hold there, and when at one point it looked as if this might not happen, as countries such as Ghana and Egypt, who were also recipients of Western aid, joined the non-aligned movement emanating out of Yugoslavia, Brezhnev dramatically reduced the funding for African scholarships in the late 60s and early 70s. It was only when Angola and Mozambique began to collaborate with Cuba and the USSR to reduce Portugal's hold over Lusophone Africa, and Haile Selassie's long hold over Ethiopia fell to a Marxist government, that the USSR upped its funding for African students again. And what about the students returning to African countries fluent in Russian and friendly towards Communist ideology, only to find themselves viewed with suspicion by a government that had now

made stronger ties with Britain or America after those covert assassinations of the country's Communist-leaning leaders?

My search for Afropea once again led me to the hinterlands, an hour's ride south of the centre of the city, where I emerged from the Metro and on to the humongous rectilinear Miklukho-Maklaya, a street flanked by imposing high-rise student accommodation and stretching off for miles into the pale, foggy distance. Until then, after ten or so days in the country, I could count the number of black people I'd seen in Russia on two hands, but there among the snowy out-lands were small groups of African men and women who had been turned into tiny silhouettes, their dark skin contrasted against the oversized off-white urban expanse. On my European trip I'd never seen so many black people together looking so miserable; in Clichy-sous-Bois there was anger, in Rinkeby there was banter, but here the overriding feeling was a sort of resigned sadness, and I wondered if this was a response to the sternness of the culture that surrounded them (I, too, had stopped smiling in public) or if they were as deeply unhappy as they looked in this unforgiving Russian limbo-land.

Hunched over, leaning into the cold breeze flowing through the open street, I wondered how the students hung on over deep winter, but of course I knew the answer; this was better than war, famine and poverty under any sun, beside any palm tree, by any river or ocean. The vision of the Motherland I carry in my mind is one of tropical beauty and warmth of people and climate because it is the Africa I've experienced on previous trips, but my African blood is full of yellow fever, rabies and hepatitis antibodies, is insured and ensured by a British education and consulate, as well as a return ticket to London. I felt sure that these students weren't European passport holders or the sons and daughters of powerful diplomats you find in British and French private schools, because those people go to British and French private schools. Most probably it was the desperate circumstances and pressures of home that were getting them through the harsh frozen winter here in Moscow.

I felt this disjuncture between feeling *Afropean* and then those who were more intelligibly *African in Europe* powerfully as I slid on the campus forecourt, which had practically turned into an ice rink, and tried in vain to make conversation with numerous African students. The imposing Soviet modernist university building was closed, so I wandered around the student accommodation on the other side of the street, where a huge, optimistic billboard promoting the university covering an entire side of the high-rise depicted a proud-looking African man next to an Asian woman, both in the traditional dress of their homeland, with the words 'The People's Friendship University of Moscow Welcomes You', but this scene was in stark contrast to the reality of student life beneath it. The men and women I saw were dressed in thick jackets and woolly hats, too cold to look prideful and conscious of keeping out of the way of the Slavic drunks and junkies proliferating in the area, whose alcoholism and drug use often came with missing limbs, thanks to heroin from Afghanistan and a flesh-eating home-made drug called Krokodil. Despair-induced addiction was killing way more Slavic people than Nazis were killing Africans; more than 30 per cent of all deaths in Russia are attributed to alcoholism.

I saw a Muslim man lay out a small rug on the snow in an empty field beside the uni and begin to quietly pray on his hands and knees. A receptionist at my hostel had spoken of mosques popping up everywhere and attacking Russian culture. Not only is this not true – the number of mosques in Russia, and particularly Moscow, is disproportionately low for the number of Muslims there, with only four official mosques serving more than a million Muslims currently resident in the Russian capital – but my experience of Islam throughout Europe was generally that it was a humble, meditative religion mostly experienced silently and out of sight, behind doors or in makeshift corners. There was no extremism or threat here, in a depiction we don't often see, just a lone man kneeling in the ice in silent communion with his god, and in this unforgiving landscape, faith in a god that frowns upon intoxication is better than drinking yourself to death. I found something even more productive that had helped brown-skinned people get by in Moscow: desperation to get out. A small internet café-cum-convenience store was the only thing open, and I watched students that appeared to be from both East and West Africa come and go, and I tried to make conversation a few times, but most of the people I spoke to weren't interested, and when I tried to speak politically, as if to say, *I'm black, you're black, and I want to hear your story*, I realized that blackness wasn't such a huge conundrum to them. They had been in Russia studying for maybe a couple of years, and in the country they had come from were politicians, policemen and teachers who all looked just like they did, which meant that on a day-to-day basis being 'black' was largely as banal as being white in Europe. They weren't black students, they were just students, on tour and studying in a bit of a horrible place to get qualifications they needed to pursue their chosen career paths, and though it's true that *I* saw these students as black, it made me feel less sure of my own blackness than ever before, and less sure about the usefulness of any label when searching to understand my own identity or that of a community.

After ordering a hot chocolate at the internet café and watching everyone huddled in tiny plasterboard capsules surfing the net on filthy old PCs, I eventually made conversation with Fraser from Benin and Michael from Ghana, and they both agreed that Moscow was not a place they wanted to stay. 'We must come and get our grades and move on to get a good job and support our families,' said Fraser, and Michael added, 'It's cheap here, that's why everybody comes, it's a good standard and we can afford it.' When I asked about racism, like everybody else I tried to chat with on the campus and near the accommodation, they both said they hadn't noticed any problems, and the main reason was because they kept their heads down. Fraser said, 'Not too much trouble. We just stay here and study, work hard, sleep and work more. There are no parties here, no distractions, there is nowhere to go and it is usually too cold anyway. I never see the evening here, I am always in my room before it gets dark,' and then Michael said that they had to go and study, and both men disappeared into a huge concrete slab of a building. I wandered around in the snow some more and, though there were plenty of students around, there was no buzz; this wasn't freshers' week at Leeds Uni, or spring break at Berkeley. There was no milling, and everyone strode purposefully to their destination. When I approached they were cagey and elusive, looking as if they were serving a sentence and stoically sitting it out until being released into the world with qualifications and, you would hope, career opportunities.

Part of the divide, I felt, was because the students I saw weren't tuned into that Afropean frequency that resonates somewhere between Africa and Europe like I and many of my friends were; they were from Ethiopia, Angola, Ghana or Nigeria, and that was that, but if they hung around, the children of these first-generation immigrants *would* need to understand their cultural identity in different, possibly more complicated terms. When I emailed Caryl Phillips for some tips before visiting Russia, he had replied, 'It's a different place from when I was there in the 80s, but it will still be cold as hell.' Caryl had visited the university when it was still named after Patrice Lumumba, but what he describes seeing in Soviet Russia then could have perfectly described what I was seeing now: 'Out in the street an African woman pushed hard at a pram in which a small baby was wrapped up like an Eskimo. Snow fell – it already lay a foot high on the ground . . . how would the child's mother retell the tale of their Soviet sojourn, and her struggle with six-month-long Soviet winters, once back in her native Angola or Mozambique? After all, the child would have to live for ever with the distinction of having to write Moscow, USSR, under place of birth.'[3]

There is a possibility, of course, that the mother wouldn't retell the tale – a certain generation blocked out painful memories in the struggle to survive – but I wanted to ask different questions about the child Caryl mentions, which were perhaps those of a different generation, where being black or African and writing a country such as Russia as a place of birth isn't quite as strange as it was in the early 80s. I wondered where that child was now; he or she would be about my age. And what if the mother had stayed on in Russia and attempted to take part in Russian society? How would the child retell *their* stories growing up in Russia as a second-generation black Muscovite to a mother who had been born and bred in a particular part of Africa and who would always have a simpler answer to the question 'Where are you from?'

As for me, there in the cold and dark of the Moscow hinterlands, I felt stranded, even among the black students. I also felt as Western European as I ever have, and couldn't wait to leave.

MARSEILLE AND THE FRENCH RIVIERA

Interlude in Rome

It was strange to have been picked up in the sullen snow and, after only a couple of hours, plonked in the south of Europe, where I found warmth and respite. Before going to Russia I'd felt the continuity of the continent beneath my feet, seen how each country morphed gradually into the next, making every landscape seem expansive but connected. Flying in and out of Russia, though, felt hollow and isolating, breaking the spell of my journey by land.

I landed in Rome, allowing myself to become a tourist for a few days, visiting the Vatican City, the smallest officially recognized state in the world. Walking through St Peter's Square, I was surprised to see a large presence of black nuns and clergymen, though I shouldn't have been; it's estimated that, by 2025, one fifth of the world's Catholics will be of African heritage.

The display of divine power on show, channelled through human minds and hands, particularly the masterful work of Michelangelo on the roof of the Sistine Chapel, made me proud to be human, yet it all also quietly suggested that I was less than that. Like the rest of the art on display in the Vatican City, it was ferociously white, a world of pink flesh and golden resplendence, depicted in a way that made the two virtually indistinguishable. I was walking through the pinnacle of everything I'd ever been taught to value by almost every source of official authority I'd been placed in the care of as a child, from school to Church to museums and galleries, and indeed I did find the work awe-inspiring. These aesthetics had been implanted so deeply within that when I saw the various paintings of a blue-eyed, bearded white man above the clouds, I knew that not only was that white male the omnipresent, all-powerful eternal creator of existence we know as God, but that he was the exact God I'd prayed to as a child, the God I attempted to draw as a five-year-old when my primary school teacher set me the task of drawing heaven, the God I saw when my eyes were closed. I entered the Sistine Chapel to look at perhaps the most famous image of this white God in the history of mankind, Michelangelo's *Creation of Adam*, a portrayal of the birth of humanity centred around the fingers of two white men, Adam and God, with that silver beard, surrounded by a clinch of blond-haired cherubim. This was the nucleus of the vision that had seeped into my brain, that was part of my social conditioning.* Though Jesus was, of course, not a white European like this depiction suggested, but a man from the Middle East, I could forgive all this – the Vatican wouldn't be the first place imagining its own as the chosen people – but much of what I was seeing was the brainchild of Pope Nicholas V, a major figure in the Roman Renaissance of the fifteenth century, under whose watch (along with the popes who succeeded him and enacted his vision) the Vatican City in its current form was assembled. These were the same men who gave a blessing to the start of the trans-Atlantic slave trade as we know it, and this narrative of white godliness gave morality and justification to its form, for it suggested that all this white purity was at stake.

When the war-mongering king of Portugal Alfonso V sought to expand the riches of his country and crusade through the Muslim world, he sought holy approval and moral authority from Pope Nicholas V, who, at war with Islam, issued a papal bull called the *Dum Diversas* in 1452 in which he granted to the king the right to 'invade, search out, capture, and subjugate the Saracens and pagans [black people] and any other unbelievers and enemies of

---

* There have, of course, been numerous interpretations of this famous painting – even a *Simpsons* version. When African-American artist Harmonia Rosales drew God as an older black woman reaching out to a young black Eve, however, it caused uproar online, so unthinkable was it to white society.

Christ wherever they may be, as well as their kingdoms, duchies, counties, principalities, and other property . . . and to reduce their persons into perpetual servitude'. Two years later, seeing the successful effects of this slavery, the bull was revised to include not only lands already conquered but any lands that may be conquerable, which ultimately meant 'permission to enslave the peoples of Africa'. The bull signalled the expansion of Europe throughout North and West Africa and, under successive popes, the creation of similar conditions under the name of Catholicism in the Americas. The beauty of this basilica was connected to the terror of slavery, and I felt that my own lineage belonged to the Vatican's shadow side. Yes, yes, I know Africa and Asia had slavery, too, but I'm talking here about a specific incarnation of slavery based around constructions of race that still informs and underpins, even if on a subconscious level, the hierarchies in Western civilization and throughout the world. It was a particularly barbaric and virulent form of slavery because it sought not only to enslave people but to justify the enslavement to itself by reducing its subjects to non-humans under the eyes of God.

This fair-skinned and often blond-haired interpretation of the sacred was even out of tune with the Italians I saw on the streets of Rome, with their dark curly hair and olive skin, which hinted at ancient Rome's long, sometimes blurry history with North Africa, particularly the Phoenicians of modern-day Libya, the Roman Empire stretching as it did all across the Mediterranean and well into the African continent. I wondered how many people in Italy or indeed Africa thought about that history as young brown-skinned men and women make a similar trip from Libya to Italy today, dying in an attempt to make a better life for themselves, vilified by the right-wing press and deemed illegal by authorities, with NGOs attempting rescue operations to save drowning men, women and children coming under attack. In 2015 alone over 2,000 people lost their lives trying to make this crossing, fleeing from civil war and poverty, journeying through deserts with little food or water and past armed border guards to make the treacherous boat ride across the Mediterranean on ill-equipped rafts manned by unscrupulous smugglers. All this instability came after the fall of the divisive, anti-imperialist go-to scapegoat General Muammar Gaddafi, at the hands of rebels backed by Western powers. When Gaddafi used strong-arm tactics to maintain control and a certain stability at the expense of people's lives, he was a butcher and a dictator; when the West allows the same people to die, they are as passive and innocent as Michelangelo's cherubim.

On my last day during my brief stay in Rome I saw a dog lying on the street, panting and with its eyes open but acting strangely, not moving as people walked around it. Relaxed restaurant-goers grew concerned, waiters and waitresses abandoned their duties, tourists and office workers joined them and formed a little group around the dog, which still wasn't moving. Some started panicking, frantically asking for assistance, and just when a restaurant manager called a vet the dog got up on its feet and sauntered off through the piazza. While this was going on I saw a blind Roma woman with an infant holding out an empty cup, skinny West Africans in tattered shoes trying to sell fake Fendi bags and poverty-stricken immigrants of all shades living under less charitable conditions than a dog would be forced to endure.

Joseph Mobutu's
Roquebrune-Cap-Martin

For a moment I was part of an art deco poster, there on a speeding train coasting along and tunnelling through the Riviera, crossing the border near Ventimiglia, before France announced itself with the hilly, creamy villages of Provence through the right window and a glittering turquoise sea stretching off into Africa through the left. It was no wonder that James Baldwin and Josephine Baker chose to spend their twilight years in this part of the world, leaving Paris behind to enrich their melanin with vitamin D and sooth the angst of a lifetime against the Mediterranean breeze. As consecutive glasses of Gavi were left undisturbed by the smooth motion of the train passing over the tracks of a route once taken by *le train bleu* (a luxury express born in the roaring 20s and serving celebrities in style until the early 00s), I read Baldwin's classic collection of essays about tales of life in 30s and 40s Harlem, *Notes of a Native Son*. Despite being so far away from Harlem, the cool prose strangely matched the mood of the train – there was a worldliness and an elegance, any anger, emotion or poverty crafted and elevated into a dignified, compelling and clear-sighted analysis. He could have been sitting opposite me or anyone else on that train, and over a bottle of wine, convince and charm the entire carriage of people into his way of seeing the world. If only he were really there on board.

The pleasant cosmopolitan atmosphere was interrupted, abruptly, when a bunch of inebriated red-faced English football fans on tour boarded in Menton. There were seven of them, and one was so drunk he was being carried on to the train over the shoulders of another. They were between the ages of around twenty-five and fifty, mostly towards the older end of that scale, dressed in ill-fitting football shirts, and one of them said, 'Anyway, if we don't win she's getting it in her arse when I get back.' The two tables of drunk men laughed and one of them said, 'Facking hell, I bet she's rooting for us more than you are.' They were the reactionary brand of cockney, and from past experience I knew that if there were two things groups like this bunch had contempt for, it was women and wogs. I tried to avoid eye contact, but when I heard one of the men say, 'Look, Gaz, it's one of your best mates,' followed by laughter and 'Ya, mon' in an offensively bad Jamaican accent, I knew I'd been spotted. I ignored the comment and a few moments later saw that they were covering the younger, comatose man who'd been carried on the train and was now slumped next to a window seat with cream from a chocolate éclair – British 'banter' at its finest. One of them stumbled down the train carriage, stood over me with what was left of the éclair and said, to sniggers and giggles from his mates, 'Hey, Mr Afro-man, want some dessert?' I told him that I didn't and he turned to his mates and said, 'Facking hell, he's English!' and one of them muttered out of the side of his mouth, 'Not on my fucking watch.' This swaying middle-aged mess then turned back to me and said, 'Thing is, if you refuse, me and my mates will take offence,' so I took the éclair. The belligerent forty-odd-year-old man standing in front of me, wearing a football shirt two sizes too small for him, his hairy belly hanging out over his jeans, shit tattoos on his sunburnt arms, threatening me if I didn't take his éclair, was somebody's husband and, worse, somebody's father; the twenty-something slumped in the corner covered in cream turned out to be his son.

These men didn't see anything wrong with what they were doing, of course, because as arrogant and ignorant Brits abroad, influenced by the mass sociopathy countries with huge histories of imperialism often suffer from as tourists (and which affects even those members of society who can't conquer their own bladders – I noticed that the younger man had a wet patch around his crotch), forgetting that Britain's empire and international prestige had long since shrivelled away, they were just 'havin' a laaarf'. It didn't matter how uncomfortable their actions made other people feel, the most important thing was that nobody stopped them from imposing their culture as they saw fit and that they had to give absolutely zero leeway to other people's feelings. As far as they were concerned, they could have spat at me and called me a nigger, and if I protested they'd claim they weren't being racist and that I couldn't take a joke, that I was part of a snowflake PC brigade ruining the world by being an oversensitive *social justice warrior*, another term for what I call being a decent human being. Yet the biggest 'snowflakes' of all usually turn out to be right-wing 'free speech' advocates, who are the first to emotionally overreact when somebody tries to defend themselves from the bullying or speak freely themselves; to those used to a certain kind of privilege, equality can feel like oppression.

In some ways I did feel sorry for these men. Seeing them on this train among a sensibly dressed young woman who I imagined was a student working on a laptop, a young man reading a novel, two middle-aged women talking quietly to each other, all of us trying to ignore their idiocy, it struck me that it was *their* culture that was the flimsy one, lost in a maelstrom of misinformation from Britain First memes on Facebook, overly attached to the failure or success of a football team and a pint of beer. That was it. As human beings they were infinitely complicated, like the rest of us, but the culture that contained and confined them – neoliberal capitalism – really hadn't allowed them to develop much of a culture of their own.

V. S. Pritchett once wrote about these types of men, about 'the unhappy traveller':

> He is travelling not for pleasure but for pain, not to broaden the mind but, if possible, to narrow it; to release the buried terrors and hatreds of a lifetime; or, if these have already had a good airing at home, to open up colonies of rage abroad . . . and when

they return from their mortifications it is to insult the people and the places they have visited . . . with the zest so sore that we conclude travel for them is a continuation of domestic misery by other means.[1]

Claude McKay spoke of the unhappy traveller, too, through one of his characters in the Marseille-set novel *Banjo*: 'He sees everything, but he learns nothing. And I don't think he is capable of learning. He carries abroad with him everything that should be left back home. Everything that is mean, hard-boiled, and intolerant.'[2] Clearly, the journeys that need to be made are mental ones and, as the old proverb goes, 'A fool doesn't see the same tree a wise man sees': as I tried to appreciate the glorious view of the Côte d'Azur and plot my trip to James Baldwin's house, the middle-aged Brits were pissed out of their heads, spreading cream over the carriage and splurging out racist and xenophobic slurs.

The tree proverb was about to apply again in a very different way, because, had I not been looking for black Europe, I'd have been blinded by one of the most stunning stretches of coastline in the world, one that hid black narratives other than Baldwin's. The Riviera didn't just attract famous writers, artists, movie stars and architects, but – as I was about to see first hand – ruthless kings, murderous oligarchs and corrupt African dictators.

I alighted one station before Monaco to collective jeers from the cockneys – 'Bye, Ruud'; 'Cha, mon, enjoy your cake, mon' – and left the stink of alcohol on board for the jasmine-scented tranquillity of Roquebrune-Cap-Martin and a small café-cum-beach shack called Le Cabanon down by the rocky, hidden and gloriously beautiful cape.

I paid a quick visit to a minimalist white villa called E-1027 built in the 20s by Irish designer Eileen Gray and later developed by Le Corbusier, which as well as being the site of his death (he drowned in the cape below), had, like quite a few of these prime

Riviera properties, also been the scene of a murder. In 1996 the last private owner was stabbed to death; he himself had been suspected of killing the owner before him. Some of the underlying stories emanating out of these beautiful homes were worthy of Hercule Poirot; much of the Riviera had a murderous history.

Over in a neighbouring and equally beautiful coastal village called Villefranche-sur-Mer lay Villa Leopolda, owned by a philanthropist called Lily Safra, who inherited it after her husband,

Edmund Safra, was murdered by his male nurse in Monaco in the 90s, a crime the nurse still vehemently denies, observing that, the year before Safra died, the bank he was a principal shareholder of made a report about a vast Russian money-laundering operation. Villa Leopolda went up for sale recently as the most expensive villa in the world, and when the latest billionaire buyer pulled out at the last moment, he lost his deposit; a cool 36 million euros. The malevolent mood of Villa Leopolda didn't begin there, though, because it was one of a few properties originally built by King Leopold II of Belgium with his Congo blood-money, helping to establish the region as a playground for the rich and famous. In an ugly mimicking of the old colonizer, a more recent leader of the Congo had bought a similar villa right where I was, just a stone's throw away in Roquebrune-Cap-Martin. Next door to the Eileen Gray house was a huge, frilly, baby-pink building that I knew was home to one of the world's richest and most corrupt African dictators. It was the Villa del Mare, just one of twenty such luxury properties across the world owned by the former Congolese president Joseph Mobutu.

While the Congo – then Zaire – crumbled, defaulting on crippling debts it owed to Belgium, the old colonizers it had made rich still had their hands around the region's throat a hundred years after King Leopold II, and Mobutu was being nursed after having surgery for prostate cancer in this luxury villa, sitting on billions made by selling off the Congo's natural resources and pocketing international aid meant for his people. As someone with enslavement in my heritage, I can't help but feel haunted by these journeys of old money and the histories of inheritance, and how they are sometimes still fuelling, even if at times only in seemingly whimsical ways, power and success; such as that famous actor who was put through private school by the fortune his great-grandfather amassed through plantations in the Caribbean. Someone, right this minute, is sitting on money King Leopold II attained from massacre, and money that Joseph Mobutu acquired through the assassination of Patrice Lumumba and the eventual economic destruction of an entire country. These sinister energies had been transferred into quietly nestled beauty draped in bougainvillea, surrounded by manicured gardens, with the Mediterranean Sea lapping at the doorstep. When Mobutu died in 1997, many of his assets, including the Villa del Mare, were eventually sold off, with the proceeds heading straight to Swiss bank accounts owned by the Mobutu family. One of Mobutu's sons, then serving as prime minister and set to inherit his father's fortune, blocked the Congolese government from cooperating with a Swiss investigation aimed at retrieving the money and giving it back to the people. The last I heard, the Mobutu family had sold this villa to a Russian billionaire.

I circumnavigated the perimeter of the house, sticking my camera over a gap in the fence. The photograph revealed a Segway and a bunch of gardening equipment in the gate house, with a long drive leading into the plush grounds of the estate. Then I walked along the beach, past wealthy old men and women with shiny plastic faces and drooping, leathery bodies, and up a side-alley by a small stream cascading down the hill into the sea. This was another flank of the villa and, balancing precariously on a wall, perched on my tiptoes with my arms raised at full length, I took more photographs over the fence, to see a bunch of stone heads and an old statue of a lion, similar to the ones you can see in the abandoned remains of Mobutu's 'African Versailles' palace in Gbadolite, the Congo. I peered through any holes I found in the fence, got on my stomach to look under gates, circled the perimeter once more, becoming obsessed with and spooked by my proximity to a building connected to such troubling and far-flung stories in this tranquil and exclusively aloof inlet in the south of France. When a helicopter began to hover ominously and conspicuously low overhead and then, its noisy rotors chopping through the air, circle the periphery of the estate, I decided it was time to leave. I'd disembarked the train and made this little sojourn to see the result of corruption with my own eyes, because it was unfathomable to me before, no more real than a James Bond movie, and there still exist Mobutu apologists who claim he wasn't as corrupt as he seemed. But the Villa del Mare is real, and an African dictator from a desperately poor and failing country really *had* once owned it in the midst of its turmoil.

James Baldwin's Saint-Paul-de-Vence

I'd decided to take my time travelling along the Riviera, which was surprisingly inexpensive because the sun, the sights and the seaside strolls were all free of charge, and my Interrail pass had already been paid for so I could train-hop at will. I briefly visited Villefranche-sur-Mer, which, like so many other areas across the world that houses the super-rich, was twee, geographically impressive and empty, the homes gated, antisocial and often unoccupied, serving as just one of many residences owned by their proprietors – beauty is wasted on billionaires. After wandering its sleepy off-season backstreets and coastal paths towards Cap Ferrat to visit Villa Leopolda (one of them strewn with invitations to a private party thrown the previous evening by a Russian diamond company), or rather the entrance to its vast grounds, I carried on to Cagnes-sur-Mer, where I caught a small, winding bus to Saint-Paul-de-Vence, a lofty, golden-brown village that only made the brow of the hill overlooking the Côte d'Azur more scenic. There was huge wealth here, too, but it wasn't oligarch wealth, it was rock-star, artist, movie-star wealth, and that meant it had a subtly artsy, literary ambience, with small galleries, old bookshops, a friendly square and 'normal' people in the form of tour groups, which, for the first time on my trip, I was somewhat relieved to see.

I was in town to visit the last home in which James Baldwin lived before he died in 1987, a house that has become a place of pilgrimage for many writers over the years, so much so that a group was recently set up in an attempt to turn the property into an artists' colony or some sort of cultural centre in honour of Baldwin's legacy. Baldwin had other residences across the world during his lifetime that haven't quite captured the imagination in the same way as the Saint-Paul property and, as I entered the village, surrounded by vineyards at its base, and climbed the small, sun-baked streets leading to its medieval summit I immediately understood why; who wouldn't want a writing residency in Saint-Paul-de-Vence? Perhaps the Saint-Paul property also symbolized that rare thing: a happy ending for a black writer. For a poor, gay black kid born into the Harlem ghetto in 20s America who fled to Paris with only $40 in his pocket to end his life here, picking figs and peaches in a ten-acre garden, hosting A-list celebrities and writing to the blissful twitter of blue tits under the shade of a palm tree suggests a perfect trajectory for a life story of true emancipation.

Though it isn't signposted, it's not hard to find the Baldwin property on route de la Colle – locals are used to directing renegade culture tourists to it – and after a short walk from the quaint town centre I found the boarded-up gatehouse at the entrance to the premises once known as Chez Baldwin. There are tragically few opportunities to get close to history's great black writers through the properties they owned, often because they didn't end up owning any property, and still fewer are officially opened to the public.* When you visit the place a famous writer chose as a home, you hope to see, to paraphrase Frantz Fanon, a 'constellation of postulates' in the surroundings that speak of their inner lives, or be awestruck at how, say, a frugal desk or a small room could be the stage set for the birth of an epic fictive landscape or a call to arms that galvanized an entire political movement. James Baldwin's old home wasn't open to the public, but this was super-lax France and I easily broke into the unguarded grounds.

* In an article for *Vice* magazine, out of over seventy writers' properties opened to the American public, the writer Matt St John could locate only four properties once inhabited by African-American writers, those of Frederick Douglass, Alex Haley, Martin Luther King and Langston Hughes, whose property was only recently saved from being turned into a Starbucks.

Baldwin was perhaps the most coherent literary voice of the civil-rights struggle because he managed to present black people as *humans* in his fiction and essays rather than mere actors in a polemic to hammer home a moralistic or political message. He helped America see that there was no hope of an American Dream for anybody unless it included everybody. In an unfinished work of non-fiction he wrote, 'You give me a terrifying advantage ... you never had to look at me. I had to look at you. I know more about you than you know about me. Not everything that is faced can be changed, but nothing can be changed until it is faced.'[1] Unlike some of his contemporaries, he never grew to hate white Americans, but was sometimes frustrated by them because he knew that they were living a candy-coated lie until they faced up to America's history and the inequality in its society, feeling that a reconciliation with the truth was the healthiest route forward for any human being, regardless of race, which echoes Frantz Fanon's belief that subjugation was just as mentally damaging for the subjugator as the subjugated. And like the best writers, Baldwin was unflinchingly dedicated to the truth, even when it had painful ramifications.

His homosexuality, not formally announced in the early days but never really hidden, meant a series of humiliating rejections, none more so than from the black community he was faithfully trying to serve. Because of his sexuality he was refused membership to a club his mentor Richard Wright belonged to, kept at arm's length by Martin Luther King and Malcolm X, who admired and drew inspiration from his mind but were wary of what they saw as his effeminate manner, ostracized by some members of the Black Panthers, and scorned in a homophobic rant by one of the Black Panther Party leaders, Eldridge Cleaver, in his seminal memoir *Soul on Ice* as having a sycophantic love of white people and a 'sickness' that made him hate his own blackness. As American scholar Henry Louis Gates Jnr, who spent time at Villa Baldwin, wrote, 'if someone has anointed a black intellectual, rest assured that others are busily constructing his tumbrel'.[2]

This position of being American but on the periphery of American national identity, and of being black but often denounced by the foremost shapers of black – especially black male – culture, may not have been a position of privilege exactly, but it allowed Baldwin an insightful, almost liminal position amid charged race relations, something that resonated with my notion of 'Afropean'. He once said, 'It was my great luck to be born poor and black in America because it meant that I couldn't lie about what America really was,'[3] and you wonder if his sexuality afforded him a similar 'luck' when observing a black community overly hinged on masculine notions of blackness as a response to the subservient 'Uncle Tom' depictions of African-Americans of the previous generation. There is a certain clarity at the periphery, and when a writer taps into a more objective truth and accuracy their work has a way of being prescient and prophetic, so it's no surprise Baldwin's writing has aged better than perhaps that of any other writer of his generation. The evidence of this can be seen in his influence on a new generation of black writers such as Ta-Nehisi Coates and Teju Cole, the intersectional energy of the Black Lives Matter movement, whose members use him as an icon, and how America, once again dealing overtly with its racist history, is drawing heavily upon Baldwin's articulations of black life and the American Dream to understand itself.

When Baldwin first left Harlem for Paris in the 40s, it was to follow Richard Wright and carve out a writing life for himself beyond the claustrophobic climate of America, but he later returned to America for well over a decade to take part in the struggle for civil rights. By the 70s, though, exhausted by and ostracized for his efforts, and distraught at the deaths of Malcolm X, Martin Luther King and his good friend Medgar Evers, and carrying the belittling label 'Martin Luther Queen', he'd had a nervous breakdown, and this time his return to France was not to make a name for himself but to disappear and recuperate here in the south.

In Saint-Paul-de-Vence it would be proved to him that people *did* care, and that he *did* still have friends in the black community. To enter this provincial property is to walk in the steps of some of the most important African-American thinkers and artists of the twentieth century. Baldwin was known for throwing dinner and garden parties and hosted a wealth of celebrities, from Miles Davis to Nina Simone, Josephine Baker to Maya Angelou, Sidney Poitier to Ray Charles. Caryl Phillips was a regular visitor, too, and if I was right, and this was the same palm tree at the side of the house where Caryl mentioned the interview taking place, then I was standing in the exact spot in which Baldwin told Caryl, in a 1984 interview for BBC Radio 4: 'When I was young, looking for a job, the moment I appeared they put a broom in my hand. So I had to defeat the world's intentions and the only way I could do that was to make it very clear that I am not at all what I seem to be to you. I know what you are seeing but I am not that person, and I will make you know it, that I'm not that person.' Sitting in the shade of that palm tree in the south of France with his own chauffeur, a chef, an assistant with their own detached quarters, and as the toast of the town with movie stars and musician friends, must have seemed like powerful evidence of his success in having truly lived out his statement of intent. As a black working-class writer trying to 'defeat the world's intentions' myself, it was easy – and comforting – to imagine James Baldwin and all the legendary guests I mentioned, now all dead, who had often endured difficult childhoods in racist America and had put their careers on the line for civil rights, cavorting together in this patch in the south of France in the twilight of their lives. End credits.

This version of events, though, doesn't tell the entire story of Baldwin's south of France paradise. Baldwin, as it turned out, never ended up owning this plot of land. It was instead owned by an old woman called Jeanne Fauré, a landlady born into a wealthy white French colonial family in Algeria who was, by most accounts, a racist who particularly loathed Algerians and was persuaded to take Baldwin in only because she enjoyed the kudos of having celebrities as lodgers. Baldwin being Baldwin, over the years the two grew close, but she was often reported as saying he was the 'only Negro' she knew and liked and, despite attempting to buy the house in instalments, when Baldwin died he was deeply in arrears, and the property was ultimately inherited by members of Jeanne Fauré's family.

This period in the Riviera wasn't a terribly prolific time for Baldwin, either, who, in his seventeen years in Saint-Paul produced just two novels, which received a lukewarm reception from critics, four slim volumes of essays, a children's book and a book of poetry. In the previous seventeen years, despite and possibly because of segregation, the politically charged atmosphere of the civil rights movement, being broke, listed by the trigger-happy FBI of the 60s as a 'person of interest' and finally vilified by his own community, he'd produced four hugely important novels, including his most definitive work, *Go Tell It on the Mountain* and the supremely brave and controversial *Giovanni's Room*, written and published in the conservative 50s, about romantic love found between two white men. During that time he also produced three books of essays, including his classic *Notes of a Native Son*, two plays and a collection of short stories. In a biography of Baldwin's life in the Saint-Paul-de-Vence years, Jules B. Farber chronicles how he spent much of his time there drinking and chain-smoking himself to death, surrounding himself not just with well-wishing celebrities but also with gigolos, gold-digging lovers and hangers-on; people he'd never met before would turn up at his door and would stay for weeks on end free of charge. His sister Gloria was so traumatized by her stay at the house that her hair started to fall out and she decided to leave, rarely returning, because it brought back bad memories. Baldwin was often depressed here, hung over, facing writer's block, owing money to his landlady and his publisher, and paranoid that he was under the surveillance of French intelligence, which he may well have been.

I'd been powerfully unsettled by my proximity to the houses of

Mobutu and King Leopold II, which had been perfectly preserved, feeling a certain doom in their presence. Try as I might – too hard, really – to feel something near Baldwin's residence, it left me cold, with neither pathos nor poignancy, nor even anger that it hadn't been better preserved; the wreckage of the house wasn't particularly depressing because it was, after all, a beautiful provençal wreckage, more *wabi-sabi* than stark dereliction, crumbly and overgrown with vines in a way that was picturesque. In the end, I wondered whether we who make the pilgrimage aren't all just hangers-on, too, wanting to take our seat at what Baldwin called his 'welcome table', despite being uninvited, hoping Baldwin, beyond the grave, might extend some sort of hospitality, that we might be moved by his muse or somehow touched by his magic. Or, in physical terms, take from him a cultured weekend in the south of France, a few hundred words of prose, or even a fancy writers' retreat. It would take over 10 million euros to save this prime piece of real estate from being turned into apartments, but to what end? For middle-class writers and academics to crank out a couple of hundred words each day then go and lunch in the local Michelin-starred restaurant? They are, after all, usually the only people who would know about and apply for a residency. It struck me that money raised in Baldwin's name might be better spent on some sort of grassroots institute in the type of place Baldwin himself grew up, which contained the energy that charged his best writing in the first place.

The grounds at the route de la Colle address were beautiful, but it was Baldwin's charm, intelligence, elegance and wit that filled the place with such importance for all who visited him – had I not known this was Baldwin's place, it would have just been one of many beautiful provençal ruins in the area. I found an old pepper grinder in the soil and peeled off a broken tile of the exposed bathroom: silly mementoes, because Baldwin couldn't be found in the soil of Provence; there was nothing there that could truly articulate who he was, in the same way neither America nor even Harlem could ever sum him up entirely. I'm not convinced that he ever really found a home; rather, the home he found was ultimately on the road, between places. Curiously, Saint-Paul-de-Vence – or a place that might resemble it – doesn't appear in any of the fiction or non-fiction that was published during Baldwin's time there, other than in a commissioned piece when he was specifically asked to write about it, in what may be his final essay before his death from stomach cancer. Only a couple of paragraphs in that short essay, published in a 1987 issue of the *Architectural Digest*, mention how the place makes him feel – it's old, he says, takes a lot of upkeep, which he quite enjoys. This is telling, because the bulk of the text is dedicated to the concept of 'home', and to Baldwin's life as a 'Transatlantic commuter' between New York, California, Sierra Leone, London, Istanbul and Paris. He wrote:

> A house is not a home: we have all heard the proverb. Yet, if the house is not a home (*home!*) it can become only, I suppose, a space to be manipulated ... I have lived in many places, have precipitated here and there. The beginning of my life rather recalls a shipwreck, and the shipwrecked can find it difficult to trust daylight or dry land.[4]

I left Saint-Paul-de-Vence, taking James Baldwin with me, not because I'd found him there in that pretty little village, but because, just as it had earlier on the train, his spirit lay in a book in my backpack.

Frantz Fanon's Toulon

Further along the coast, an hour south-east of Marseille, sits Toulon, a modest mid-sized city that is sleepy in its off-season state, with a large naval base and a pleasantness that is underwhelming when pitted against some of its more glamorous neighbours along the Riviera, especially those I'd just visited. Bombed heavily in the Second World War and an epicentre for the extreme right for a couple of decades in the 80s and 90s (Toulon was one of only three cities nationwide to vote for a Front National majority in the 1995 local elections), a response to and an exacerbation of a general social and economic decline. It is currently undergoing an ambitious rejuvenation of its centre, which hasn't quite yet erased a slightly faded feeling.

On 8 May 1945, however, amid the wreckage of Toulon, there were massive street parties, packed dance halls, heroic parades and a general feeling of huge relief as the city celebrated the final surrender of the German armed forces in France that signalled the end of the Second World War. Toulon had been liberated from German occupation the previous year in one of the war's key battles, Operation Dragoon, which was overshadowed by – but considered equally as important as – the Battle of Normandy by many historians. This southern invasion wasn't as sexy as the American-led landings immortalized by Robert Capa's blurry and atmospheric photographs in the north of France; it was a nine-day siege that included among its men large numbers from the Free French Colonial Infantry Division – Algerians, Malians, Mauritanians and the Senegalese Tirailleurs – which, under General Charles de Gaulle, eventually helped liberate the strategically important port towns of Marseille and Toulon within the space of two days. De Gaulle, leader in exile of the French resistance, initially struggled to drum up support, as Marshal Pétain's Vichy government complied with the Nazi occupation of France. But the French colonies, seeing themselves as defenders of and beholden to their distant 'motherland' were often only too keen to join the resistance against the Germans, and in the end made up two thirds of de Gaulle's now-celebrated army.

One of the most important thinkers and revolutionaries of the decolonial struggle, Frantz Fanon, was among those men from the colonies answering de Gaulle's call. Despite being part of a black Martinican middle class and having been schooled at an elite level (one of his teachers and mentors was that giant of Francophone Caribbean literature and leader of the Negritude movement Aimé Césaire) with relatively good local career prospects ahead of him, he jumped on a warship at the age of eighteen without any hesitation. Fanon had already had his ideas of France as a bastion of righteousness challenged when, at the outbreak of the Second World War, Pétain sent white Vichy troops to govern Martinique and many middle-class black Martinicans suddenly found themselves forced to endure overt racism (rather than colonial patrimony) for the first time in their lives. By joining the Free French Forces, Fanon was considered a 'dissenter' by the colonial government in Martinique, and even his fellow white dissenters subjected him and his fellow black soldiers to racist taunts as soon as the boat left Martinique to aid in the war effort. It wasn't until Fanon experienced France first hand, though, that the seeds of a revolutionary were planted.

The first time he ever laid eyes on the country was when his regiment disembarked in an eerily deserted St Tropez, and he spent the next two years of his life in dire circumstances, being wounded in battle twice, fighting in the freezing-cold climate of Alsace – extra treacherous for someone who grew up in the tropics – and performing feats of bravery that would see him awarded the Croix de Guerre. During this time he became ever more disillusioned with French society. In a letter dated April 1945, he wrote to his parents, before undertaking what he thought would be a lethal final mission, 'If one day I don't return and you learn of my death at the hands of the enemy, comfort yourself but never say "he died for a good cause".'[1] It would be in Toulon that the reality of France's rejection of black men would sting most deeply, as his brother Joby Fanon recounted, 'In Toulon, where he was transferred, there were many parties. Frantz was an excellent dancer, but the French women wouldn't dance with a Negro, even one wearing the uniform of the liberating army. This wounded Frantz deeply, even more than the mortar shell wound he received in the Doubs.'[2] Not only did French women refuse to dance with him, instead chasing the American GIs, some even preferred to dance with the fascist Italian prisoners. Fanon mentions this painful experience in *Black Skin, White Masks*: 'When I was in the military service I had the opportunity to observe the behaviour of white women from three or four European countries when they were among negroes at dances. Most of the time the women made involuntary gestures of flight, of withdrawing, their faces filled with a fear that was not feigned.'[3] In the same book he famously talks about a young child recoiling in fear upon seeing him, pointing and saying to his mother, 'Look Mama, a Negro!' The racism of fellow soldiers was one thing, but white civilians being physically afraid of a man who had put his life on the line to save their villages and fight for their culture, a culture that he had been taught from birth he was a part of (according to Joby Fanon, the first three words a child from Martinique learned in school were *Je suis français/e*) struck Fanon to his psychological core. For so many colonial subjects the PTSD they suffered after the Second World War was less connected with the deaths and destruction they witnessed during the war and more with the death they experienced in peace – the death of the French dream. Fanon would turn twenty shortly after VE Day, and what he and his friends experienced as they struggled in Toulon to join in with the celebrations of the end of the war they'd just won was an acute feeling of rejection that many others have continued to feel in a French society that proposes as its central motto 'Liberty, equality and fraternity'. Fanon spoke for all people from the French Caribbean when he wrote the following passage, but he must have felt it viscerally himself. There are few better examples of what French colonialism did to the psychology of its subjects:

> Cultural imposition is easily accomplished in Martinique. The ethical transit [white colonial] encounters no obstacle. But the real white man is waiting for me. As soon as possible he will tell me that it is not enough to try to be white, but that a white totality must be achieved. It is only then that I shall recognise the betrayal – let us conclude. An Antillean [Caribbean] is made white by collective unconscious . . . [but] the colour of his skin, of which there is no mention in Jung, is black. All the inabilities to understand are born of this blunder . . . At the age of twenty . . . the Antillean recognises that he is living an error. Why is that? Quite simply because – and this is very important – the Antillean has recognised himself as a negro, but, by virtue of an ethical transit, he also feels (collective unconscious) that one is a negro to the degree that one is wicked, sloppy, malicious, instinctual. Everything that is the opposite of these negro modes of behaviour is white . . . in the collective unconscious, black = ugliness, sin, darkness, immorality . . . hence the Martinican custom of saying of a worthless white man that he has 'a nigger soul.'[4]

Perhaps some of the eagerness of France's colonial troops to put their lives on the line was born out of this mixture of learned pride and the subconscious desire to prove themselves as noble and honourable members of French society, to prove that they didn't have 'nigger souls'. And yet, despite doing as much as humanly possible to show that they were noble French citizens during the war, they were robbed of the country's most glorious moment. Frantz Fanon, like many colonial soldiers, was in Toulon and not Paris on Victory in Europe Day for a very important reason. When you look at footage of this crowning moment in the French capital, when the victory of the Allies in the Second World War was officially proclaimed, you won't see a single non-white soldier celebrating in the most symbolic record of French resistance, despite the fact that two thirds of those soldiers had brown skin. Why? Because of a great bleaching, or *blanchissement*, of the Free French Forces. General de Gaulle's armies were felt to be the true French war heroes, and it was important for de Gaulle and French morale that his soldiers were the ones to be seen across the world to liberate Paris. The uncomfortable fact that most of those French soldiers were brown-skinned men was not lost on Western powers, who had long calculated who the war should appear to have been won by. In a confidential document sent to General de Gaulle dated 28 January 1944, Walter Bedell Smith, General Eisenhower's chief of staff, wrote: 'It is most desirable that the division mentioned above consist of white personnel, and this would indicate the second armoured division which, with only 1/4 native personnel is the only French division operationally available that could be made 100% white.'[5]

But there is an earlier letter, dated 14 January 1944, from the British Lieutenant-General Frederick H. Morgan to the Supreme Allied Commander:

> Both General Ismay and I have impressed upon Colonel de Chevene that we would with reluctance accept anything here other than French metropolitan troops, it is unfortunate that the only French formation that is one hundred percent white is an armoured division in Morocco . . . every other French division is only about forty percent white. I have told Colonel de Chevene that his chances of getting what he wants [French troops to take Paris] will be vastly improved if he can produce a white infantry division.[6]

It's unclear exactly how compliant General de Gaulle was with this plan, and in any case his hands were tied; if he wanted his French soldiers to be the face of the Allies seen to reclaim the French capital back from the Nazis, then he had to produce an all-white regiment. Black soldiers were turned away from the capital, stripped of their uniforms and sent to holding camps before being shipped back to their respective countries. Fanon boarded an under-rationed ship called the *San Mateo* and was unceremoniously carted off back to Martinique with his fellow black Caribbean soldiers while the Europe they were effectively kicked out of was still rejoicing. De Gaulle got his wish to have a French division lead the liberation of Paris, even though the shortage of white troops meant that many of these men were Spanish, America's D-Day had been immortalized, and Winston Churchill became an icon. It wasn't just that the right side won, but that the right side were *seen* to have won. The colonized had helped to liberate their colonizers, only to realize they hadn't liberated themselves.

While Fanon was having that dud Victory in Europe Day in Toulon, over in Algeria, a territory that had been colonized by boats setting off from that very French port the previous century, this sense of disillusionment was most strongly expressed. When Germany's final retreat was made official, Algerian protesters took to the streets to voice their grievances, which ended in what has become known as the Sétif massacre, resulting in the deaths of thousands of Muslim Algerians at the hands of the colonial French military police. The end of the Second World War in France, then, marked the beginning of a severed relationship that would lead to the Algerian War of Independence just under ten years later. From 1959 pensions for servicemen from France's overseas possessions, who had put their lives on the line for the country in the Second World War – even those living in France – were cruelly terminated after the date their country of origin became independent.

Despite the humiliations of the war, Fanon himself was still keen to continue his relationship with France, albeit now in a more critically engaged capacity, devoted to making this great nation, which was letting itself down, achieve its full potential. He wrote:

> What is all this talk of a Black people, of a negro nationality? I am a Frenchman. I am interested in French culture, French civilisation, the French people. We refuse to be considered 'outsiders', we have full part in the French drama. When men who were not basically bad, only deluded, invaded France in order to subjugate her, my position as a Frenchman made it plain to me that my place was not outside but in the very heart of the problem. I am personally interested in the future of France, in French values, in the French nation. What have I to do with a Black empire? . . . An authentic grasp of the reality of the negro could only be achieved to the detriment of the cultural crystallisation.[7]

Only a couple of years after the publication of this passage in *Black Skin, White Masks* in 1952 Fanon would find himself fighting against the very culture he had so desperately tried to take part in. France had a national hero on its hands, and its rejection of him because of his race, and the mistreatment of its colonies, particularly Algeria, had transformed Fanon into an enemy by the time he wrote his decolonial opus *The Wretched of the Earth*. A psychiatrist by trade, he had by now decided that 'violence is a cleansing force. It frees the native from his inferiority complex and from his despair and inaction; it makes him fearless and restores his self-respect'.[8] This was the final work published in his lifetime and, in the introduction, one of Fanon's mentors, Jean-Paul Sartre, wrote, 'To shoot down a European is to kill two birds with one stone, to destroy an oppressor and the man he oppresses at the same time.'[9] It is this same desperate conclusion which, suffering from participation fatigue, many other French nationals forced into outsiderness still tragically arrive at.

McKay's Marseille

When nation-wide riots set France alight in 2005, one of the few big French cities to abstain from the violence and destruction was Marseille. This backed up Almamy Kanouté's claim in Clichy that the Paris riots weren't in fact riots at all but revolts, because for the sons and daughters of Marseille's immigrants to firebomb this city would be to torch a place where their own families, businesses and communities have been allowed to coexist with relative success for years. Marseille has its problems, of course; as it is a port town, drug dealers maintain a certain presence and old Mafia families play a hand in controlling a corrupt local government. As I would see, the Quartier Nord houses deprived estates similar to those on the edges of other big French cities. But as soon as I left Saint-Charles station I saw working-class, often brown-skinned men and women occupying the centre of the city with a self-assured poise that was largely missing not just in France but across Europe.

I'd heard mixed things about Marseille (mostly from Parisians), but hadn't ever experienced such a dramatically beautiful entrance to a city from a train station. Pigeons scattered out into the sunset, disturbed by kids kicking a football on this wonderfully balmy February evening, their ethnicities mirroring the mix of their heroes in the French national football team. Against the burnt-orange hue of the city, the players were all dressed in the complementary colour-wheel tone of sky blue, ubiquitous in the city because it is the colour of Olympique de Marseille, the city's only major – and dearly loved – football team.

I walked through their lively game, which had nothing resembling goal posts, and descended an ornate marble staircase adorned with statues of African and Asian muses, lions, flowers, grain, fruit and wine, indicating that Marseille was both a land of abundant natural riches and also the old French gateway to Africa and the Orient. The staircase, first inaugurated in 1848, had been bruised by its life as a functioning part of the city, and its faded stone, darkened in its crevices by pollution and covered in seagull shit, only made it more picturesque. It spilled on to a long, drooping boulevard of pink limestone buildings set aflame by a low sun, a lava flow of brake lights, and the inner glow of heaving Algerian and Tunisian cafés splaying out on to the sidewalks. In the distance, past this glowing labyrinth, lay the Mediterranean Sea, stirred gently by the throb of a full moon rising, and beyond its straits the physical land of the Maghreb – Algeria, Morocco, Tunisia – and it was clear straight away that Marseille itself housed much of that same North African energy. Yes, Marseille is physically in Provence, but they say here that it turns its back on France to stare lovingly at Africa and the Mediterranean.

As I walked down towards the main thoroughfare, La Canebière, parts of the city centre reminded me of Francophone West African cities with their faded modernism shoehorned into French colonial-era buildings, DIY shop signs and boutiques and pâtisseries that hadn't changed their shopfronts since the 60s. Later, in Le Panier, the oldest district in all of France, with its tiny, winding streets tied together by criss-crossing clotheslines and whizzed through by kamikaze mopeds, I was reminded of the Marrakech medina. Italians and Corsicans had brought a culture of pizzas, piazzas and great ice cream and coffee and, naturally, Marseille wasn't so un-French that it refused to embrace the fine old tradition of first-class independent *boulangeries*, *épiceries*, pharmacies and *fromageries* – *that* would be taking things too far.

I was staring in awe at the illuminated gilded Mary Magdalene statue perched atop the basilica Notre-Dame de la Garde in the distance, guarding the city as dramatically as Christ the Redeemer does in Rio de Janeiro, but my benediction came from a louche old white man with a face mapped by deep wrinkles wearing a flat cap and a well-worn 80s Le Coq Sportif tennis shirt I nearly made him an offer for. He snapped me out of my reverence for Mary and Marseille by asking where I was from, in the specific type of shouty French the Marseillais are famous for, informed by Italian and Arabic expressiveness. When I told him I was British he grabbed my shoulder and said, 'Maybe, but you are *métis*,' and, having heard this pretty-sounding – if old-fashioned – French term for 'mixed race' before, I told him that yes, my mom was white and my dad black. He looked me in the eye and said, 'Marseille is *métis*. This place, it is for you – everybody here is a mix. Me? *I* am *métis*! From Corsica and Italy with some Arab, but one hundred per cent Marseille!' Then he let go of my shoulder, wished me a *bonne soirée* and proceeded to get into an argument with another old man he recognized, and I heard him shout '*Vafanculo!*' (Italian slang for 'fuck off') before bobbing off down a side street.

It's true, Marseille is a mongrel of a metropolis, and all the things that made other people turn their nose up at it made me feel at home. It was love at first sight, and the love was both romantic and familial. Other than when it had been forced to play host to an international football tournament or Champions League match, this multicultural bohemia had a history of welcoming wanderers while keeping bumpkins at bay – David and Janet from suburbia, who like to travel south with their *Daily Mail* in hand and their Marks and Spencer's cooler bags and can be heard moaning, after insisting themselves upon France's beauty, 'The weather was nice, but they don't speak a word of English, and some don't even speak French, if you know what I mean.'* Those people only made it as far as toy-towns like Arles or Avignon, because

---

* I experienced this exact couple talking about this exact topic on one of my many trips back and forth between London and Marseille after the first draft of this book was completed. And during that time on the six-hour Eurostar trips I witnessed variations of the same couple saying variations of the same thing and, thankfully, never alighting with me in Marseille.

Marseille's rats are too big, the skin of its inhabitants is too brown, their faith too Islamic, their temper too Mediterranean and their politics too left wing. They would gasp at the 'antisocial behaviour', and yet they are the most antisocial – David and Janet call Jeremy Corbyn a 'loony lefty' if he so much as expresses concern about the ramifications of nuclear war – but a proper socialist, the Moroccan-born politician Jean-Luc Mélanchon, was the overwhelming vote for the Marseillais in the last French election. All this meant that, despite the ancient beauty, the 300 days of sunshine each year, the stunning sea views and proximity to Cannes, Monte Carlo, Paris, the Amalfi Coast, Barcelona, Morocco and even London without having to fly, Marseille was still working class, not touristy and surprisingly resistant to the whims of awful expats and bourgeois Parisians. It was artsy but unself-conscious, the creatives I met during my time in the city saw themselves more as tradesmen and -women or community raconteurs, and the word 'artisanal' hadn't yet been colonized by mini-capitalists turning noble old skills into photogenic lifestyle brands, so the city was also somewhat resilient to the scourge of gentrification. During my time in Marseille I noticed fewer hipsters per square mile than anywhere else in Europe.

I found my hostel down by the old port which is also the city's epicentre (Marseille's heart is on its sleeve), a down-to-earth social space I've learned to love for its mediocre buskers, constantly colonized as it was by ageing body-poppers, a Senegalese man just about holding the notes of *History*-era Michael Jackson songs and emcees free-styling in French to old-school hip-hop beats. Hip-hop looms large, and all four elements of hip-hop culture, as defined by Afrika Bambaataa, are ubiquitous in the city; as well as the breakdancing and emceeing, most of the buildings are covered in at least a tag, but many in layers of years' worth of colourful sunbleached graffiti. There are turntablism and beatboxing workshops led by youth workers for disenfranchised kids, part of a big social entrepreneurship scene at local level. It is not surprising that a city like Marseille gave birth to France's most legendary golden-era rap crew, IAM (Imperial Asiatic Man), a group that found an international audience when they collaborated with the Wu-Tang-affiliated Sunz of Man and produced a European hip-hop anthem, 1997's 'La Saga', after establishing themselves as political commentators and elite lyricists on the domestic scene. Their early stuff was juxtaposed against the more mainstream sound of Paris's most famous son, MC Solaar and, though I always loved their flow and their beats, it wasn't until visiting Marseille that I truly understood that their style was powered by a unique and very specific culture. With their appropriation of Egyptian mythology (all but one of the crew are named after pharaohs – Akhenaten, Kheops, Imhotep and Kephren – a spin on Khafra – with ancient Egyptian symbology and lyrical punchlines frequently found in their work), I presumed they were merely mimicking the way the Wu-Tang Clan used ancient Chinese culture and kung fu movies as inspiration and escapism. Not only do IAM pre-date the Wu-Tang Clan by a couple of years, but North African history and mythology is an obvious choice for kids responding to Marseille's cultural heritage and rebelling against heroes of French imperialism by asserting Arab and Nubian culture into mainstream French discourse using complex rhyme schemes in the French language. While the members of IAM have heritage from Italy, Réunion, Spain and Algeria, they carry similar intentions as Jacques Audiard, who made the acclaimed film *A Prophet*, partly set in Marseille, about a young, scared, naive Arab kid who gradually becomes an underground kingpin to create that rare thing: an empowering Arabic icon and anti-hero in popular culture, producing liberating revenge fantasies for working-class Arabs in the way that Jacques Mesrine, Michael Corleone and John Wayne have done for working-class whites. It all follows in the tradition of Marseille's self-mythologizing as a place of rebellion, as a way to both stand up for its maligned culture and keep rampant Western capitalism at arm's length.

Yet there is a long history of tolerance for foreigners of any race, as long as they are willing to be guided by the culture of Marseille, like sail boats pushed along by the mistral wind that blows through the city and along its coastline. When you look at the way the urban sprawl has been built up organically by waves of new arrivals and undesirables from all over the world since Phocaean sailors set up base here in 600BCE, often arriving broke at the port and never quite making the twenty-minute walk up to the train station to find anywhere else to live, you see that multiculturalism is embedded in the fabric of almost every arrondissement, and especially in the city centre. From the first night I laid my head down in Marseille, I was completely intoxicated.

I awoke to a scene of citrus colours on a sunny morning at the Hello Hostel as shafts of light lit up the bright yellow walls and green plastic plates of the kitchen, making everything appear luminous and jolly. I was feeling refreshed and rejuvenated by now, with days' worth of French breakfasts comprising simple but delicious luxuries for a traveller: a third of a freshly baked baguette from the local bakery, a croissant still soft and warm from the oven, freshly squeezed orange juice, a ripe and refrigerated piece of seasonal fruit – a pear or a kiwi – and proper coffee from an Italian stove-top espresso maker. It had been an odd, chilly journey to get here, which had often meant wet clothes, loneliness, instant coffee, worry and work, and when, on the rare occasion the golden tryptic of a day of good meals, a walk in a vast area of nature – in the woods, by the sea, through a park – and a sound night's sleep came together, I realized that that was all I ever really needed for some emotional stability. Marseille had all three. It had cheered me up and given me warmth and a groove. It also gave me an Egyptian nomad called Ibrahim Awad Mohammad.

The hostel was more trendy apartment than hostel, and coming from the urban-chic lounge was an animated voice that was part American, part Middle Eastern. It belonged to a middle-aged black man with long, mottled dreads the colour of charcoal and ash and a beard so long that it, too, had turned into long dreads, hanging from his face like stalactites. He had a comical physicality that reminded me of the high-brow clown Avner Eisenberg who played Al-Juhara in *The Jewel of the Nile*, and wore an old peach-coloured T-shirt tucked into cargo trousers that were so high around his paunch the belt must have been above his navel. When he spoke it was with his arms and his body, and the words that came out of his mouth sounded almost as if they had been scripted, as though he'd held an audience with this exact performance and these same words many times before.

Today's audience consisted of disparate groups of young Americans: three Chinese-American women, a young, earnest white couple, two bitchy, tech-obsessed young men on their gap year and me, a US citizen who'd never lived in America. He said, flailing his arms into the air, 'I call it United Sheeps of America, because Americans really are like sheep! They just go with whatever the president says, nobody thinks for themselves – that's why America has such big problems.' I nearly protested and then saw that all seven of the Americans around me were smiling and nodding in approval. It was something to do with his delivery, authoritative but jovial – you couldn't help but listen to and like him. When he noticed me, he said, 'Hello, what's your name?' I told him and he said, 'I am Ibrahim, please, John, take a seat,' and then he carried on controlling the centre of the room like an eccentric professor, though I had arrived at the end of his lecture, and after he'd finished chastising the Americans I half expected him to get a round of applause, as three of the group gathered round and asked to take a selfie with him. After the photographs he grabbed a seat, sat by me and said, on the breath of a sigh, 'Americans have a good heart but they don't use their minds.'

Ibrahim knew that he was interesting, and to save people time he'd obviously become his own biographer and gave me very precise details about who he was and the life he'd led. He was just passing through Marseille; he liked the city – it served as an entrance to the rest of the world, he said.

'I am born and raised on the Mediterranean so, for me, this feels like home. It's not so different to where I am from.' Ibrahim was born in Alexandria in Egypt on 22 November 1952, but with heritage from the south of Egypt, ancient Nubia, which accounted for his dark, elegant, almost Eritrean features, and what he said reminded me that Mediterranean culture was more than Italian spaghetti and Greek salads and also included Egypt, Morocco, Algeria, Croatia, Syria, Albania, Bosnia, Israel and Slovenia, linked by the ancient Phoenician travellers, influenced by the Ottoman, Egyptian and Roman empires, serving as a cultural link between Asia, Africa and Europe. If you take the inland cities of countries that have Mediterranean coasts, you find vast differences – Cairo could never be mistaken for Paris – but the cities of these disparate countries actually on the Mediterranean have a certain bond, the 3,000-kilometres coastline linked by ancient cultures and superstitions, evil-eye charms and Tarot cards, a shared cuisine and a history way deeper than what most people mean when they speak of 'a Mediterranean lifestyle'. It had been cultivated by curly-haired sun-people whose sense of expression came in on the winds of the sirocco, the levante, the ostro, the libeccio or, in the case of Marseille, the mistral. It was one of the things I loved about Marseille: its geographic location in Europe but its intrinsic connection to other cultures.

Ibrahim used Mediterranean gestures when he told me his incredible life story, leaning forward, raising his shoulders with his palms open when he wanted to make a point. He'd left Alexandria in 1975 at the age of twenty-two and hadn't stopped travelling since. You know someone has really travelled when they find it easier to tell you where they haven't been. Ibrahim had been to every country in Europe apart from Greenland, Iceland and Ireland, has visited all fifty states of the US, the Commonwealth of Puerto Rico and St Thomas and St John in the Virgin Islands. He'd been to all ten provinces in Canada, and the Yukon Territory, the Dominican Republic, all over Mexico and to every country in Central America apart from Belize, every country in South America except the Falkland Islands, to Guyana, Suriname and Paraguay. He'd backpacked across Asia: Thailand, Malaysia, Singapore, Indonesia, Cambodia, China, Macau, Hong Kong, Vietnam and Laos, and in the Indian subcontinent, through Nepal and India. He'd just arrived by boat from Tunisia the day before I met him and was moving on to Barcelona, along the coast, next, saying, 'I wanted to stay in Tunisia longer, but my stomach couldn't handle it. Every night I was bent double and having to go to the toilet every five minutes. Tunisia grows great fruit but sells all its best stuff to Italy and keeps all the shit for themselves – there is a big problem with food poisoning,' and I thought of Saleh in Stockholm: 'Tunisia is where Europe gets all its best fruit.'

Ibrahim was the ultimate nomad, travelling for fun and out of inquisitiveness, and it had made him see himself and his heritage beyond the confines of a category. He was critical of North African governments, atheist despite his despairing Muslim family back home and, when he asked what I was doing in Marseille and I told him that it involved some research about black Europeans, he said, 'Why? We are all the same! If there is one thing I have learned on my travels it is that human beings are human beings – you know, Africans enslaved Africans long before the trans-Atlantic slave trade. The same with Egypt – all around North Africa they call me "Nubian", and not in a kind way. I have faced as much discrimination in Africa as anywhere else. As soon as an Arab sees me and looks at my dark skin, he looks down his nose at me until I speak, and they can tell that I'm from Egypt, then they are all "Brother, brother". It is all economic. Humans enjoy killing humans and, as soon as they have power, they exploit it, no matter what colour they are.' He wasn't theorizing or historicizing, he was speaking of his lived experience as a black traveller, moving not out of forced immigration or economic necessity but to assert his freedom outside nations and other constructs. During my five-month trip I had met only a handful of fellow black backpackers, and Ibrahim was the only one I met who had been born and raised in Africa, and to see the world through his eyes was liberating. He'd travelled with many of the same issues I had to travel with and had freed himself from many of them because he wasn't invested in the idea of home like I was; if Europe imploded, his life, which he carried in a single backpack, wouldn't. I wanted to know if he had any tips for me, one black backpacker to another.

'No tips! That's my tip. I personally am not bothered about seeing any sites, I just like to hang out and drink my coffee and see how the real people live. I'm an adventure seeker and I go wherever, whenever I feel like it. I have absolute freedom, nothing to tie me down or rush me along, no rules. I am simply looking for the most complete experience of the world.' He quoted a saying that I knew he'd stolen from Paul Theroux (or, who knows, maybe Theroux stole it from Ibrahim) – 'Tourists don't know where they've been, travellers don't know where they're going' – and then said, 'Although I know where I am going now: to the toilet!' I asked Ibrahim if we could meet up later – I had many more questions – curious about whether he had any children, which surely were a part of having 'the most complete experience of the world'. I also wondered how he had funded forty years of carefree travel, but when I tried to pin him down to a time he responded with a non-committal 'Let's see.'

Thankfully, I saw Ibrahim again that same evening on the hostel computer. He'd just managed to find a cheap way to get to Barcelona by bus, a journey that took eighteen hours and cost only five euros. Seeing me looking on, he said, 'People see me travelling the world and say, "He must be rich," but I say, "No, not rich, just organized!" ' and it turned out that him saying he didn't have any tips was merely a way of being contrarian and pithy, because over the years he had developed an ingeniously thrifty system of survival, albeit one that was not for the faint-hearted.

'I will pay for absolutely anything if it is good, especially food and travel, but I can't stand paying for accommodation. It is very rare that you will catch me in a hostel like this. I'm here only because I needed it after my experience in Tunisia. I prefer to sleep outside, and it's so easy when you're in a warm country, which I usually am all year because I follow the sun.' Over forty years of travel he had developed an international network of old friends which meant that he was never too far away from a warm bed if he was desperate, but he said he rarely took up the opportunity because he hated small talk and the feeling of being indebted to someone, and I started to think that part of his nomadism was because he had chronic commitment issues. For someone who had essentially slept rough for the last four decades he looked remarkably healthy, his clothing was well worn but bright and clean and he looked nourished and in fairly good shape for a man in his sixties. How did he manage it?

'For a start, I don't drink or do drugs. I have no vices. In Amsterdam, people asked me if I paid to be with a woman and I say, "No! I just do window-shopping." If I know I'm going to stay around for a while I will join a local fitness club – I pay thirty euros or dollars for a month, and for that I can work out if I want to, but more importantly I get somewhere to go where I can have free coffee every day, filtered water, newspapers, magazines – I can usually tell you all about what's in the latest issue of *Vogue*! I also use their showers and rest on their sofas. I spend a lot of time in public libraries and universities too – at a lot of the unis in the States you can use facilities no problem. And airports – they are the best places to sleep!'

I still wondered how he managed to fund the trip to the airport, or find the thirty euros for the gym, and Ibrahim told me that sometimes, especially somewhere like America, which he found particularly expensive, he'd had to work, and when I asked what this work was, he said, without sorrow or boastfulness, 'I beg! Sometimes I can make two or three hundred dollars a day. I had a real job once, at Lipton Tea, was a good worker and they offered me a promotion, but people are so small-minded – they got jealous of me and I decided to move on. Some people had been working there for years, it was their life, but I have to say I think they are insane for working a nine-to-five job. I have one life and it will be a life lived free of shackles at all costs – that's why I have never and will never have a wife or children – too much responsibility, and the world is over-populated anyway.' Possibly because of his obsession with remaining unencumbered, Ibrahim also said that he thought nationality and religion were the two most stupid ideas ever invented.

'Even though I find religion mumbo-jumbo, I will wander the world freely as a humanist and, regardless of anyone's beliefs, I will call them my brother and sister, and if they don't like me, well, I will just move on and never look behind. If they do like me, I will add them on Facebook!' After wishing him *bon voyage* before he set off to Barcelona I added him on Facebook and over the next few months enjoyed seeing him post photographs from all over the world, from Walnut Creek in California to Chernivsti in Ukraine, and always with a smile on his face, surrounded by young back-packers with their arms around him.

Walking along the Vieux Port, I imagined that many of the people around me were sort of cultural nomads who had washed up at these shores and ended up under the sun, by the port, drunk or stoned, broke but well fed, with good friends, contented in a blasé sort of way, looking at the past, saying, *C'est la vie*, or the future, thinking, *Insha'Allah*. Children were loud and unruly as they ran around semi-derelict playgrounds with the odd bit of smashed bottle here, some dog dirt there, perhaps a loitering drunkard, but they looked to me to have grown up happy and streetwise under marine light, by the beach, with friends of many colours, looking more *vivant* than vitamin-D-deprived London or Parisian kids with overstressed parents. They were also 'raised by the city', to paraphrase the old African proverb; the community, not just the parents, raised Marseille's kids. Life here was

communal, underachieving, unfashionable and present. I noticed
that few people walked around staring into their phones; they were
too busy arguing on street corners, bantering in cafés, playing
football in pedestrianized squares, swimming in the sea, lazing on
the beach, and in that way the entire city was a throwback. Without the odd tell-tale clue, most of my photographs of it could have
been taken any time in the last thirty years, or perhaps even further back.

Flanking the north side of the Vieux Port is a tiny opening linking the port to Le Panier, the old town, called passage de Claude

McKay, after the Jamaican poet who summed up this mood of Marseille most vividly in his 1929 novel *Banjo*. I spent my evenings reading it at the Bellevue bar overlooking the port to the background lilt of a live reggae band, and it struck me that not much had changed in the last hundred years. Lincoln Agrippa Daily, the novel's protagonist, is an African-American sailor who arrives at the port of Marseille broke with a banjo and, describing the main character, Claude McKay might have been talking about Ibrahim Mohammad: 'Banjo was a great vagabond of lowly life . . . his life was a dream of vagabondage that he was perpetually pursuing and realizing in odd ways, always incomplete but never unsatisfactory . . . Banjo had no plan, no set purpose, no single object in coming to Marseille.'[1] Of another character, McKay wrote:

> The sentiment of patriotism . . . to him . . . was a poisonous seed that had, of course, been planted in his child's mind, but happily, not having any traditional soil to nourish it, it had died out with other weeds of the curricula of education in the light of mature thought. It seemed a most unnatural thing to him for a man to love a nation, a swarming hive of human beings bartering, competing, exploiting, lying, cheating, battling, suppressing and killing among themselves; possessing, too, the faculty to organize their villainous rivalries into a monstrous system for plundering weaker peoples.[2]

Banjo falls in with a motley group of 'beach boys', black vagabonds from all over the African diaspora who found themselves, for one reason or another, at the shores of the old port, working odd jobs, playing music, chatting up equally disreputable women and generally living life as it came to them. Among these beach boys is Malty Avis, the good-natured West Indian ringleader; Ginger, a 'chestnut-skinned' hippy; Dengrel, a somewhat eccentric Senegalese man estranged from his own Senegalese community; Ray, a Tolstoy-admiring intellectual and writer in the making from Haiti (a character who appeared in McKay's first novel, *Home to Harlem*);

Taloufa, a Nigerian 'race-man' (political, a Garveyist) by way of Cardiff; Bugsy, a cynical, dry-humoured bruiser always ready for a fight, verbal or physical; and Latnah, an Arabic lady of the night handy with a switchblade, generous with her cooking, her francs and her body. This 'picturesque black rabble', as McKay calls them, spend their days swimming in their underwear and their evenings in the seedy bars of 'the ditch', a small area between the port and the old town, getting into arguments with haughty 'mulatto' sea-men, or fist fights with Italians, begging and busking, then spending all their money on copious amounts of cheap wine. Not only did McKay paint an extraordinary portrait of immigrant life in 20s Marseille, but he subtly extolled the virtues of Pan-Africanism and socialism; a new arrival – a mixed-race sailor – enters the port and looks down upon Banjo and his friends, saying they are an embarrassment to the black race and, attempting to go it alone, quickly falls foul of the Marseille underground, getting swindled of his cash and thrown into jail by the corrupt police force.

For those who found their place and engaged with the life of the city, Marseille at that time was a thrilling and thriving hub of activity, if we're to believe McKay:

> They were all on the beach and there were many others beside them – white men, brown men, black men. Finns, Poles, Italians, Slavs, Maltese, Indians, Negroids, African Negroes, West African Negroes, deportees from America for violation of the United States immigration laws afraid and ashamed to go back to their own lands, all dumped down in the great Provençal port, bumming a day's work, a meal, a drink, existing hand to mouth, anyhow any way, between box car, tramp ship, bistro and bordel.[3]

The port today is home to newer waves of immigrants – Romanians and, certainly, Algerians displaced by the Algerian War – while others have moved on, and the Vieux Port is no longer industrial, as it once was. The working docks have given way to consumerism and shifted further along the coast towards L'Estaque, but I saw the general mood of McKay's Marseille everywhere. He describes how 'Squabbling and scuffling came natural to them, like eating and drinking, and bandying, and did not have any bad effect upon the general spirit of their comradeship,'⁴ and that was the same in Marseille now. During my time there I'd often see huge road-rage rows, which sometimes even got physical, and it almost always ended in a shaking of the hand and some sort of good-humoured banter. Once, in the North African market hub Noailles, after catching a heady whiff of apples and incense and seeing men bathed in the red light and smoke clouds of a shisha bar, I took some photographs and was spotted by an Algerian man who rushed out and followed me down the street, shouting. He had the almost military-style haircut of many Algerian men, cropped severely on the sides with a little tuft on the top of his head, and wore tracksuit trousers so slim fitting they looked almost like leggings, which was another Arab-Marseillean fashion state- ment and again somehow contributed to an overall look that was brutal. 'You 'ave problem whiz me?' he shouted, in a vicious but complementary mix of Arabic and French twangs. 'No problem,' I said, and then he asked why I had taken a picture of him. I pro- duced my old BBC pass and told him I was working on a piece celebrating the true culture of Marseille and, after examining it carefully, his aggressive frown turned into a big smile. 'Aaah, BBC? I am sorry, I thinking you 'ave problem . . . maybe police?' He laughed and put his arm around me 'Please, you are welcome. Come make photos as you want . . .'

Marseille is a place that needs to be charmed, takes some warming up, but when locals and shop owners who were once frosty get to know you they frequently throw in a few freebies with your *pain quotidien*, the city rewards you for trying to take part and kicks you in the *cul* if you don't make an effort. Though Marseille does have its secrets, layered as it is with long, deep histories and corruption – members of Mafia in council seats, an underground economy and trafficking of all kinds – you don't need money or social capital to fit in in Marseille, you just need to be up for a chat and a pastis every now and then. Despite gaining billions of euros' worth of investment in 2013, when it was the European City of Culture, you get the sense that Marseille is still a city of modest aspirations. It is certainly still poor; a quarter of the population lives below the poverty line and, though it is France's second-largest city, unemployment is higher than the national average. The city stretching out from the south of Le Panier, the warren-ridden old town, is whiter and wealthier than the north, but the way communities sit side by side would still feel familiar to McKay's Banjo.

Following in the footsteps of Mark Twain, who visited Marseille in *The Innocents Abroad*, writer Irma Kurtz noticed that 'Nationalism is second to community and neighbourhoods persist. Someone said "oh it's not really a melting pot because you can see all the groups are distinct, the Italian group is distinct, the North African group is distinct," but that *is* a melting pot. It's [just that] the ingredients haven't broken down yet, they're still bobbing around in the heat . . .' I might go so far as saying the better metaphor for Marseille, then, is not a melting pot but a transcultural tagine, the separate ingredients having soaked up the same North African spices, sitting under the same roof.

Like many writers and artists over the years, Kurtz also said that Marseille reminded her of New York in the old days, in the way that New York was American but not America; so, too, she thought, was Marseille French but not France – and in that way it was the perfect setting for Claude McKay, a writer connected to the Harlem Renaissance. While Marseille had a similar energy and ethnic composition to Harlem, for McKay it was also a way of distancing himself from the constant pressure to 'uplift' the Negro race in a capitalist society. Marseille offered a possibility to suggest the virtues of black socialism in a peripheral setting where characters weren't reduced to avatars for it.

Though there was, ultimately, a mutual respect between the two writers, W. E. B. Du Bois frequently turned his nose up at McKay's work, once saying, of an earlier novel, that 'every art and emphasis paint drunkenness, fighting, lascivious sexual promiscuity and utter absence of restraint in as bold and as bright colours as he can'.[5] These things are certainly prevalent in *Banjo*. A huge concern for some black intellectuals at the time of the Harlem Renaissance was to distance themselves from the savage stereotypes often forced upon them by a society still coming to terms with the legacy of slavery. I see McKay's novels as a celebration of the quest for an authentic lifestyle against a backdrop of racism and discrimination – they were hip-hop before hip-hop – black culture creation despite limited opportunities, refocusing on the modest inner hopes and social lives of black men and women rather than allowing them to be defined merely by heroic moralism or their reaction to racism. A celebration of the beauty that emerges out of the slums of oppression or, to use an analogy that frequently appears in the African-American tradition, from Ben E. King's 'Spanish Harlem' through Tupac Shakur's poetry and Aretha Franklin's collaboration with Lauryn Hill; the appreciation and celebration of the beauty of a rose that, though dirty and dishevelled, manages to somehow bloom through a crack in the sidewalk. Black power and beauty from the street up. In a stinging reply to W. E. B. Du Bois, Claude McKay defended himself against the former's criticism with:

> Nowhere in your writings do you reveal any comprehension of esthetics and therefore you are not competent nor qualified to pass judgment upon any work of art ... You have been forced from a normal career to enter a special field of racial propaganda and, honorable though that field may be, it has precluded you from contact with real life. Therefore I should not be surprised when you mistake the art of life for nonsense and try to pass off propaganda as life in art![6]

This mirrored some of my feelings about the way black Europe has frequently been written about within the academy.

James Baldwin once said that, despite the poverty of Harlem, it was 'a life which had produced me and nourished me', and what Marseille and Harlem also had in common in terms of their nourishing capacity was summed up by another writer who spent her formative years as a New Yorker and could have been speaking about Marseille when she imagined what an ideal city might entail. In Jane Jacobs's *The Death and Life of Great American Cities* (1961), a classic in the subject of urban studies, she suggests that what makes a city successful is how it encourages a proximity of very different people, businesses and communities and binds them together in a way that casually enforces cultural exchanges, something London was once famous for. She believed that neighbourhoods should be a mix of new buildings to attract businesses and a certain amount of wealth, and old buildings which, carrying embodied energy and long since paid off, could offer lower rents to poorer tenants. Jacobs believed in the type of dense neighbourhoods that are all over Marseille, and especially in Le Panier, writing, 'The whole point is to make the streets more surprising, more compact, more variegated, and busier than before – not less so.'[7] This created what she termed 'social capital': 'respect in the deepest sense – strips of chaos that have a weird wisdom of their own not yet encompassed in our concept of urban order'.[8] The idea is that in small districts people can look out for each other and recognize when something isn't right, asking questions like 'Have you seen Mabel recently? Shall I pop round and check on her?' or 'I saw a strange man outside David's house, should I give him a call?' Such questions could easily turn into gossip in the monocultured countryside, but Marseille is a mid-sized city of about 800,000 citizens, a series of small villages that have over time been integrated into a dynamic whole, and it's very easy to live in Le Panier, socialize in St Victor or get away from it all by finding one of many beaches or calanques to escape to. Harlem had the compactness and the community, but America never had that sense of escape, which is probably why so many Harlem Renaissance writers, at the first opportunity, ended up decamping to France – a meeting place in the middle of a continent, and perhaps the most densely variegated country on Earth. Reading McKay in Marseille gave me a powerful sense of the virtues of a translocal movement. The people in Le Panier likely had much to talk about with those in Rinkeby and Clichy-sous-Bois, in Bed–Stuy and Peckham, in Dwarzak in Freetown and Rocinha in Rio. As I'd seen first hand it would be easier said than done, but thinking of it this way seemed to justify my journey and the shaping of it into the form of a book connecting the disparate people and locales of black Europe in a single narrative, allowing each area and community to 'speak' to one another on digestible terms.

Many of Jacobs's concerns when she wrote her seminal text were in response to postwar urban planning rooted in a functionalist modernist movement heavily inspired by Le Corbusier, whose *pièce de résistance* ironically sits in the south of Marseille. His building Cité Radieuse – or Unité d'habitation – is considered by many to be the most definitive building of the twentieth century and now houses an art gallery, a hotel and Jonathan Meades. When I wandered around I could see why it turned heads, full as it was of groundbreaking features, each flat having dual-aspect orientation and a sea view, due to a clever interconnected stacking system on each floor. A school is integrated into the building, as well as a 'high street' on the third floor lined with shops and boutiques, and a swimming pool and terrace on the roof. For all this, the corridors are long, silent, dark and impersonal, and standing on its roof or looking out of an apartment window, the stunning views of the Côte d'Azur offered are imbued with a subdued, antisocial and alienating atmosphere. It feels as if you're stranded at sea on a cruise liner.

As a tourist attraction (it was given UNESCO World Heritage status in 2016) and as an experiment in architecture, a beautiful one-off, it adds to the city of Marseille, but thank God it stopped with a single building. I saw the ultimate realization of Le Corbusier's vision when I visited an entire city he master-planned, Chandigarh in India's Punjab region, and the public squares were huge expanses of concrete, the boulevards wide and vast, built on a grid, each area given a bland, formal and monotonous name – Sector 17, Sector 22, and so on – and it completely sucked the famously colourful and communal Indian city life out of the atmosphere. What Marseille (and once Harlem) had in abundance was incident and atmosphere, allowing struggling creatives to connect with each other often, to offer each other a network of help, advice and support and, more than anything, a place where being poor and black didn't completely rule you out of taking part in city life.

Though Unité d'habitation is the only major work of Le Corbusier in Marseille, since its construction lesser buildings by lesser architects inspired by it have popped up in the north of the city and have now become some of Marseille's roughest estates, and the impersonal vastness has led not to creativity but to social unrest. One of the most notorious and massive of these estates is La Castellane, a place featured in the television series *Extreme World*, presented by British actor and TV presenter Ross Kemp, complete with dramatic music and moody cut-aways. One of the first things I did in Marseille was take a two-hour-long walk north along the coast to make a pilgrimage to La Castellane, partly to compare it to Clichy-sous-Bois in Paris – which had become a sort of measure against which I'd judge other areas of high immigration – and partly because it was the birthplace of perhaps the greatest footballer of all time, Zinédine Zidane, who once said, 'Every day I think about where I come from and I am still proud to be who I am: first, a Kabyle from La Castellane, then an Algerian from Marseille, and then a Frenchman.'[9] Wandering alone, wearing an Olympique de Marseille football shirt and with my Afro out, I walked into the giant fortress-like maze of La Castellane and was left alone, spotted some kids playing in a youth club, an old woman hanging out her rugs on a balcony, girls chatting and watching some boys play a lively game of football. I wasn't trying to buy or sell drugs, or a TV actor with a skinhead, body-guards and a film crew looking for drama, so I didn't get any, got bored and caught a bus back to my hostel.

On the way back to the Vieux Port I got chatting to the bus driver, Brian, who started speaking to me in good English when he heard my accent. Brian – who had been raised in Marseille and was of Algerian heritage – told me that he loved Marseille, even though he thought it was a crazy city. As he sped through the streets (the bus-driving in Marseille is as crazy as the city), he said, 'As a bus driver, sometimes you don't know who you're talking to, maybe some passengers have Mafia connections, maybe not. But if you are cool with people, they are cool with you. Marseille is a great place. I grew up just there, in the Quartier Nord, not far from La Castel-lane, and my father is my hero, because he always used to say to us kids since we were very young, "I know this is not a nice place for you to live, but I promise you that one day I am going to get you out of here." And he did, *al hamdallah*. He worked so hard for his family and he moved us to Cinq-Avenues, in the 6th arrondissement, near to Palais Longchamp, the most beautiful park in the city.' Brian's English was so good because he had done a lot of travelling, working as a rep all over the world, had spent a year living in Lon-don, then worked for six months at a resort in Montego Bay, another six months in Senegal, a big resort for French tourists, and in Bulgaria. He loved to travel but said that it had made him realize what he had on his doorstep, that the natural beauty in Marseille had not yet been beaten. His story reiterated to me again that, when a degree of upward social mobility is made possible for hard-working people like Brian's father, the next generation identify more with the place that has made it possible. I don't know how Brian's father did it, but so many second-generation kids saw their parents work all hours of the day, to the detriment of their chil-dren's interpersonal development, and then end up with nothing.

Marseille's chequered history of crime, socialism and immigration, its working-classness and industrial heritage reminded me of the specific multicultural area of Sheffield I grew up in, in the 80s and 90s, before it lost its identity to vapid capitalism – and I began to think of the city as Firth Park-on-the-sea. But unlike Firth Park, Marseille came with a history of literature and art (Dumas set one of his most famous novels, *The Count of Monte Cristo*, in Marseille), it was a place for writers and scholars and troublemakers who put the richness of casual conversations, poetic spaces and meetings with the muse before business and gated new builds.

Early in this book I mentioned how Alain de Botton spoke of status anxiety – and that discomfort can be endured when it isn't accompanied by humiliation. At the end of that book, the author proposes bohemian culture as a possible solution to status anxiety. Bohemians, de Botton says, shun fame and fortune and gaudy symbols of success (capitalism) and orientate their goals around art, community and craftsmanship: 'An insight of bohemians has been that our ability to maintain confidence in a way of life at odds with mainstream culture greatly depends on the value system operating in our immediate environment . . .'[10] De Botton shares a party invite drawn by the bohemian poet Brian Howard in 1929, the year McKay's *Banjo* was written. It has a list of likes and dislikes. The things disliked contain stuff like 'People who worry they can't meet so and so because they've got a bad reputation' and 'Public [private] Schools'. The 'likes' column includes jazz, the Mediterranean and Picasso, three things intimately connected to Marseille, and Marseille began to strike me as a sort of black Bohemia – a place that could sustain my Afropeanness over the long term. A place where I could be black and not worry about what car I drove or whether or not my trainers were fresh.

Picasso, who spent the latter part of his life living at various places in Provence and along the Riviera because of the perfect marine light and died half an hour away from Marseille, where his ashes were spread, once said, 'I want to live like a pauper with lots of money.'[11] I felt that you could live like that in Marseille. It had a bit of Harlem in the 20s, Sheffield in the 90s, splashes of Rio and Marrakech, with Arabic, Italian, Corsican, African and French culture intertwined in the lifestyle. I'd called it a mongrel, talked about the cacophony of its architectural styles, but that's not to say that Marseille isn't its own thing, coherent and distinct, and in that way I felt I'd found a physical embodiment of Afropea. It is a city of simple pleasures and one where young and old, rich and poor, black and white, Christian and Muslim – or what McKay summarized as 'colorful miscellany' – occupy the same beautiful old port and enjoy the same glorious sunsets and sweeping views of the basilica. Simple, yes, but wildly magical. Ibrahim Mohammad was living an authentic life that I found somewhat alluring, certainly more so than the nine-to-five life my mates from back home were living. His was a black freedom quite different to the unfreedom afforded in consumer society, which suggests liberty through the possession of objects and social status. Had I met him anywhere else, I might have entertained the idea of following in his footsteps for a bit, extending my travels and making the world my home for a year or two. But in Marseille I had found a place I could exist in Europe without any questions of belonging. I knew immediately that I'd found an Afropean Mecca that I would one day return to and make my home, in a bid to end up like one of the characters in Claude McKay's *Banjo*, Ginger, the 'chestnut-colored' seaman who, after losing all his money, settled in Marseille and 'remained on the beach to become a beach bum and a philosopher'.[12]

LISBON

The Night Train to Lisbon

I'd stayed longer in Marseille than scheduled, which meant having to breeze through Barcelona and whizz through Madrid, where I spent a single evening in Lavapiés before moving on to Portugal. This area, known for its ethnic diversity (32.5 per cent of the population are classed as 'foreigners' – more than double the Spanish capital's average), its creative community and sloping streets full of colourful stencils, had more CCTV cameras installed than anywhere else in Madrid. It was also currently under siege from a number of random police raids, nearly always directed towards people with brown skin.

The area had its issues, mostly petty offences such as pickpocketing, no more so than other poor areas of Madrid, but then this wasn't as much about crime as it was a sort of ethnic cleansing: the stringent initiatives had a not-so-hidden agenda to get rid of immigrants. There had been reports of police demanding ID from black men and women on their way to do grocery shopping, without any evidence that the person in question was about to commit a crime, and in some cases stories of people going out to buy some bread and simply disappearing, never to return. Two teenage African manteros – or street vendors – had been shot at and then beaten up when they ran away from officers for fear of deportation.

Like the stop-and-searches, the cameras, which were conspicuous and surrounded by spikes, were less about watching what was going on – such as the group of Bangladeshis having a lively game of cricket in a concrete square, or the crowds chatting outside a Senegalese restaurant called Baobab, or even the small unofficial Moroccan flea market selling second-hand clothes and desperately cheap obsolete technology – all the things I witnessed on my brief visit. They were more about making anybody who wasn't an official part of the Spanish discourse on identity feel uncomfortable and unwelcome. The area was following the usual pattern of gentrification: poor immigrants re-creating a bit of back home where they stood, usually in a downtrodden part of town, followed by open-minded creatives who found the layers of culture and low rents agreeable. This mix of culture and creativity was attractive to the more adventurous type of traveller, who brought with them disposable capital, which in turn created a tourist economy and a vested interest by the state, using the creative and multicultural heritage of Lavapiés to promote the area while systematically destroying what had really fuelled it. Pasted on the wall of a side street in Lavapiés was a manifesto written by a grassroots socialist organization called the Lavapiés Popular Assembly, set up to counteract this troubling trend in the area. A snippet read:

> Every day in our neighbourhood we see raids and racist police at checkpoints in which people are identified and detained simply because they are poor and have certain physical characteristics. We won't let the police run amok in our neighbourhoods nor sequester certain people based on the colour of their skin . . . The criminals aren't in the streets of our neighbourhoods, they don't carry blankets over their shoulders, they don't sell flowers, they aren't poor. The true criminals are in the offices of multinational corporations and in parliament. They suck poorer countries dry, leaving them bereft of resources, obliging people to come to our country to make a living . . . We, the workers of the world, know damn well who our enemies are and we are disposed to defend ourselves against them. We don't have arms, but we have our voices, mutual support and, if need be, our shoes.

This last comment alluded to an incident in which police, who had grabbed hold of a non-violent Senegalese man, were pelted with the footwear of Lavapiés locals of all ethnicities, and has since served as a symbol of unarmed resistance.

Had I read this impassioned manifesto at the beginning of my trip, it might have struck me as a tad naive, but now, as my travels were coming to an end, and having seen first hand how working-class solidarity might empower both black Europe and white, working-class Europe, I read the words with a new understanding. My dismissal of such ideas before was a product of the very fracture between the international and the working class. Being part of a generation that came of age after the fall of the USSR and the rampant capitalist dreams that infected working-class identity, from the ghetto-fabulous hue of hip-hop (get rich or die trying) to the introduction of the National Lottery (get rich without trying: 'It could be you!'), I'd been conditioned to believe that anything other than getting rich was of no value, taught that distancing myself from others in my class and my locality was the only sensible, viable option to lead a good, meaningful life. The mantra for this type of path is best summed up by the title of the hugely successful 00s self-help manual by hip-hop mogul Russell Simmons (complete with an introduction by Donald Trump): *Do You! 12 Laws to Access the Power in You to Achieve Happiness and Success.*

Now this manifesto – and Marxism in general – struck me as something that everyone who isn't in the top 2 per cent of income earners should re-evaluate – that old idea that if working classes of all cultures, currently so divided by political spin, came together, they could make their lives better and defend their local areas, not from immigration but from the kinds of grossly mismanaged global business that pits the poor against each other in order to compete for scraps. Lisbon would prove to be a valuable case study.

As the *Lusitania* train-hotel shuttled me out of Madrid and west through the Iberian peninsula, I read Pascal Mercier's *Night Train to Lisbon*, a book bought randomly on the day I set off from London. I'd lugged it around Europe for months, just to have the silly satisfaction of reading it on an actual night train to Lisbon, which I'd always planned to be the final train of my journey. The novel's title suggested a Hitchcock-style thriller was in store, but it turned out to be more Jean-Luc Godard, a thriller without thrills, moving along as slowly as my nine-hour train ride snaking up and through the dark, winding hills of Salamanca. Yet I found poetry in the sentences, which again jumped out of the pages in ways they wouldn't have five months earlier:

> Buried under all the mute experiences are those unseen ones that give our life its form, its colour, and its melody. Then, when we turn to these treasures, as archaeologists of the soul, we discover how confusing they are. The object of contemplation refuses to stand still, the words bounce off the experience and, in the end, pure contradictions stand on the paper. For a long time, I thought it was a defect, something to be overcome. Today I think it is different: that recognition of the confusion is the ideal path to understanding these intimate yet enigmatic experiences.[1]

The term 'Afropean' was my own object of contemplation, serving as a departure point of investigation and what I hoped would be my destination – a coherent, shared black European experience – but the black Europe I'd travelled through had refused to stand still, and I'd begun to think of the myriad experiences of black Europeans as the whole point; 'Afropean' was an opportunity to build bridges among various histories, cultures and people, but it certainly wasn't absolute or monolithic. In *Night Train to Lisbon*, the protagonist, Professor Gregorious, lives vicariously through the differing life experiences of a dead author, Amadeu de Prado. Where Gregorious is lonely, unassuming and studious, Prado's life was one of revolution and passionate love, and the two men connect across space and time through their human experiences, as Gregorious ponders, 'Was it possible that the best way to make sure of yourself was to know and understand someone else? Even someone whose life had been completely different and based on a different logic than your own?'[2]

This book within a book, the author tells us, was written in 1975, and is an account of life in Portugal under a very real Estado Novo government that eventually collapsed in 1974, four years after the death of its founder, a former university professor named António de Oliveira Salazar. Quietly spoken, meek in appearance, from a humble farming family but highly educated, Salazar wasn't your typical dictator, and his legacy is hugely divisive – some credit his leadership with keeping Portugal a politically stable place for decades, steering the country through the Great Depression and the Second World War (a political neutrality that kept Franco's Spain from siding with Nazi Germany). For many who lived through it, though, his tenure was marked by insularity, economic stagnation, fascism and ruthless autocracy, particularly towards Portugal's long-suffering African colonies in Mozambique, Angola, Cape Verde, São Tomé and Guinea-Bissau, places Salazar never set foot in, despite having had a stint as minister of the colonies before assuming power.

For a country with such a hugely rich, violent, influential history, Portugal flew under the radar for much of the twentieth century and so its colonial history hasn't entered the global imagination in the way French and British colonialism has, despite pre-dating and outliving both. As one of the oldest and most picturesque cities in Europe, the Portuguese capital, Lisbon, remains a somewhat mysterious place, hasn't been as vociferously committed to celluloid or the world's imagination as other big cities with less beauty and history. Most of the world's mainstream knowledge of Portuguese culture is second hand, tinged with African influence through Brazilian samba, football and carnivals, or Mozambican recipes (where peri-peri and the Nando's restaurant chain has roots), and the Portuguese accent most of us put on if we're giving it a go is also Brazilian; it can be quite a shock to hear *Portuguese* Portuguese, which sometimes sounds Eastern European in intonation to English ears and is rarely heard outside of Portugal. The author of a seminal though out-of-print book about the history of Portugal in the twentieth century, Tom Gallagher, described Salazar as a hermit leader attempting to keep Portugal a hermit country, something he largely succeeded in doing until his death in 1970. When once asked by a journalist why nothing ever seemed to happen in Portugal, Salazar was quoted as saying, 'Happy countries have no history,'[3] a telling reply that underpins why colonial history remains particularly elusive in Portuguese schools.

In truth, Salazar's answer disguised a kind of violent PR campaign monitored and maintained by a secret police (PIDE – Polícia Internacional de Defesa do Estado) legendary for its ruthlessness, using torture methods to gain information and detaining anyone merely *suspected* of dissent without having to bring charges against them. Another element of Salazar's PR campaign was imbuing in the collective Portuguese imagination of a certain generation the idea that its specific brand of colonialism was a condition under which black and white populations lived in harmony. It was based around a concept called Lusotropicalism developed by Brazilian sociologist Gilberto Freyre, which conveniently overlooked massacres and gross inequalities and highlighted Portugal's own mixed heritage, which has old roots in North African, Jewish and Iberian cultures. It suggested that the Portuguese had a unique skill in blending in with the tropics and pointed to the mestizos, a small middle-class mixed-race intelligentsia born of black and white parents (or sometimes the descendants of white Portuguese men who'd had their way with enslaved black women). His ideas were all the things those embracing the word 'Afropean' should be deeply wary of: a blindly optimistic branding of connectedness that suggests racism doesn't exist.

The reality of life under Portuguese colonialism for most black people was as miserable as life under any other European power.

With a provision known locally as Xibalo, African 'Indigena' (natives), who weren't granted full citizenship like their white counterparts, could be forced to work under the Portuguese or sent off to mine South African gold without pay, or pay so low that, once forced to pay taxes to the Portuguese state, they were essentially working for free, a dressed-up form of slavery endemic to Salazar's time in office. As Amílcar Cabral, the Guinea-Bissau liberation leader and intellectual who played a key role in the Portuguese colonial war and was later assassinated, once said, 'They made us leave history, our history, to follow them, right at the back, to follow the progress of their history.'[4]

Under the indigenous people's rule and Portugal's supposedly spectacular talent at mixing with Africans, a whole 1 per cent of the black and mixed-race population deemed 'European in character' were awarded honorary status and chosen as beneficiaries of Portugal's Lusotropical propaganda. The standards that had to be met, as quoted in a pamphlet published by the International Defence and Aid Fund just before the collapse of the Portuguese Empire, were:

- To be eighteen years of age and to be able to speak Portuguese
- To earn sufficient income for oneself and one's family
- To be of good character and possess those qualities necessary for the exercise of the public and private rights of a Portuguese citizen
- Not to have evaded military service or have been declared a deserter.

These were qualities many whites wouldn't have measured up to, judging by the rate of desertion from the Portuguese army, but were nearly impossible for a black African to achieve in a system geared endlessly towards their subjugation, even if they were of 'good character', a judgement open to racist subjectivity. However, a minuscule number of outliers – black men and women who managed, somehow, to miraculously navigate their way into such a position – were granted assimilation through further education, language instruction, courses in Christianity and, finally, full citizenship. Many were sent to largely white colonial schools before the heart of the colonial motherland beckoned with an opportunity to study at one of Lisbon's prestigious universities. Many of these African students, however, found themselves at the centre of a political maelstrom.

As the winds of African independence swept through the world in the postwar period, Portugal clung on to its colonies, with Amílcar Cabral astutely observing, 'If Portugal was economically advanced, if Portugal could be classified as a developed country, we would surely not be at war with Portugal today.'[5] There was indeed more colonial kickback from Salazar's Portugal than other European countries for that very reason. Like other Western powers, Portugal had vested economic interests in its territories – 25 per cent of Portugal's exports were from the colonies, which also contained a large captive market, as well as a vast store of minerals and raw materials, largely untapped by Estado Novo but embodying future collateral. The problem is that Salazar didn't have the infrastructure or economy to create the type of neocolonial dependencies or soft power relations of France or Britain who, though weakened by the Second World War, still had the economic power to ensure they took a behind-the-scenes role in the governance of their former overseas territories. Salazar's claustrophobic rule – one that portrayed itself as embodying the best of capitalism and communism but through gross inequality and crippling bureaucracy actually embodied the worst of both – resulted in the economic stagnation of the country, which meant that the end of Portuguese colonization would really mean the end.

During this period Portugal witnessed the greatest exodus of people in its history, but the exodus was shrouded in secrecy, enacted in the same fearful way as those fleeing the USSR or the GDR in the 70s and 80s. In *A Seventh Man*, John Berger's masterful, prescient collaboration with photographer Jean Mohr, originally published in 1975 and about the displacement of poor white migrant workers across Europe in the postwar years, there is a description of how treacherous leaving Portugal could be under Salazar:

> Until recently most emigration from Portugal was illegal. Both the Spanish and French frontiers had to be crossed clandestinely. Smugglers in Lisbon arranged such crossings. Their fee was $350 per person. Having paid this sum, many would-be migrants were cheated. They were led into the mountains just across the Spanish frontier and left there. Totally disorientated, some died of starvation and exposure: some found their way back $350 the poorer. ($350 at this time represented as much as a year's earnings for the average Portuguese peasant; in 1964 the average per capita income in Portugal – an average which included the incomes of the upper class – was $350.)[6]

There were even more eyes on the African students in Lisbon – their successful assimilation was key to proving the theories of Lusotropicalism and maintaining power over the African colonies. An increasingly paranoid Salazar deployed the Portuguese secret police to spy on and infiltrate the burgeoning underground student movements, and there was particular scrutiny of the activities of black students. It wasn't just the atmosphere of suspicion directed their way that led them to consider their position in Lisbon but also the growing feeling among these men and women – particularly those students who were signed up to the Portuguese army – that they would be sent to fight against the liberation movements growing out of their own home countries. Indeed, that was a very real possibility, considering young white men wanting to fight in the colonies continued to dwindle dramatically throughout the 60s and 70s. When the Angolan War of Independence kicked off in 1961 and between 20,000 and 30,000 Angolan civilians were massacred in that first year alone, followed by similar reports coming out of other Portuguese territories in Africa, the position of black students in Lisbon became morally and politically untenable. In the end, the catalyst for change in Portugal would not be in Lisbon but Luanda, Portuguese atrocities in Africa bringing international attention and changing the sentiment among ordinary Portuguese citizens, who'd started to perceive the war as something of an 'African Vietnam'. This resulted in a peaceful coup now known as the Carnation Revolution, in which Estado Novo was finally usurped.

One particular group of sixty African students studying in Lisbon played a major role in the liberation of Lusophone Africa and the downfall of Estado Novo. With the help of the Methodist Church, the World Council of Churches and Cimade, a French ecumenical organization with a track record of on-the-ground action (it had helped to smuggle Jewish children out of occupied Europe in the Second World War), they arranged a dramatic escape from Salazar's clutches and went on to change the course of African history. Hearing about the plight of Africans in Lisbon through church gatherings, international connections were made and Cimade put together a 'rescue team' led by a Frenchman called Jacques Beaumont, who'd worked as a message carrier for the French resistance, and Chuck Harper, an American member of the organization.

In order for the plan to work, the students had to travel separately to an agreed location in Porto, having been given elaborate details both strict and vague which couldn't be written down in case any of them were arrested and interrogated or tortured by the Portuguese secret police. Joaquim Chissano, who would go on to become the president of Mozambique, was one of those students who fled Lisbon and sums up the palpable atmosphere of fear and tension in his memoirs. Full of nerves and following the instructions, he took a street car, then a taxi, making sure he wasn't being tailed by the PIDE or any of the many informers operating at street level, then, after nearly missing a connection, travelled by train to a location specified by Cimade.

Chissano met a fellow African student on the way to Porto and, when they arrived, they were told by a stranger walking hurriedly past them to go to a specific place at a specific time to meet a driver who would then take them to another secret location. On the way, they convened with all the other students, who'd used various routes and methods to avoid the suspicion travelling as a group would have elicited, and together they headed off to meet up with a professional smuggler who, though usually a smuggler of coffee, not humans, would be waiting for them at the Spanish border. Even before the border crossing the students had to dodge patrol guards and wait in a shack until the early hours of the morning, and were then guided down a steep path in pitch-darkness to the water's edge and, four or five at a time and in complete silence, had to navigate the strong currents flowing through the narrow but treacherous River Minho. This was made all the more difficult because the boat that was used was leaking and slowly filling with water and, as quietly as possible, the students had to scoop out the contents with whatever they had on them, which wasn't much because they'd had to dispose of anything that could expose their true identity, including clothing with Portuguese labels. After making it on to the Spanish side of the river the students scrambled up another steep bank and spent eight hours cramped inside an abandoned barn that still stank of its previous occupants – sheep.

They had to navigate many close calls, crashing into ditches, being stopped by policemen, driving through the crowded streets of a carnival and, as they were in a car full of black men and women, had locals draw attention to them by shouting, 'Pele! Pele!' through the dusty windows. They hid in church houses, made their way past barking dogs as they trundled through tiny villages at dawn, sneaking past sleeping policemen. Perhaps the most hair-raising moment was when one of the cars was detained by Spanish police. The students were interrogated, their false passports revealed and connections to Cimade exposed – a major diplomatic incident was on the cards. The army deserters in the group could be shot, the French and American drivers tried as kidnappers, with everyone facing long stretches in prison, at the very least. Though they didn't know it then, Salazar had been alerted to the detainment and demanded the return of the students to Portugal, and among those members of the group who included this experience in their memoirs, there is still uncertainty as to why they weren't ultimately sent to Lisbon in an armed convoy. All that happened, in the end, was a couple of anxious nights spent in a Spanish prison, after which an officer, seemingly left-wing and perhaps sympathetic to African independence, gave the students a speech about international solidarity and, miraculously, let them go. The journey still wasn't quite over – the cars broke down after the heavy-handed usage, which forced the group to find a bus to hire. Pictures exist of this beaten-up bus standing in Galicia, skinny young black students who would become some of the most important thinkers and revolutionaries of African independence in Portuguese territories cramped inside, moonlighting as religious tourists making a pilgrimage to Spanish religious sites.

The bus travelled a further 1,300 kilometres through Spain from San Sebastián to Pontevedra until finally entering France and thus safety, thanks to those on it having been granted political asylum by Charles de Gaulle, who at that time was said to have been furious with Salazar for allowing mutineers in the Algerian War to take refuge in Portugal. In Paris the students lived in limbo-land for a little while, before some flitted once again, this time freely, under the influence of Kwame Nkrumah's Ghana, via East Germany, from where they were then flown to his newly independent country to get shown what African independence looked and felt like first hand. Some went on to train in guerrilla warfare in Algeria, others went to America on scholarships, while still more ended up in places as far flung as Czechoslovakia and China. A few of the students even went on to study in Moscow, at Patrice Lumumba University. This all hints that, beyond ambitions of self-governance, the students didn't all have a shared vision of Africa and were about to attempt to restore a continent that didn't itself have a shared vision of what it wanted to be, having been spliced by colonial powers along unnatural lines for decades or, in the case of much of Lusophone Africa, centuries, with old intertribal rivalries and grudges rising up from the past almost as soon as the colonial wars had been won.

The one thing that did connect the men and women on the bus fleeing Lisbon was the studiousness it took to achieve a place in Lisbon in the first place, and then the refusal to turn a blind eye to the plight of their countrymen for their own advancement. Their experience in Lisbon enabled collaboration across the Lusophone African diaspora, and a connection to the young white thinkers of the left, and all this produced a hotbed of talent. Many African leaders who managed to survive the FBI's hit list had to make hugely corrupt neo-colonial compromises with the West or, in their fending off of the West ended up mimicking the colonizers and becoming ruthless dictators. Angola, in particular, is currently rampant with corruption, its oil making billionaires out of Russians, Brits, Americans and elite Angolans while most of the country languishes in poverty. But that small group of students contained more than a few genuine success stories. Joaquim Chissano has since won the coveted Mo Ibrahim Prize for good governance, a prize awarded so far only to four men, for his role in bringing peace to Mozambique after decades of a violent civil war that succeeded the war of independence; and another of those sixty students who fled Lisbon, Pedro Pires, went on to become president of Cape Verde and also won the Mo Ibrahim Prize. Henrique 'Iko' Carreira was one of the students who spent the night in a Spanish jail and he later became a war hero in the Angolan civil war before serving as the country's defence secretary for five years. The students in the sixty who fled also included Pascoal Manuel Mocumbi, who became prime minister of Mozambique, Manuel Rodrigues Boal, who was the regional director for Africa in the UN's World Health Organization, José Eduardo Araujo, Cape

Verde's minister of justice, and many more who went on to senior positions in African governments.

Chissano told the *Guardian*:

> The suffering in the Portuguese colonies was untold. We had to learn many things from nothing. We were not allowed to conduct politics because there was a fascist regime that other countries' colonies did not have. They had colonialism but not fascism. Even the apartheid regime was less cruel in my view . . . so when we became leaders we had to liberate the people with the dignity we used to speak about.[7]

That group of students escaped Lisbon and altered the course of history in their homelands, but they also played a role in

changing the very fabric of the city they dramatically fled. When the train I was on pulled into Oriente station the next morning the sun was rising over the Portuguese capital, a new day spilling over the horizon and illuminating another patch of Earth I'd never seen before. I stepped off the train as the city woke up for a Monday back at work and saw how the commuters were as mixed as anywhere I'd been on my trip. If I was to fashion an average skin tone and hair type, it would have been my own. If there was anything to that concept of Lusotropicalism, it was being put to the test – albeit inversely – in real life, right now, in twenty-first-century Lisbon.

A European Favela

The well-thumbed, out-of-date Lonely Planet guide in the lounge of my Lisbon hostel as I waited to be checked in read:

> Imagine you are given a blank canvas to paint a city. First the backdrop: cobalt skies, seven hills (a different view for each day of the week), a blue splash for the river. Hmmm, now for the details: candy-bright houses, twisting alleys, grand plazas where locals relax in the sunshine . . . It's beautiful, but lacks icons, so you add a likeness of San Francisco's suspension bridge, swirly Manueline turrets, ivory-white domes and – as an afterthought – a Moorish castle on the hillside. Perfect. Now stand back and observe your masterpiece: Lisbon.

I wanted to add: . . . *of course, funding all this will be a problem, so let's have a splash of forced labour and begin a trans-Atlantic slave trade followed by and overlapping with centuries of ruthless colonialism. Oooh, and how about an unofficial favela-like settlement with its own underground economy, where we can shunt away the families and descendants of cheap Cape Verdean labourers?* Lisbon may be a masterpiece, but look closer at those broad brushstrokes and you'll find some troubling details.

After giving me the tour and handing over some locker keys, João, the hostel manager, who had studied sociology and personified many of the young, socially conscious Portuguese people I met, said, 'You're staying in our "Lagos" room! It's the Portuguese word for "lakes", but Nigeria's Lagos takes its name from a town of the same name . . . I'm glad that Nigeria is now the more famous namesake . . .' Portugal's Lagos is located on the lip of the Algarve and faces North-west Africa. It is where King John I of Portugal set sail from in 1415 to lay siege to the Moroccan city of Ceuta, a key battle that is considered by many to have kicked off Europe's age of exploration, marking the beginning of the globalized world as we know it and, ultimately, the trans-Atlantic slave trade. A square called Mercado de Escravos (Slave Market) in Portugal's Lagos became the gateway for the very first African slaves in Europe; there, they were bought and sold and dispersed around the continent. When he took control of the country Salazar was inheriting over 600 years' worth of Portuguese dominion and, as evidenced by Lisbon's medieval Moorish castle, the line between Africa and Europe had long been blurred in Iberia.

Lisbon pre-dates London, Paris and Rome and was the first and last capital of colonization, and I could feel Africa all over it. Towards Largo do São Domingos, Angolans and Cape Verdeans – each in their own groups and dressed in gleaming white cotton or vivid primary colours in patterns – debated intensely as Arabs roasted and sold old chestnuts, the leftovers of winter, and the ubiquitous Romany gypsies, dressed in rags and scarves, were, as was often true, begging. I was semi-outraged when I saw an old black man crouched over an ancient boot-polishing kit, cleaning a white businessman's shoes, but over the following couple of weeks I saw that this wasn't some gross old colonial power dynamic being enacted but came in various configurations; old white men cleaned black businessmen's shoes, too. Every day I'd pass the same homeless and comatose drunks lying under a sign that read, 'Lisboa, City of Tolerance' and, though the juxtaposition was amusing, on the surface, at least, there was a relaxed, multicultural atmosphere in the heart of a city that had the soul of a village.

One afternoon, on a climb up to the Moorish castle on the Costa do Castelo, I saw a group of black men charged with the tedious task of repairing the intricate mosaiced streets I'd been walking on and admiring all over the city since I'd arrived – made up of small pieces of stone around seven centimetres square. The men were shirtless and their graft and poverty had given them centrefold torsos: wide backs, six-packs, strong arms, lean muscle, dark skin shining with sweat under the sun. In another setting they might have had a crowd of admirers around them, but because it was menial work people strode by oblivious as the workers methodically and gruellingly set each small stone down individually by hand and hammer, with thousands more to do. It was easy to tune out of their toil. The city was the centrepiece, the stone buildings and winding staircases covered with graffiti in thoughtful colours, oranges, pinks, peaches and yellows that climbed winding staircases like colourful vines or Virginia creepers, matching the hues of local peach trees, small orange groves and the early blossom of spring, and the clothing lines of faded washing in pastel colours draped overhead. The religious iconography, the rosary beads and madonnas in windows and the potholed façades of cramped buildings and crumbling staircases made me feel like I'd stepped into a city of shabby chic, but I'd begun to mistrust its quaintness, which was being maintained today, as throughout history, by invisible people in invisible corners.

For all the talk about mixing and miscegenation, Portuguese culture had long had a way of keeping a white elite in luxury and shunting the poor to the sidelines in extreme ways.* *Favela* is a Portuguese word for a tree native to Brazil, and was given its current meaning when disenfranchised veterans on the losing side of the violent civil war of Canudos in the late nineteenth century were forced to construct homes that formed a desperate DIY settlement on a hill populated by the favela tree. To me, the favela signified a

---

* When I was at the 2014 World Cup in Brazil, the first time I'd ever been to the country, I'd been suckered by the type of Lusotropical PR the rest of the world receives – I was expecting a multicultural carnival but was sickened by the corruption and inequality I saw. I'd never experienced such segregation, and it was only when I bumped into some fellow Brits in Rio, who turned out to be Etonians, that I was exposed to a world of supreme wealth – private parties sponsored by luxury watch brands next to hugely impoverished favelas: completely different worlds separated by skin colour.

very specific Portuguese form of disenfranchisement: the careful framing of a picture, with denial about what lay beyond it, rural poverty without infrastructure, people disconnected from the life and economy of the city but also exploited by it for tourism and cheap labour. This wasn't just an issue with territories abroad that had Portuguese heritage, it had become an issue particular to Portugal itself. In the 60s, while the rich grew richer, poor white farmers and workers couldn't keep up with the rising rate of inflation and shanty towns known as *barraca* began popping up all around Lisbon, the economic heart of the country, and were riddled with the type of diseases usually only found in the developing world, like kwashiorkor and pellagra. These barracks still exist, though they now house a different demographic.

The first reasonably sized wave of Cape Verdeans came to Lisbon in the 40s, mostly as students. Some got their degrees and never went home, and their educated, middle-class offspring can be found taking an active role in the centre of Lisbon today. For a number of reasons, the biggest flow by far happened around the time of Cape Verdean independence in 1975. There were serious droughts in 1968 and 1973, as well as political instability as leaders tried to undo centuries of colonial oppression, and in the early handover of government a small window of opportunity appeared for those born or with a family member born or living in Portugal to obtain Portuguese citizenship. This didn't just provide access to a richer country but the possibility of access to the wider European labour market and later the EEC, an earlier incarnation of the EU, which Portugal officially became a part of in the mid-80s. The move also meant that Cape Verdeans who migrated would keep the state pensions and social benefits they had been paying into since the early 60s. This was a combination of push and pull factors created by colonialism – the push of political tumult and poverty in Africa, and the pull of a relatively thriving Europe that had built huge wealth to the detriment of Africa.

Then there was another factor: the thirteen-year war and the subsequent loss of its African possessions had been extremely costly for Portugal, and the country needed cheap labour, the type that could be found in the Cape Verdean countryside – unlike the mixed-race *miscagem* and the educated *assimilado* outliers, many of these immigrants were poor, illiterate and exploitable. They came over to Portugal to work in construction or as cleaners and found themselves in the paradoxical position of building a city that precluded them from having their own homes, so they salvaged building materials from the leftovers and waste of the sites they were working on and created unofficial settlements. These impoverished areas on the edge of Lisbon became places that cultivated the kind of safety, community and social capital Cape Verdeans had at home, things that could be leveraged against their situation as impoverished outsiders in a European society. That's how Cova da Moura, or, in English, 'the Moorish Pit' was born, a place constructed by poor Cape Verdeans on the outskirts of Lisbon in the 70s on vacant land that has, over the years, grown into a fully-fledged community and transitional space for Cape Verdeans moving into Lisbon.

I should mention at this point that some of my travels around the continent had involved a community that isn't entirely visible in my narrative. There are now over 10,000 people connected to the Afropean.com website that I set up to give and receive information about the Afropean experience. As I travelled, I knew no ambassadors, had no runners or fixers, no team of researchers, and the publishing deal came later, so a lot of my itinerary around Europe was fuelled by the collective knowledge of this exponentially growing online Afropean community, and the power of the group was invaluable in helping me get access to Cova da Moura. I put a call out and, lo and behold, somebody put me in touch with a friend of a friend who knew someone who might know someone.

That contact was Nino, and he arranged to meet me in downtown Lisbon, at Roccio Square. Via text, I'd told him what I was wearing and, eventually, in the distance I saw a tall, well-built man who had a particular Afro-Portuguese look about him walking towards me; distinct, but I'd have guessed Brazilian if I'd seen him on the streets of London. 'Shawnee?' he asked with a warm smile and a hand stretched out. He had a young man's face but a wise man's eyes, with deeply set crow's feet beside them, and in some ways he had the same aura as Saleh, the Tunisian bouncer I'd met in Stockholm – alpha, free of insecure posturing – and it was no wonder then that he, too, had in the past made a living as a bouncer. We got in his car, which showed signs of him being a committed family man – it was an unglamorous station wagon with children's toys on the back seat. He had two toddlers, he said, and apologized for the mess before breaking the ice: 'So, my big brother told me to look after you, and about Afropean – I like this idea. I have a strange story that is maybe a little different. My father, he is a white Mozambican, it is my mother who is black, so I am kind of torn. After the revolution and independence he was forced to leave a country that his family had been connected to for generations. One day they just said, "You must go home now, you must go back to where you came from," but Mozambique was the only home he'd ever known. He was forced to move to Portugal, a place he'd never even visited! I was born in Mozambique but moved here when I was a tiny baby.'

After a bitter fight for independence, years of further resistance surfaced in a newly decolonized country underneath which there was a power vacuum. An entirely new communist regime was put in place which immediately began asserting its authority and expelling white Portuguese citizens who sometimes became poverty-stricken refugees known as *retornados*; they comprised over a million people from the former Portuguese colonies.

'My father was forced to come to Lisbon, but he always says to me that Mozambique is in his veins – he doesn't like the culture or the weather in Portugal, he had a good life in Mozambique, fell in love there and started a new family. For him it will always be home.' Nino personified how complicated a modern-day Afropean identity could be, formed of the various ways European and African cultures had interconnected with each other through both negative and positive experiences. Would Nino's father lay claim to being Afropean? I wondered. He was, after all, born in Africa, married to a black woman and had produced brown-skinned children. He could certainly play a part in the production of knowledge under the Afropean banner, yet it was his son's blackness, not his whiteness, that had been otherized by this invention of races. He was born in Africa and doesn't feel at all connected to Europe, but because of his race he is considered more European by society than his son will ever be. The truth is that race is often forced to embody and speak for certain ideas, despite the fact it can't ever hold in both hands the full spectrum of a human life and the cultural nuances it creates.

I asked Nino where home was for him, and I have to confess that his answer contained a bit of a bombshell. 'I was only a baby when we left Mozambique, so of course it's Lisbon. That's why I think it will be so interesting to visit Cova da Moura – I have lived in Lisbon all my life yet I have never been!'

We fell silent for a minute or two and, as we neared the dusty outskirts of the city, where the pretty tiles and ancient fountains had given way to a high-rise bleakness outside the pages of Lonely Planet, I think Nino sensed the change in atmosphere, and said, 'I don't know Cova da Moura, but don't worry, we are meeting my friend who knows everyone from there – he will be able to take us in. His name is Jacaré, which in English means . . .' He couldn't remember the word: 'You know, the animal, the one with the big teeth?' Tiger? Shark? Crocodile? Alligator? 'Yes, yes, alligator.' He laughed loudly and said, 'It's funny. When I think about it, I don't even know his real name!'

We pulled up outside a huge tower block and parked next to the only life that seemed to be there: three young black men leaning against a railing. Nino pointed to one of the men and said triumphantly, 'There is our guide to Cova da Moura!' We got out of the car and Nino and Jacaré greeted each other like old friends, with big hugs and banter. Nino shook the hands of the other two guys, who he didn't know, and introduced me in Portuguese, as though he was a boxing announcer hyping me up to the audience: *Holding a professional record of seventeen wins, two losses and one draw . . .* I heard the words *jornalista* and *fotografo* in there, and shook everyone's hand, leaving Jacaré until last. He was about my height, with a similar build and complexion, but carried an edge in his eyes that I lacked, and he looked straight at me, weighing me up. Jacaré wasn't aggressive exactly, but he carried himself with a certain swagger, and though he smiled and teased everyone around him, when he looked into my eyes there was, at least on that first meeting, a deep suspicion of me. Just as the three of us got into the car, another man sneaked up to Jacaré and shouted, in English, 'Criminal!' and started laughing. The two men embraced and exchanged some words, and then Jacaré said he was ready to go, and I began wondering just who would be guiding us around Cova. Jacaré spoke no English, so Nino translated, in what I felt was a slightly guarded way. I asked how they knew each other. Jacaré laughed and talked in long sentences and big gestures, pointing to his friend. Nino edited and perhaps censored the translation: 'Haha, he is a joker. We know each other working for a nightclub, how you call it in English? We tell the people who can come in.'

The terraced roads disappeared and, instead of the usual hinterlands where the city becomes taller and greyer, after we passed a huge Ikea store the architecture shrank again, the tarmacked roads began to crumble and, within the space of a kilometre, I was in a landscape reminiscent of Rocinha, the famous Rio favela, but then it was also similar to a South African township. In essence, I had entered what has over the years been called everything from the Global South to the Third World – right there in Europe.

Because of the potholed road, Nino slowed down and we ambled into Cova da Moura, a low-rise sprawl of wrought-iron roofs and crumbling concrete covered in colourful and accomplished murals which suggested a truly global idea of blackness: images and quotes from Martin Luther King, Tupac Shakur, Nelson Mandela, Portuguese-Mozambican football hero Eusébio and Amílcar Cabral shared wall space. Despite knowing that Cova da Moura dated all the way back to the 70s, making it almost as old as Milton Keynes, I was still surprised at how established this *barraca* was. From a distance, it looked as though it would blow away in the breeze; close up, I saw that, while many buildings were just a few foundations away from being shacks, most were well built out of solid materials and had the feeling of permanency. Unlike the solemn tower blocks we passed, Cova da Moura was densely populated and I felt eyes firmly fixed on the back seat of the car, where I was sitting. Jacaré mentioned something to Nino, who then said to me, 'He say don't worry about the staring, when somebody who is new comes into town they know straight away, so they are just curious,' but I could see that Nino himself was a little on edge. Now not translating what Jacaré had said but speaking, I assumed, from his own experience as a doorman, he added, 'It will be fine because they can tell you're not Angolan – in Lisbon there are some problems between the Angolan and Cape Verdean guys. They don't like each other.'

When we pulled up and emerged out of the car this time, we were surrounded by life. Younger children looked happy and carefree, with little girls playing a skilful game of Double Dutch with a skipping rope and boys practising their football skills in the hopes of becoming the next Nani – the former Manchester United star is a local hero, born in a neighbouring town similar to Cova da Moura in Amadora which has since been demolished. Old men nattered in doorways and, outside on the street, elderly women cooked sizzling chorizo sausages on skillets over small, blackened home-made grills fashioned out of rusty gas canisters. A lilting guitar strummed inside one of the cracked and colourful stone huts, in which every window or door was filled with people hanging out washing or chatting from balconies to passers-by below, where noisy, stuttering motorbikes and scooters zoomed by.

Jacaré told me I could take photographs if I wanted and, though there were interesting images everywhere, the vibe in Cova da Moura was strange and unlike anything I'd experienced. The creolized Portuguese, the handmade side streets, the ominous messages I was getting from the glares of young men of a certain age, it was all a riddle to me and taking photographs felt awkward, as though I was on some sort of culture safari. When I mentioned this to Jacaré, he said, 'Please, is no problem! The thing is, people aren't used to outsiders. It's why police can never come here. There are many things happening that are considered illegal. But as you can see, it is like a big family, so nobody will talk, and everybody looks after each other – they have to, no one else will.'

Cova da Moura is, by its very existence, illegal, and at the time of writing is still not recognized as an official part of Lisbon. It was in some ways a place of what Doug Saunders in his excellent book *Arrival City* (2010), about immigrant enclaves on the edges of big cities, calls 'failed arrival':

> If left to its own devices, and deprived of access to the larger political system, the arrival city will generate a defensive politics of its own. In Brazil, it took the shape of the drug gang. In Mumbai, it is Hindu nationalism . . . The arrival city wants to be normal, wants to be included. If it is given the resources to do so, it will flourish; without them, it is likely to explode. The arrival city is not a static, fixed place. Rather, it is a dynamic location headed on a trajectory. It is within our power to decide where that trajectory leads.[1]

It would be unfair, though, to suggest that 'failed arrival' was the overwhelming mood of Cova da Moura, and I got the sense that, if given a hand, it could be somewhere that thrived, producing citizens that contributed to the masterpiece of Lisbon in a more meaningful way. I don't want to be romantic about life in Cova da

Moura, but it was certainly alive. When Nino translated what I said Jacaré looked at me with pride and replied, 'Believe me, they have made this a home over many years, when the government would have had them homeless. It was never a dream of people to live like this, but now a lot of the people you see here wouldn't leave even if they could. You will see, there are a lot of myths about this place, and a lot of spirit that doesn't get spoken about beyond the area.'

We walked past one of the old women cooking chorizos on a griddle crusted with bits of black gunk, and when she saw me looking she offered a big, toothless smile, sliced off a bit and handed some over on a fork. Any hesitancy about the cleanliness of the grill gave way to the fact that I knew these women had been feeding and nourishing the community this way for decades. I bit off a piece and burned the roof of my mouth, but then the meat and the spices melted on to my taste buds – I could have eaten a huge tub of it. Just then Nino said to me, 'Shawnee, look around you, what do you see?' In a reverie after the taste of the sausage and the friendliness of the old woman's gesture, I saw his question as a prompt to quantify my experience, so my answer was embarrassingly sentimental: 'I see community . . . I see Africa!' 'Yes, okay, but take another look.' What Nino was trying to get me to look at was something far more banal and so startlingly obvious both of us felt shocked we'd only just noticed it. The buildings were humble, the people obviously on the bread line and the roads barely roads at all, but lining each one, sitting among the poverty, were rows of new top-of-the-range cars; black-market BMWs, Hondas and VWs in gaudy colours gleaming under the low sun, cars that I certainly couldn't afford and which looked preposterous against the dishevelled but dignified backdrop. In Cova da Moura, where taxis don't enter and bus routes don't reach, the cars, regardless of what they were used for or how misguided the status they supposedly bestowed, struck me as an investment of pride, freedom and independence.

Jacaré got talking to a man I placed in his late teens, full of bravado, as men are at that age. He told him that I wanted to find out about Cova da Moura and after a lot of talking the message I got was 'Look around . . . you're okay, you're only visiting, but you're lucky you're not Angolan.' I wanted to know how everybody knew I wasn't Angolan and, thinking of those Angolan and Cape Verdean students who collaborated to escape Lisbon and aid in the liberation of Lusophone Africa, where this antagonism stemmed from. Jacaré looked me up and down and said, 'Don't worry, don't worry. If anything, you look more Cape Verde than Angolan . . . in Cape Verde you get strange mixes because it was a stop-off point on the way to South Africa, and all the sailors from all over the place used to mix with the locals, so sometimes you can get dark skin but with European features or African features with blue or green eyes, freckles and gold hair.'

I was led to a building that housed the Associção Cultural de Juventude, an award-winning community centre and organization originally set up by locals in the 80s, as a library for children and a centre for women's rights. Over the years it has produced a local gazette, secured funds for a dedicated building, which is perhaps the most impressive in Cova da Moura, founded a kindergarten for working parents, a citizens' advice bureau and a recording studio, and uses what it calls 'participatory citizenship' to improve and maintain sanitary infrastructure. It also offers literacy courses, had recently established official guided tours and was responsible for commissioning the enlightened graffiti I saw all over Cova da Moura which acts as positive affirmations – semiotics at their best. The quote under Amílcar Cabral's mural outside the building felt particularly resonant: *As crianças são as flores da nossas lutas e a razão do nosso combate* ('The children are the flowers of our struggles and the reason for our fight'). I spoke with Avelino, a long-time resident of Cova da Moura who was in his fifties and helping to run the association. When he saw Jacaré his reaction was the same as that of everyone who knew him – an exaggeratedly physical embrace, this time in the form of playful shadowboxing. Avelino had helped Jacaré turn his attentions from gangs to youth work as a young man, and he immediately struck me as the wise, calm voice of Cova da Moura in among the external scaremongering and the internal posturing of local gangs. I asked him why it wasn't safe for Angolans in Cova da Moura, and he said, 'That actually isn't true, and I can tell you that because my wife is Angolan and we live just over there, behind the association building. But I admit there are some issues.' The real problem, Avelino told me, dated back to the early twentieth century, when the German government briefly took control of Angola in a small war against Portugal for the territory to expand what was at the time German South West Africa. Even after the war, Germany maintained a friendly connection with the Angolans who'd allied with them to get rid of the Portuguese, and later supplied Angolan independence movements with weapons. Cape Verdeans, on the other hand, were always considered the jewel of Portugal's African colonies, especially under Salazar, and were used as a poster-country for Lusotropicalism. Because of this, it is said that Cape Verdeans traditionally and culturally consider themselves more Portuguese than other Africans.

The rivalry revealed how the lines could get blurred: you had Nino's father, who was white and felt Mozambican; and some of the older Cape Verdeans, who were black and felt Portuguese. I use the word 'black' even though I object to the idea of blackness as a 'race' in an absolute sense (for brevity, I also sometimes use 'mixed-race', but this, too, is problematic because it suggests that I am forged by two entirely independent 'pure' races rather than two vastly diverse and complex DNA journeys), but 'blackness' is a useful term to draw upon because of the excellence that has been produced under its artificial banner and to identify issues levelled historically at those considered 'black'. Still, it is important to remember that it is a construct and there are many hierarchies and much shadism within such a contentious notion. Salazar's preference for the Cape

Verdeans had made some members of the community haughtily think of themselves as superior, just as French preference for Martinicans did in France, and it made me angry to think that what often lay at the heart of this division – white colonial bias – was still making black communities harbour prejudices against one another.

After a tour around this impressive centre at the bluff of a hill, we looked out at some of the depressing tenement buildings, suspended in the hazy pollution of a dimming sky – they were the same ones we'd passed on the way to Cova da Moura. Avelino turned to me and lamented, 'Once, they were areas just like Cova da Moura, but now they've been demolished and replaced by these.' I asked if what Jacaré had told me was true, that, even if given the chance to live in a modern building, the inhabitants would want to stay where they were. 'When people first came here, they had no land, no money, no rights. So they tried their best to re-create the home they knew in Cape Verde – not because they didn't want to fit in with Lisbon, but because they couldn't.' He looked down at the lifeless concrete high-rises. 'If they razed Cova da Moura it would destroy our community, and that is what we have here, a real community, and the government can't afford to rehouse enough people anyway. Cova da Moura is here to stay. We can even receive post, but only by certain postmen, of course.'

When slums that have been organically grown by the community over time are destroyed, the natural logic of the place which has been nurtured for decades is also destroyed – the DIY system of networks, commerce, social spaces and what cartographers might call 'subaltern geospatial intelligence', the innate unofficial understanding of how to move through and thrive within a space built on years of local, home-grown knowledge. Surely there was a way to invest in these communities in a way that didn't crop them so severely. Avelino had mentioned that Cova da Moura's future was secure, but in a leaflet he handed me, published by the centre he worked for, I read a different story, and one in which the future didn't at all sound so certain:

The neighbourhood was constructed illegally in the late 1970s in the Lisbon Metropolitan Area. The houses were built by the people who still live here now. It is a place where a sense of a 'good proper way of life' is growing stronger and stronger, and the concurrent desire to combat the image of poverty, crime and social exclusion that have been associated with the area. At the same time, and because it is situated near Lisbon, the area has been coveted by real-estate speculation with real threat to the neighbourhood.

When you combine this information with a recent article entitled 'The Six Cities We Want to Move to in 2017' in the high-end men's fashion journal *Mr Porter*, the displacement of those living in Cova da Moura is a very real concern:

Cheap rents, solid tech infrastructure such as fast fibre broadband and healthy venture capital mean the City of Seven Hills is entering a new golden age . . . Labour costs are approximately a third lower than Berlin, which means startups can now be found in grand 16th-century palazzos that were built when Lisbon was the richest city on Earth, or in the vast industrial neighbourhoods along the Tagus River.[2]

That's what is happening all over the world, isn't it? An educated elite can work remotely from home or use Dad's capital to start up a business in a new territory, with a compliant government encouraging commerce and capital which only in small ways would benefit the local working classes, and in many ways would crush them.

In Cova da Moura there was a sense of community: people worked together, everybody knew everybody and looked out for each other in a way that was impossible in the high-rise outposts of other big cities. Jacaré led Nino and me down to a small café-cum-bar where a band was playing a subversive iteration of a traditional Cape Verdean music called coladeira. It sounded like

Afrobeat and morna music mixed with the blues, and the band playing was incredible; numerous people, young and old, male and female, were packed on to a small makeshift dance floor cleared of tables and chairs. The bar sold ice-cold bottles of beers for a euro and, when I tried to buy a round, Jacaré, who I could tell by now had warmed to me, motioned his thumb across his neck, and Nino said, 'You pay, you die!', a perfect threat to quell my bashfully British insistence, so I sat down and enjoyed the music while Nino and Jacaré supplied me with endless beers. The guitarist of the band was doing his best Jimi Hendrix impression, epic solos, playing behind his head and with his teeth, while some middle-aged men sat nonchalantly chatting and smoking at a nearby table. An old woman who looked in her seventies, was probably in her fifties but danced like she was in her twenties was doing all the traditional Cape Verdean dancehall moves that are usually done with a partner. Looking at her, and some of the older guys, I thought that among them were likely some of the very first settlers to Cova da Moura, setting up this arrival city from scratch as a gateway on the periphery of a big city, perhaps with the dream of one day making it as an official urbanite. That goal was unattainable for most, who could only hope to build a foundation for the next generation.

Jacaré reiterated something Almamy Kanouté had told me in Clichy-sous-Bois, at the beginning of my journey; that many young people grew up seeing their parents' best efforts go largely unrewarded. 'That is the problem. You grow up and your parents never have time for you because they are working so hard for the future, but that future doesn't come, they end up with nothing! The new generation see gangsters with flashy cars and it makes them think, *Fuck it; money is easier than integration!*'

When Avelino told me that most people wouldn't want to leave Cova da Moura even if they could, I'd imagined he was talking about the older people, but after what Jacaré had said I wondered if it was the younger generation whose identities are more deeply

woven into the social fabric of the area. Looking around at the faces of these older men and women, made wise by their tough lives, I couldn't exactly work out if I could see contentment or resignation in their eyes. They knew their place, who their friends were, what they might realistically expect from life, and now they sat around, sipped on beer and coffee, smoked their cigarettes and enjoyed the music that whisked them back to the island of their youth, probably the countryside surrounding Santiago, the capital, where I was told most of the residents had heritage.

As we watched the Cape Verdean Jimi Hendrix perform more acrobatics with his guitar, still with the old woman dancing, Nino turned and said, 'This is crazy. People in Lisbon never get to see this kind of thing from Cova da Moura. All you hear about is drugs, guns and violence.' Unfortunately, when we left the bar, tipsy and in good spirits, we were confronted with a wilderness outside that had earned the reputation Nino was talking about. Dusk was settling and the just-set sun made all the creamy, crumbling homes look a pale purple, and there was a kind of unpredictable crepuscular energy about the place, way more men on the streets. There were whispers in Creole, sudden movements, and when a kid drove past on a sort of mini-quad bike something spooked Jacaré and he stared at us with stern eyes. 'We shouldn't stay here. Things are gonna get a bit crazy now.' We didn't ask any questions but, when we were back in Nino's car, he said that somebody had a gun on them and that 'something big was about to go down'. As we snaked our way upwards through the dark blue, barely lit streets out of Cova da Moura a heavily armoured police van containing about twelve officers gingerly and quietly trundled by us in the opposite direction.

I'd been told that Cova da Moura was a no-go zone for police and, despite seeing that this obviously wasn't literally the case, I could tell by the expressions on the faces of the officers, who were dressed in riot gear and clinging to guns, that they weren't about to be welcomed. I caught the eye of one particular officer who couldn't have been more than about twenty-five, and he had a look of sheer terror in his eyes, and as the truck disappeared into Cova da Moura I almost pitied them, though the pity would have been misplaced – Cova da Moura has frequently been subject to brutal night-time police raids. As ENPAD, the European Network for People of African Descent reports, between 2000 and 2014, 'about 40 individuals were killed by policemen under nebulous circumstances and . . . a disproportionate number of those individuals (one third) were black youth; such as the 14-year-old Kuku and the 15-year-old Musso'.[3]

Shortly after leaving we drove past the huge Ikea department store I had seen on our arrival. Many people in the community told me a familiar story: when Cova da Moura is named as a place of residency on a job application, employers won't consider the applicant. But I'd heard that many people had found work at the Ikea here, and it was odd to think that a young man serving you Swedish meatballs or scanning your flatpack shelving unit would finish work, de-robe from his blue-and-yellow uniform and go back to living in what many Lisbon residents called a slum. It was indicative of a concealed narrative all over Europe: taxi-drivers, waitresses, shop assistants, cleaners and security guards were inhabiting the same spaces as consumers but living in an entirely different world most of those consumers don't have to think about. And that's what Cova da Moura was; a hidden world that forced you to question identity and the structures behind the grand visions of Lisbon. But this vision can't be upheld for ever. If the West continues to vilify or close its eyes to global poverty, gross inequality and the necessary environmental and economic migrations currently taking place, Cova da Moura is what most of Europe may look like soon enough.

An Afropean Odyssey

It was Carnival time across Portugal, which meant a series of epic parties over the best part of a month that only ended when people felt like it. But Carnival was a celebration of the passing of the seasons; the chill of Northern and Eastern Europe was already a distant memory, the spring equinox heralding the end of my trip.

The train out of Lisbon left at six in the morning, just before the weather took a turn for the worse. The April showers had arrived early and it rained ceaselessly for the rest of my trip. Watching the train cruise past cork trees hanging in the spring mist, I dozed off, and other than changing for a connection in Faro, pretty much slept until Seville, where I arrived at seven in the evening. From the comfort of my own home months earlier, with my feet up, probably, sitting by a burning radiator, I'd decided that the last two days of my Interrail pass would be sufficient to make it from Lisbon to Gibraltar, where I saw myself concluding my trip heroically at Europa Point, from which, on a clear day, it was possible to stare at the shores of Africa from the shores of Europe. In order to save time and money, I'd decided my future self wouldn't need anywhere to sleep in Seville. That I'd be fine hanging out in the streets until the first coach left for Algeciras the next morning, but of course I hadn't factored in any variables: the rain and fog which had hung over the passing landscape since Portugal, a hangover from the night before (I'd boarded my train straight from a final blow-out at a huge Afrobeat party), or the seedy Sevillians of the night. I wandered around the empty streets of this pretty Andalusian city, which looked as though it was floating among low-flying clouds and, beautiful as it was at that time of night, Seville was also surreal and unsettling. An aggressive, incoherent, drunken old Spanish man picked a fight with me, a middle-aged kerb-crawler mistook me for a male prostitute and tried to pick me up, and at about three in the morning I saw the diffuse red glow of some handbrake lights in the distance – a lone, gleaming white Porsche 911 was idling at a deserted intersection; the driver had fallen into a drunken stupor at the wheel, slumped forward from his leather sports seat, his window down and all the doors unlocked.

You're reading all this in the form of a neat little package, an edited book, probably with a fairly assured-looking author photograph of me on the back cover. But there and then in the early hours of the morning in San Sebastián station, and after five months of self-funded budget travel, my hair was starting to dread, my shoes were falling to bits, I'd begun talking to myself and some of my late-night travel notes were becoming increasingly oblique. As a solo traveller in search of black Europe I'd started to get used to strange places at strange times occupied by strange people because my search often led me to black people who were forced to work unsociable hours, or living out on the periphery, or forced into travelling on the cheap coach at stupid o'clock in the morning, regular men and women shunted by prejudice into the surreality of poverty, educated immigrants sharing work shifts and geographies with alcoholics, addicts and criminals. It has been reported that there are abnormally high mental-health issues among black communities in Europe, but my travels had been largely sustained by a very steadfast sanity which so many black men and women had managed to maintain despite often living under such bizarre conditions.

A Moroccan man called Abdel Wafi guided me to the correct bus stop, and by the time the bus arrived as the first hint of dawn tinged the morning I was the only non-Arab waiting to board. This wasn't a surprise. I was headed to that historic grey area between Europe and North Africa, the southernmost tip of the continent along a coastline with place names such as Algeciras, Cádiz, Tarifa, and, more specifically Jabal Ṭāriq, or, to use its Spanish derivative, Gibraltar. All these places were found in the area once known as the Islamic Iberia, now known collectively as Andalusia, from the Arabic Al-Andalus, land of the vandals.

The legendary Moroccan traveller Ibn Battuta, perhaps the most famous non-white travel writer in a genre saturated by white men, visited the area on his pilgrimage through the Muslim world when much of southern Spain was under Islamic control and, despite extensive journeys through Africa and Asia, including the Far East, Andalusia was the only area of Europe he ever set foot in. Battuta, who by this point had already travelled half the globe, making the Hajj at the age of twenty-one and not returning until nearly a quarter of a century later, was in his mid-forties – a man entering old age in the fourteenth century – and journeyed to Gibraltar with a bunch of volunteers to support the Islamic army as it fended off an attack from the Christian King Alfonso XI of Spain. We were thankfully spared a tale of military heroism or martyrdom because, by the time Battuta and his colleagues arrived on the shores of Gibraltar, the threat of an invasion had been killed off by a plague ravaging much of Spain. So instead we have something rarer and, I would argue, more valuable, an account of a North African *flâneur* and sightseer travelling for fun, knowledge and adventure. He described a Muslim European landscape of groundbreaking and intricate architecture based on mathematical theorems, of an intellectual, artsy and literate Islamic society whose knowledge and contributions to Spain for a period that lasted over 700 years have been systematically oppressed, with books destroyed in the hundreds of thousands when Islam was overthrown. It's a history that was later written out of European textbooks, the type that we take for granted. Books that, even if written as an objective piece of social science, were often the product of an individual, someone with hang-ups, with a certain past and probably a Western education, who sat down at his desk and wrote works with lofty titles such as 'The African Situation' or 'A Concise History of Europe'.

Ibn Battuta's account is priceless because it is a view of the world forged outside of the normalized narratives of Greece and Rome, which, as I'd seen at the Vatican City was the worldview most of us in the West (and, increasingly, outside the West) are powerfully exposed to most of the time. History, as they say, is only told by the victor, and if you look at any travel section of a bookshop you might add: *and the victor's descendants*. People who, to quote Henri Cordier in the introduction to Dunn's book 'wrote the history of their little world under the impression that they were writing *world* history [emphasis my own]'.[1]

The medieval Islamic world, seen through the eyes of one of its own intellectuals, was a cosmopolitan counterpoint to its depictions in the hands of others as a land of brutal Saracens, made compelling by the author's own right to snobbery, hyperbole and poetic licence, not mere anthropological study but offering subjective opinion from a rarer, more human position, all of Battuta's bitchy brags about having travelled more than such-and-such an Arab scholar proof of his humanity. He picked ripe oranges in Málaga, which was back then free of the remnants of Western civilization; used condoms scattered on beaches by young men and women having a last hoorah on hen and stag dos, commenting that 'it is one of the most beautiful capitals of al-andalus, and combines the advantages of inland and maritime cities. Its figs and almonds, its fine ceramics and gold porcelain, are exported to the furthest corners of east and west.' He bathed in hot springs in Alhama de Granada, feasted in the grounds of Islamic palaces and markets in the stunning Moorish city of Granada and collaborated with Muslim creatives and noblemen he met along the way. Battuta held Gibraltar as a sacred place in his heart because it provided an important military location for the Islamic world, swearing he'd guard and defend it until the end of his life. But Gibraltar, too, has changed.

Melvin Van Peebles once said, 'A bed's not much when you've got one, it's everything when you don't,' and after an evening without sleep, sitting at the back of the stuttering old bus to Algeciras that smelled of sick, in a seat with a half-licked lollipop stuck to it that I had to peel off and a bed of crumbs and wrappers covering the floor, I was so relieved to be warm, indoors and able to recline slightly that it felt like the lap of luxury. I drifted off immediately, waking intermittently, due to the seat coming loose from its hinges and sometimes jolting me towards the floor as the bus trundled and wound its way over and through the granite shadow of a storm cloud laid over the hills of Sierra de Grazalema like a translucent veil.

Algeciras finally appeared in the gloom like a typical North African town, populated by Africans, and considering how drab the weather was, it all struck me as strangely dynamic – men and women were going places, the ferry port was an exit and entrance point to and from Africa, people populated downtrodden internet

cafés to call home, or arrange and connect with contacts on the continent. I was disappointed to be only passing through, especially so when I finally arrived at Gibraltar, which I'd chosen over Algeciras as the end point of my trip. There was something perverse about having circumnavigated the continent to the south, only to end up back in the UK that I had liked when I was planning the trip, and being able to see the northernmost tip of Africa from it felt vaguely allegorical. I had exactly four hours to get there, see Africa and get out in order to be able to make all the train connections I needed to and get home using the last day of my Interrail pass, connections I couldn't afford to miss.

In Gibraltar I really was *back* in Britain, a pastiche seaside Britain of the 80s, mean-spirited and pissing it down, fish-and-chip shops with Union Jack flags set amid browny-grey postwar architecture, and unless a miracle happened, there was no way I was going to be able to see Africa in this weather.

Liberating some annoying sterling shrapnel I'd had jangling around with the euros in my wallet since leaving the UK, I bought two 'hopper' tickets for £2.40 from a bus driver who spoke the kind of Spanglish the British Gibraltarians had demanded of him, like something out of a racist 70s sitcom – 'Owight, mate, where we gah'in? Two ticket you like for you, yeah, mate?' – and caught a big daft red double-decker bus whose terminus on the front read 'Morrisons'. It took me along Winston Churchill Avenue, and I half expected to pass a statue of Margaret Thatcher made out of, I don't know, Branston Pickle jars and bottles of HP Brown Sauce, along with the red postboxes and the Angry Friar Pub.

I had to get off and make a change at a McDonald's, where I took refuge from the rain and ate a late lunch, and as I sat by the window eating a Filet O Fish and a hot apple pie, listening to GBC (Gibraltar's radio service, which basically seemed to be playing reruns from BBC Radio 2), looking at a view of a William Hill betting shop and a NatWest bank in the drizzle, I knew I was definitely back in Britain. I found all this mildly amusing because it was as though I was experiencing the final piss stain of a British Empire that had once ruled the world, and what Gibraltar reeked of was a nostalgic pathos Paul Gilroy calls 'postcolonial melancholia'. That's what all this silliness was; the sometimes overt, sometimes subconscious sadness of the death of empire and its perceived greatness, an obsession with Second World War-era Britain because it was the last 'good' thing to happen to the nation. In Britain, what people really meant when they said they wanted their country back was that they wanted other people's countries back, which was the lifeblood to making that other *Daily Mail* trope happen: making Britain *great* again. I have to admit, though, that as I handed in my British passport to enter all this, even I felt a vague and brief wave of reassurance wash over me, no matter how hard I tried to shake it: all this British bollocks still felt something like home. There in the downpour, as I made the final stretch of my trip through the wet sadness of Gibraltar, feeling a conceited and self-congratulatory mix of exhaustion and relief, I could almost hear my experience and the condition of Gibraltar and the British Empire at large being poignantly scored to the sound of 'The Last Post'.

The bus I caught to Europa Point had gradually shed all its passengers as the strange familiarity of British-built terrace houses and pubs finally relented, and the bus ambled up a small road that wasn't really designed for a bus and emerged dramatically at the rocky coast, with me as the sole passenger left on board. I had cut my journey so finely that this bus, which stayed idle at the Europa Point terminus for twelve minutes before making the return journey, was the same bus I needed to be on to make my own return journey. The driver pointed me in the direction of a lighthouse, and I saw that Europa Point was a building site, under renovation but deserted by the workers because of the bad weather. I ran through the rain and the greyness, gusts of wind blowing wildly like the impasto brushstrokes of a painter, brooding storm clouds overhead, obscuring the spire of the large, modern and impressive Ibrahim-al-Ibrahim Mosque perched dramatically at the edge of the rocky outpost. Everything was monochrome, and I could barely see a few metres in front of me, never mind across the straits and into Africa.

Perhaps I'd wanted to feel the proximity of the two continents I felt most connected to, but the more I thought of it, looking out at sea, being drenched by fatefully bad weather, amid unglamorous scaffolding and dormant work tools, the more I realized I didn't need to see the landmass of Africa looming emblematically in the distance to end my travels, because Africa was right where I was standing. All this time it had been dominated by nostalgic, imperial iconography and, much like black Sheffield and other such areas in Europe, hadn't been exported. This created the illusion that black Europe was a place without culture, history or geography, which, as I'd now seen first hand, I knew was utterly untrue. As well as experiencing the black European landscape, I'd connected with the knowledge production of its myriad communities, learned about bold, empowering black and working-class traditions that I'd been kept at a distance from my whole life, despite being black and working class myself. These scattered fragments of Afropean experience had formed a mosaic inside my mind, not monolithic, but not entirely amorphous either; rather, the Afropean reality was a bricolage of blackness and I'd experienced an Africa that was both *in* and *of* Europe.

I looked once more into the fog hanging over the sea, obscuring Africa, and closed my eyes for a moment to feel its presence as the wild surf spritzed my face. Then, turning around to face the tumultuous old continent where I'd been born and raised, I went back to where I came from.

Notes

INTRODUCTION

1. 'Thieves in the Night', *Mos Def and Talib Kweli are Blackstar* (Rawkus: 1998)
2. Aimé Cesaire, *Cahier d'un retour au pays natal*, trans. Seth L. Wolitz, 'Black Poetry of the French Antilles', Fybate Lecture Notes: 1968, p. 18
3. Frantz Fanon, *Black Skin, White Masks* (Grove Press: 1967), p. 111

PROLOGUE: SHEFFIELD

1. Alain de Botton, *Status Anxiety* (Hamish Hamilton: 2004) p. 12

A TOUR OF BLACK PARIS

1. Written and recorded for the WNYC and archived by NYC Municipal Archives WNYC Collection, date unknown. Hear the monologue here: https://www.wnyc.org/story/192767-richard-wright/

AN AFROPEAN *FLÂNEUR*

1. W. E. B Du Bois, *The Souls of Black Folk* (A. C. McClurg: 1903), p. 2

FOUR DAYS IN CLICHY-SOUS-BOIS

1. François Maspero, *Roissy Express*, trans. Paul Jones (Verso: 1994), p. 190
2. Émile Zola, *The Kill*, trans. Brian Nelson (Oxford World Classics: 2008), p. 73
3. Maspero, *Roissy Express*, p. 163
4. Ibid., p. 172

TERVUREN UNCENSORED

1. Adam Hochschild, *King Leopold's Ghost* (Pan Macmillan: 2006), p. 50
2. Eva Swyngedouw and Erik Swyngedouw, 'The Congolese Diaspora in Brussels and Hybrid Identity Formation: Multi-scalarity and Diasporic Citizenship', in *Urban Research and Practice Journal*, vol. 2, no. 1 (Routledge: 2009), p. 71

A MEETING WITH CARYL PHILLIPS

1. Adam Hochschild, *King Leopold's Ghost* (Pan Macmillan: 2006), p. 313
2. Caryl Phillips, *Revisiting the European Tribe*, in *Wasafiri*, 79, 2014
3. Caryl Phillips, *The European Tribe* (Faber and Faber: 1987), p. 121
4. Marc Augé, *Non-places: An Introduction to Super-modernity* (Verso: 2008) p. xxi.

FIGHT THE POWER

1. Grace Jones and Paul Morley, *I'll Never Write My Memoirs* (Gallery Books: 2015), p. 307
2. Joyce Moore Turner, *Caribbean Crusaders and the Harlem Renaissance* (University of Illinois Press: 2005), p. 240
3. Ibid., p. i (Preface)
4. Ibid., p. 249
5. Francis Fukuyama, 'The End of History?', in *The National Interest*, no. 16, summer 1989, p. 4
6. Turner, *Caribbean Crusaders and the Harlem Renaissance*, p. 242
7. Gloria Wekker, *White Innocence: Paradoxes of Colonialism and Race* (Duke University Press: 2016), p. 14
8. Ibid., p. 5
9. Fatima El-Tayeb, quoted in Ibid., p. 4

GERMAICA

1. Walter Rodney, *The Groundings with My Brothers* (Bogle-L'Ouverture Publications: 1969), p. 34

RINKEBY SWEDISH

1. Owen Hatherley, 'How Sweden's Innovative Housing Programme Fell Foul of Privatisation', in *Guardian*, June 2013

I WORRY AS I WANDER

1. Claude McKay, 'Soviet Russia and the Negro', *Crisis*, 27, December 1923, p. 65
2. Susan Robeson, *The Whole World in His Hands: Pictorial Biography of Paul Robeson* (Citadel Press: 1981), p. 58
3. Langston Hughes, *I Wonder as I Wander* (Hill and Wang: 1993), p. 74
4. Ibid., p. 82
5. Ibid., pp. 83–4
6. Ibid., p. 74

STRANGERS IN MOSCOW

1. Quoted in Joyce Moore Turner, *Caribbean Crusaders and the Harlem Renaissance* (University of Illinois Press: 2005), p. i (Preface)
2. Jean Van Lierde (ed.), *Lumumba Speaks: The Speeches and Writings of Patrice Lumumba, 1958-1961* (Little, Brown and Company: 1972), p. 422
3. Caryl Phillips, *The European Tribe* (Faber and Faber: 1987), p. 113

JOSEPH MOBUTU'S ROQUEBRUNE-CAP-MARTIN

1. V. S. Pritchett, *Books in General* (Chatto and Windus: 1953), p. 88
2. Claude McKay, *Banjo* (Black Classics/The X Press: 2000), p. 168

JAMES BALDWIN'S SAINT-PAUL-DE-VENCE

1. James Baldwin, 'As Much Truth as One Can Bear', in *The New York Times Book Review*, 14 January 1962, p. 11

2. Henry Louis Gates Jnr, 'The Welcome Table: James Baldwin in Exile', in *Exile and Creativity: Signposts, Travelers, Outsiders, Backward Glances*, ed. Susan Rubin Suleima (Duke University Press: 1998), p. 318

3. As told to Caryl Phillips in the documentary *No Complaints*, BBC Radio 4, 1984

4. James Baldwin, 'Architectural Digest Visits: James Baldwin', in *Architectural Digest*, August 1987, p. 124

FRANTZ FANON'S TOULON

1. Kristen Stromberg Childers, *Seeking Imperialism's Embrace: National Identity, Decolonization, and Assimilation in the French Caribbean* (Oxford University Press: 2016), p. 41

2. Ibid., p. 42

3. Frantz Fanon, *Black Skin, White Masks* (Grove Press: 1967), p. 156

4. Ibid., pp. 19–3

5. Transcript voiced from official document in Mike Thomson's *Document*, BBC Radio 4, 2009

6. Ibid.

7. Fanon, *Black Skin, White Masks*, p. 203

8. Ibid., p. 74

9. Ibid., p. 19

MCKAY'S MARSEILLE

1. Claude McKay, *Banjo* (Black Classics/The X Press: 2000), p. 8

2. Ibid., p. 118

3. Ibid., p. 4

4. Ibid., p. 35

5. W. E. B. Du Bois, 'Review of *Home to Harlem*', in *Crisis*, 35, June 1928, p. 202

6. Claude McKay in *The Correspondence of W. E. B. Du Bois: Selections, 1877–1934*, ed. Herbert Aptheker (University of Massachusetts Press: 1997), p. 375

7. Jane Jacobs, 'Downtown is for People', in *Fortune*, 1958.

8. Jane Jacobs Lecture at Harvard University, 1956

9. ZZ Top, in Zinedine Zidane interview with Andrew Hussey, in *Guardian*, April 2004

10. Alain de Botton, *Status Anxiety* (Hamish Hamilton: 2004) p. 287

11. John Richardson, *A Life of Picasso: The Triumphant Years, 1917–1932* (Jonathan Cape: 2007), p. 385
12. McKay, *Banjo*, p. 33

THE NIGHT TRAIN TO LISBON

1. Pascal Mercier, *Night Train to Lisbon*, trans. Barbara Harshav (Grove Press: 2008), p. 17
2. Ibid., p. 97
3. Tom Gallagher, *Portugal: A Twentieth-century Interpretation* (Manchester University Press: 1983), p. i (Preface)
4. Amílcar Cabral, *Revolution in Guinea* (Stage 1, London: 1973), p. 63
5. Gallagher, *Portugal: A Twentieth-century Interpretation*, p. 158
6. John Berger and Jean Mohr, *A Seventh Man* (Verso: 2010), p. 49
7. Ruaridh Nicoll, 'The Great Escape that Changed Africa's Future', *Guardian* 8 March 2015.

A EUROPEAN FAVELA

1. Doug Saunders, *Arrival City* (Windmill Books: 2011), p. 75
2. Jonathan Openshaw (Mr Porter: 2017): https://www.mrporter.com/journal/the-report/the-six-cities-we-want-to-move-to-in-2017/2082
3. Open letter: 'ENPAD Condemns the Police Brutality against Black Persons in Cova da Moura, Lisbon', 11 February 2015: http://stopblackface.com/enpad-condemns-the-police-brutality-against-black-persons-in-cova-da-moura-lisbon/

AN AFROPEAN ODYSSEY

1. Ross E. Dunn, *The Adventures of Ibn Battuta, A Muslim Traveler of the 14th Century* (University of California Press, 1989), p. 7

Acknowledgements

I returned from the travels from which most of this book emerged exhausted, after five chilly months on the road, with five tatty notebooks full of scribbles. They were covered in coffee rings from Ethiopian roasts in Rome, sauce stains from Sudanese takeaways in Berlin and oil from the cocoa butter I bought at a Surinamese market in Amsterdam to keep my brown skin hydrated during a bitterly cold European winter. I'd set off in solitude, but by the end of it all I realized that I'd amassed a tribe of sorts, who offered friendship and support and graciously pointed me and my scruffy journals in the direction of a fully formed book.

I'm deeply thankful to Cecilia Stein, who commissioned and developed this work, nurturing my better ideas while challenging any fuzzy moments with patient, nuanced, constructive and clear-sighted criticism – I felt I was in safe hands right from the start. Helen Conford enriched the project with an obvious passion for and understanding of what I was trying to achieve, and her gentle guidance and encouragement energized and elevated my writing. Sarah Day's thoughtful and vigorous copy-editing was the polish that allowed me to feel comfortable setting my work free into the world, and I'm incredibly grateful to Etty Eastwood, Jim Stoddart, Sam Voulters, Rebecca Lee and all at Penguin for the way I was allowed to keep the personal soul of the book alive, from the content to the cover.

Suresh Ariaratnam continues to act as more than my literary agent; he's also a good friend, an elegant voice of reason and literature-world translator. He took on both me as a writer and the book you're holding when we were half formed, and I owe much of the evolution that has taken place to him. To afropean.com's co-founders Nat Illumine and Yomi Bazuaye, whose tireless, skilful and selfless work forms the foundation of this book and the scaffolding that will allow the Afropean discussion to continue beyond it, I'm eternally grateful. To our frequent contributors Nina Camara, Tommy A-Man Evans and Tola Ositelu, and our tenacious and recurring intern Imani Ballard, as well as the many other contributors to Afropean.com over the years, who have helped to describe how it feels to be Afropean for many people: I hope this book serves as a meaningful extension of all the hard work and love you have put in over the years. ENAR (European Network Against Racism) continues to provide so many valuable statistics about black lives in Europe, and their funding towards my early work enabled me to create afropean.com.

Leon Hackett was a true friend and supporter from the beginning, and his belief in and ambition for this book was greater than my own. I'm indebted to the prolific and dedicated work of Sharmilla Beezmohun and the Speaking Volumes team of Nick Chapman and Sarah Sanders, as well as the Breaking Ground Black British Writers tour scribes I was lucky to frequently vibe off: Diran Adebayo, Jay Bernard, Bernadine Evaristo, Gabriel Gbadamosi, Colin Grant, Nick Makoha, Karen McCarthy-Woolf, Roger Robinson and Warsaw Shire, as well as our frequent champions and collaborators Maggi Morehouse and Elisa Joy White.

The youth workers and community leaders working with disadvantaged kids from communities like the one I grew up in are unsung heroes. Their work to provide amenities and initiatives in the midst of increasing cuts to vital funding is perhaps the single most important type of work being carried out in black communities across Europe. As a young man, I at one time or another benefited greatly from the creative altruism of the following people in Sheffield: the late Trevor Bailey, Simon Barth, Chris Bart-Williams, Sangita Basudev and the staff at Sheffield Live, Debjani Chatterjee, the late Trevor Darien, Father Tim Ellis, Mohammad Kassim, MC Nige, Uriah Renee, Desiree Reynolds, Lloyd Samuels and Dr Abdulgallail Shaif; and, in London, Carol Jacobs, Jacob Sam La Rose, Russell Thompson at Apples and Snakes, and countless others. My work has roots in theirs.

Working with, studying under or simply having enlightened conversations with the following thinkers and creatives has been an immensely rewarding experience that has enriched the content of the book: Ayo Akinwolere, Robbie Aitken, Elena Akilo, Brussels, Craig Atkinson at Café Royal Books, Edith Bergfors, Rob Berkeley, Tony Burns, Alain 'Fusion' Clapham, Tereza Cruz at the New University of Lisbon, Eleonora Cutaia, Marie Daulne (Zap Mama), Jean Philippe Didieu, the Elusive Jahnell, Cecille Emeke, Seb Emina, Hélène and Célia Faussart (Les Nubians), Tina Freeth, Paul Gilroy, Kyle Greenwood, Claude Grunitzky, Linton Kwesi Johnson, Chris Jones, Eric Kambel at Afro Europe Blog, Musa Kargbo, Bob Kilburn, my first-ever editor at *Blues and Soul* magazine ('Writing is discipline, John'), Sandra Krampelhuber, Benedicte Ledent and Daria Tunca at the University of Liège, Alanna Lockward, Marta Sofía López Rodríguez and all at Afro Europes, Kathleen Louwe and the Africa Desk at Bozar, Omar Lyefook, Florent Massot, Peter Meanwell, Ayoko Mensah, Najila Moubtassime. Rebecca Norris Webb and Alex Webb, along with Robin Maddock, helped me make sense of the thousands of photographs I came back with, Eddie Otchere, Shannon Park, Eva Ulrike Perker, Ed Petrie, Jessica Phillips, Tony Phillips, Lucy Pilkington, Kim Podemik and all at Photofusion in Brixton, Hannah Azieb Poole, Anna Rastas, Matt Roebuck, Chris 'Apoc' Rowan, Antje Sharenberg, Stephen Simmonds, Ana Sobral, Stephen Small, Mark Stein and the Transnational Studies team at the University of Münster, Alex Webb, and all at Bare Knuckle Soul and Montévidéo Marseille. I'm thankful to the welcoming staff at Café 'Cup of Tea' in Marseille, where, fuelled by Rwandan Kinihira green tea, intermittent breaks scrutinizing their Photo Poche collection and a soundtrack of Michelle N'dgeocello records, I blissfully wrote most of my second draft.

ACKNOWLEDGEMENTS

To Natasha, for sticking by me during the most unglamorous moments of the writing of this book, sustaining my work with love, wisdom and endless support, and Célia, whose birth long after my travels turned me into the kind of nine-to-five writer it took to finish the manuscript: I love you beyond words, and hope this book provides some sort of connection to knowledges and a cultural foundation I felt was missing from my own childhood, growing up in the West.

And finally, to my mentors: Chris 'Finguz' Morris, the polymath, whose intelligence, humility, creative stamina, politics, morality and parenting skills leave me in awe, Anna Bergfors, whose craft has inspired my photography more than anyone else and who has helped me find meaning in plain old hard work, and Caryl Phillips. When I first met Caryl at the beginning of this trip, I had only a loose idea of what I wanted to achieve. The first person who really believed in me and the project happened to be someone who could open so many important doors for the book. In the most literal sense, this book would not have been possible without his guidance, support, friendship and literary trailblazing.

To everyone I met on my journey, whose stories, though not all included here, helped piece together a black European narrative: this book is for and about you.

Resources:

For further information and details of black European organisations, artists, scholars, grants, musicians, community centres, book recommendations, NGOs, and businesses, please visit our ongoing project: afropean.com/map

For a wider selection of photographs from the journey, visit afropean.com/photoessay

To hear an audio exploration of Afropean culture, visit afropean.com/podcast

To share your own Afropean story with an online community, please contact submissions@afropean.com